German
With Ease

Original Text by
Hilde SCHNEIDER

Adapted for The Use
of English-Speaking Readers
by A. STETTLER

Illustrated by J.-L. GOUSSÉ

ASSiMiL
Le don des langues

B.P. 25
94431 Chennevières-sur-Marne Cedex
FRANCE

ISBN 978-2-7005-0527-6

ASSiMiL

Languages available

Optional recordings on audio and mp3 CDs are available for all courses.

The Assimil Series

Beginner – Intermediate

Arabic With Ease
Chinese With Ease volume 1
Chinese With Ease volume 2
Writing Chinese With Ease
Dutch With Ease
New French With Ease
German With Ease
Hungarian With Ease
Italian With Ease
Japanese With Ease volume 1
Japanese With Ease volume 2
Writing Japanese With Ease
Spanish With Ease

For Kids

Sing Your Way To French

Advanced

Using French

Business

Business French

On the Road

Dutch From The Word Go!
French
German From The Word Go!
Italian
Polish
Russian
Spanish

Contents

Introduction VII

Lessons 1 to 100

1 Im Café 1
2 Das Restaurant 5
3 Im Park 9
4 Wie geht's? 11
5 Am Telefon 17
6 Immer dasselbe... 21
7 Wiederholung und Erklärungen 25
8 Ein Fest 27
9 Ein Fest (Fortsetzung) 29
10 Eine Überraschung 33
11 Eine Begegnung 37
12 Wenn das Wetter schön ist... 41
13 Ich kann es versuchen... 45
14 Wiederholung und Erklärungen 49
15 Ich habe einen Freund... 51
16 Drei Stunden später... 55
17 Der Zahnarzt 59
18 Das Verbot 63
19 Mögen Sie Würstchen? 67
20 Wo ist der Bahnhof? 69
21 Wiederholung und Erklärungen 73
22 Eine schöne Wohnung 79
23 Schwierige Gäste 83
24 Verstehen Sie das? 87
25 Ein wahrer Schatz 91
26 Der Hausmeister 97
27 Wer soll das bezahlen? 101
28 Wiederholung und Erklärungen 105
29 Ein Brief 109
30 Ein ruhiger Nachmittag im Hotel 113
31 Ein Gespräch mit dem Chef 119
32 Ein Interview 123
33 Ein sympathischer Besuch 129
34 Beim „Fondue“-Essen 133
35 Wiederholung und Erklärungen 137

36 Das liebe Geld! 141
37 Ein guter Tip 147
38 Ein Ausweg? 151
39 Ein Ausweg? (Fortsetzung) 155
40 Endstation 161
41 Beim Arzt 165
42 Wiederholung und Erklärungen 169
43 Die guten, alten Zeiten 171
44 Lieber Christian! 177
45 Neues Leben 181
46 Neues Leben (Fortsetzung) 185
47 Drei Szenen einer Ehe 191
48 Wer ist schuld daran? 195
49 Wiederholung und Erklärungen 201
50 Verkäufer sein ist nicht leicht 203
51 Erinnern Sie sich auch daran? 209
52 Das neue Rotkäppchen 213
53 Das neue Rotkäppchen (Fortsetzung) 219
54 Ist Ihnen so was schon mal passiert? 223
55 Der Engel mit Schuhen 227
56 Wiederholung und Erklärungen 231
57 Wie der Vater, so die Söhne 233
58 Gemüse auf einem Spaziergang 239
59 Was halten Sie davon? 243
60 Der kleine Blonde und sein roter Koffer 249
61 Kein Wunder! 253
62 Ein glücklicher Zufall 257
63 Wiederholung und Erklärungen 263
64 Der Auserwählte 267
65 Und Sie, sind Sie schon einmal einem Nationalisten begegnet ?.... 271
66 Nehmen Sie nicht alles wörtlich! 277
67 Nehmen Sie aber bitte auch ab und zu etwas wörtlich! 281
68 Der öffentliche Fernsprecher (I) 287
69 Der öffentliche Fernsprecher (II) 291
70 Wiederholung und Erklärungen 297
71 Klein-Fritzchen 299
72 Quark und Schwarzbrot 305
73 Bitte anschnallen! 309
74 Vater und Sohn 315
75 Die Rückkehr 321
76 „Onkel“ Christoph 325

77 Wiederholung und Erklärungen 331
78 Wußten Sie schon… 335
79 Ein Volk, aber viele Mund- und Eigenarten 339
80 Der Aberglaube 345
81 Die Lorelei und ihre Nachkommen 349
82 Im Wartezimmer 355
83 Im Wartezimmer (Fortsetzung) 361
84 Wiederholung und Erklärungen 367
85 Die Pessimistin und der Egoist 369
86 Eigentum muß geschützt werden 375
87 Der Spaßvogel 381
88 Verschiedenes 387
89 Ein gemütliches Abendessen 391
90 Der Krimi am Freitagabend 397
91 Wiederholung und Erklärungen 401
92 Stille Wasser sind tief 405
93 „Aktenzeichen XY ungelöst“ 411
94 Hatschi! 415
95 Ein Zeitungsbericht - Überfall auf Heidener Tankstelle geklärt 421
96 Andere Länder, andere Sitten 425
97 Die Rede des Bürgermeisters 433
98 Wiederholung und Erklärungen 439
99 Mein lieber Matthias! 441
100 Trauen Sie niemandem! 447

Grammatical appendix 456

Introduction

German with Ease will make you familiar with the everyday German language. Most of the texts are dialogs between people meeting in the street, in cafés, at work, at home...
Even complete beginners will be able to make themselves understood and to understand a conversation in the course of a few months.

The Assimil method relies on daily involvement by the student. You will learn German by listening and repeating the sentences and, finally, speaking yourself. The most important rule is: do a little every day. It is only through constant contact that one's natural powers of learning are exploited to the full. Even if you devote only ten to fifteen minutes each day to the course, do so **every day**, and do it when you are relaxed.

During the first part of the process, the **First Wave** (Lesson 1-50), we only ask you to listen, repeat and understand. Read the texts aloud and compare them with the translation and notes. Do not pay too much attention to grammar rules. As you proceed, you will gradually assimilate the basic constructions of the language in the same way as you assimilated your native language. Don't learn anything by heart.

From Lesson 50 onwards – the **Second Wave** and active phase of the Assimil method commences – you will go back to an earlier lesson, starting at Lesson 1, and translate from English into German.

At both stages, the exercices will help you to consolidate your knowledge.

The more complex points of grammar are examined every seventh lesson (**Wiederholung und Erklärungen**). In the texts, such points are indicated by [N-] and a number. Each time you come across one of these references, read the relevant Note but **no more**. In this way, when you reach the "**Wiederholung und Erklärungen Lektion**", it will be a real review.

Do not try and do too much at once. We have tried to make things as simple as possible, so find your own rhythm, and you will enjoy daily practice.

Pronunciation

The only way to acquire correct pronunciation is to listen to the recordings. However, to make things easier in the earlier lessons, we provide German pronunciation using the nearest equivalent English phonetic transcription and not the International Phonetic Alphabet. In German the pronunciation is not too difficult because you pronounce each letter.

However, pay attention of the following points :
The **Umlaut**, **ä**, **ö**, **ü** :
ä is pronounced like "ai" in *fair* ;
ö is pronounced like "er" in *her* ;

For the **Umlaut ü**, there is no equivalent sound in English.
For those who know a little French, it corresponds to the pronunciation of the vowel "u" in French. Listen carefully to the recordings and repeat aloud ; this will be the best way of getting familiar with it.

The *ch* is pronounced in two ways :
Preceded by the vowels **i**, **e**, **ü**, **eu** *[oy]*, it is pronounced slightly less gutturally than "ch" in the Scottish word loch. We will write it this way in the pronunciation *[çh]*.

Preceded by the vowels **a**, **o**, **au**, it is pronounced gutturally. It will be written with a capital **H** *[cH]*.

The letter **ß** is used instead of ss at the end of a word or before consonants.

The "e̲" underlined is pronounced like the "e" in *open*. Please note that the stress is on the bold-faced letters.

These indications will be sufficient for the time being. Remember that nobody speaks a language without making mistakes at first...

Viel Spass! Enjoy yourself!

1 Erste Lektion *[erste lekts**ioh**n]*

Im Café

1 – Herr **O**ber!
2 Der Tee ① ist kalt!
3 – Wie ② ist der Tee?
4 – Er ③ ist kalt!
5 – Oh, Verz**ei**hung!
6 – Herr **O**ber, der Tee ist jetzt gut;
7 **a**ber die T**a**sse ④…
8 – Ja, die T**a**sse?
9 – Sie ⑤ ist zu klein! □

Pronunciation Key
*im kaf**ay** **1** herr **oh**ber **2** dehr tay ist kalt **3** vee ist dehr tay **4** ehr ist kalt **5** Oh, fert**sy**-oong **6** herr **oh**ber, dehr tay ist yetst goot **7** **ah**ber dee t**a**sse **8** yah, dee t**a**sse **9** zee ist tsoo klyne*

Notes

① In German, all nouns are spelled with an initial capital letter. You may have also noticed that nouns have a gender. They are either masculine, feminine or neuter.
Tee, *tea*, is masculine, its definite article is **der**.

② **wie**, *how?*, is pronounced *[vee]*, like *ee* in the verb *meet*. The **e** is not pronounced.

③ **er**, *he*, is the masculine personal pronoun. ▸

First Lesson 1

In The Café *(n.)*

1 – Waiter *(m.) (Mister waiter)*!
2 The tea *(m.)* is cold!
3 – What is the tea like *(how is the tea)*?
4 – It *(he)* is cold!
5 – Oh, excuse me *(pardon)*!
6 – Waiter, the tea is *(now)* good now;
7 but the cup *(f.)*...
8 – Yes, the cup?
9 – It *(she)* is too small! □

④ **tasse**, *cup*, is a feminine noun; its definite article is **die**. Please note that the "**e**"s underlined in our Pronunciation Key block are pronounced like the **e** in *open*.

⑤ **sie**, *she*, is the feminine personal pronoun.

1

Please see below the two exercises, which will accompany each lesson. The first exercise, **Übung 1**, *consists of short German sentences which you should read aloud and then translate orally into English.*

Übung 1 – Übersetzen sie bitte
Exercise 1 – Please translate

❶ Wie ist die Tasse? ❷ Sie ist klein. ❸ Wie ist der Tee? ❹ Er ist zu kalt. ❺ Peter ist klein, aber Klaus ist groß*. (* groß: tall)

Übung 2 – Ergänzen Sie bitte
Exercise 2 – Please fill in the blanks

(Each dot stands for a letter.)

❶ What is the tea like *(How is the tea)*?
. . . ist der Tee?

❷ It is good.
. . ist gut.

❸ Excuse me, (Mister) waiter!
. . . . Herr Ober!

❹ The cup is too small.
Die Tasse ist . . klein.

1

The second, **Ergänzen Sie bitte***, will help you to test your newly acquired vocabulary: we ask you to fill in the blanks. You will find the answers to the exercises at the end of each lesson.*

Answers to exercise 1

❶ What is the cup like? ❷ It is small. ❸ What is the tea like? ❹ It is too cold. ❺ Peter is small, but Klaus is tall.

❺ She is small.
. . . ist klein.

❻ Anne is small, but Klaus is tall.
Anne ist . . . . . , aber Klaus ist groß.

Answers to exercise 2

❶ Wie – ❷ Er – ❸ Verzeihung – ❹ – zu – ❺ Sie – ❻ – klein –

Remember that you are not required to learn the texts by heart. Listen carefully to the lessons and read each paragraph aloud, immediately after you have heard it. This sort of revision will help you to assimilate new words and constructions before learning a grammar rule.

2 Zweite Lektion *[tsvyte lektsi**ohn**]*

Das Restaurant ①

1 – Ich ② bin sehr m**ü**de,
2 und ich h**a**be H**u**nger.
3 Dort ist ein ③ Restaur**a**nt.
4 Es ④ ist schön ⑤, nicht wahr?
5 – Ja…, **a**ber…
6 – H**a**ben Sie ⑥ auch H**u**nger?
7 – Ja, **a**ber…
8 – Sind Sie nicht m**ü**de?
9 – Doch, **a**ber das Restaur**a**nt ist zu t**eu**er.
10 Dort ist **ei**ne Kn**ei**pe ⑦; sie ist auch schön, nicht wahr?

Pronunciation Key

We hope that the Pronunciation Key helps you to make yourself familiar with the spoken language, but do not write it down.

*dass restor**ohn** **1** içh bin zehr m**ü**de **2** oont içh h**ah**be h**oo**nger **3** dort ist ine restor**ohn** **4** ess ist shern, niçht vahr **5** yah,*

Notes

① **Restaurant** is a neuter noun, the third gender. Its definite article is **das**. Don't worry too much about this novelty; the gender of any new word will be indicated in the English translation:

m. = masculine, *f.* = feminine, *n.* = neuter.

② **ich**, *I*, the Pronunciation *of* **ch** is not easy. It is pronounced between **sh,** as in *shop* and **s** as in *sleep*. We will write it *çh* in the Pronunciation Key block. It occurs after **i**, **e**, **ü**, **eu**.

③ **ein**, *a/an*, is the indefinite article of the neuter and the masculine gender. **Eine**, as you will see later, is the feminine form: **eine Tasse**, *a cup*.

Second Lesson 2

The Restaurant *(n.)*

1 – I am very tired,
2 and I am hungry *(I have hunger)*.
3 There is a restaurant [over there].
4 It is nice, isn't it *(not true)*?
5 – Yes…, but…
6 – Are you *(also)* hungry, too *(have you also hunger)*?
7 – Yes, but…
8 – Are you not tired?
9 – Indeed I am, but the restaurant is too expensive.
10 There is a pub *(f.)* *[over there]; it (she)* is *(also)* nice too, isn't it? □

***ah**be̲r … **6 hah**ben zee owcH **hoo**nger **7** yah, **ah**be̲r **8** zinnt Zee niçht **mü**de̲ **9** docH, **ah**be̲r dass resto**rohn** ist tsoo **toy**-e̲r **10** dort ist **i**-ne̲ kny-pe̲; zee ist owcH shern, niçht vahr*

④ **es** is the neutral form of the personal pronoun. **Das Restaurant ist schön**, **es ist schön**, *The restaurant is nice, it is nice.*

⑤ **schön**: **ö** = **er**.

⑥ **Sie**, *you*, is the personal pronoun that is used to address a person in the formal way. The **s** is always spelled with a capital letter. The **ch** of **auch** is always pronounced gutturally, as in the Scottish word *Loch*. It is not the same sound as the **ch** of *ich*. This sound occurs after the vowels **a**, **o**, **u**, **au**. In the pronunciation key the guttural **ch** will be written with a capital **h** *cH*.

⑦ **die Kneipe**, *the pub*, is a place where you can have a beer or a snack. It is a colloquial word.

2 **Übung 1 – Übersetzen Sie bitte**
Exercise 1 – Please translate

❶ Das Restaurant ist zu teuer. ❷ Sie sind müde? ❸ Dort ist das Café. ❹ Ich habe Hunger. ❺ Haben Sie auch Hunger?

Übung 2 – Ergänzen Sie bitte
Exercise 2 – Please fill in the blanks
(Each dot stands for a letter.)

❶ I am tall.
Ich . . . groß.

❷ You are small (formal "you").
Sie . . . . klein.

❸ Is the restaurant expensive?
Ist das Restaurant . . . . . ?

❹ No, it is not expensive.
Nein . . ist nicht teuer.

❺ There is a café over there.
. . . . ist ein Café.

❻ I am hungry.
Ich habe . . . .

Answers to exercise 1

❶ The restaurant is too expensive. ❷ You are tired? ❸ The café is over there *(there is the café)*. ❹ I am hungry. ❺ Are you hungry, too?

Answers to exercise 2

❶ – bin – ❷ – sind – ❸ – teuer ❹ – es – ❺ Dort – ❻ – Hunger

3 Dritte Lektion *[dritte lektsi**oh**n]*

Im Park

1 – Verz**ei**hung! Ist d**ie**ser Platz ① noch frei?
2 – Ich gl**au**be ②, ja.
3 – D**a**nke! W**u**nderbar d**ie**se S**o**nne ③, nicht wahr?
4 Die Luft ist auch so gut!
5 Sind Sie oft hier?
6 War**u**m **a**ntworten Sie nicht?
7 Spr**e**chen Sie ④ Deutsch?
8 – Nein, ich bin Franz**ö**sin ⑤.
9 Ich spr**e**che nur ein w**e**nig ⑥ Deutsch.
10 – Sch**a**de!

Pronunciation Key
*im Park **1** fertsy-oong! ist d**ee**zer plats nocH fry **2** içh gl**ow**be yah **3** d**a**ng-ke! v**oo**nderbahr d**ee**ze z**o**nne, niçht vahr **4** dee looft ist owcH zoh goot **5** zinnt zee oft heer **6** var**oo**m*

Notes

① **der Platz**, *the seat* or *place*, is masculine. **Dieser Platz**, *this place*, **dieser** is the demonstrative pronoun of the masculine gender.

② **glauben**: the **au** is pronounced like the **ow** of *how*.

③ **diese Sonne**, *this sun*; **diese** is the feminine form of the demonstrative pronoun. The neuter is, **dieses**.
E. g.: **dieses Restaurant**, *this restaurant*.

④ In German, the questions are formed by inverting the verb and the noun or pronoun. Do, does, did is never translated!

⑤ **eine Französin**, *a Frenchwoman*; **ein Franzose**, *a Frenchman*. But note: **Ich spreche Französisch**, *I speak French*.

⑥ **ein wenig**, *a little*; the ending **-ig** is generally pronounced *-içh*.

Third Lesson 3

In The Park *(m.)*

1 – Excuse me! Is this seat *(m.) (place)* still free?
2 – I think *(believe)* [so], yes.
3 – Thank you! Wonderful this sun *(f.)* [shine], isn't it?
4 The air *(f.)* is so good, too!
5 Do you often come here *(are you often here)*?
6 Why don't you answer *(why answer you not)*?
7 Do you speak German?
8 – No, I am French.
9 I only speak a little German.
10 – What a pity *(pity)*! □

***ann**tvort<u>e</u>n zee niçht **7** shpre**ç**h<u>e</u>n zee doytsh **8** nyne, içh bin frants**er**zin **9** içh shpre**ç**h<u>e</u> noor ine **veh**niçh doytsh **10** sh**ah**d<u>e</u>*

4 **Übung 1 – Übersetzen Sie bitte**
❶ Dieser Platz ist nicht frei. ❷ Ich spreche ein wenig Deutsch. ❸ Sind Sie Franzose? ❹ Warum ist der Tee kalt? ❺ Die Sonne ist wunderbar.

Übung 2 – Ergänzen Sie bitte

❶ Do you speak French? *(formal "you")*
. . . . Sie Französisch?

❷ No, I speak only German.
Nein, ich . . . . nur Deutsch.

❸ Is this tea good?
Ist . . . . Tee gut?

❹ This restaurant is not expensive.
. . . . Restaurant ist nicht teuer.

4 Vierte Lektion *[feerte lektsi**oh**n]*

Wie geht's? ①

1 – G**u**ten Tag, W**o**lfgang!
2 – H**a**llo, **A**nne! Wie geht's?
3 – Gut, d**a**nke.
4 – K**o**mmst ② du mit ins ③ Caf**é**?

Pronunciation Key
vee gehts ***1*** *g**oo**ten tak, v**o**lfgang* ***2*** *h**a**lloh, **a**nne! vee gehts* ***3*** *goot, d**a**ng-ke* ***4*** *k**o**mmst doo mit ins kaf**ay***

Notes

① **Wie geht's?** or **Wie geht es?**, *How are you?* The answer is **gut**, *well/fine*, or **es geht gut** word for word "it's going good", *I'm good.*

Answers to exercise 1

❶ This seat is not free. ❷ I speak a little German. ❸ Are you French? ❹ Why is the tea cold? ❺ The sun [shine] is wonderful.

❺ I speak a little English.
Ich spreche . . . . Englisch.

❻ Do you often come here *(are you often here)*? *(formal "you")*
Sie sind . . . hier?

Answers to exercise 2

❶ Sprechen – ❷ – spreche – ❸ – dieser – ❹ Dieses – ❺ – ein wenig – ❻ – oft –

Fourth Lesson 4

How Are You?

1 – Hello, Wolfgang! *(good day)*
2 – Hello, Anne! How are you *(how goes it)*?
3 – Fine, thanks.
4 – Will you come to the café with me?

② In German, the present tense is used for the simple and the progressive forms in English and can be used when making an invitation: **Kommst du...?**, *Will you come...?*

③ We say: **Ich gehe ins Café**, *I go to the café*; but: **Ich bin im Café**, *I am in the café*. Can you notice the difference? The explanation will follow shortly.

5 – Ja, gern. Ich h**a**be Durst.
6 – Was tr**inkst du?**
7 – Ich trinke **ei**ne Limon**a**de. Und du?
8 – Ich n**e**hme ein Bier.
9 **A**nne (sie) trinkt ④ **ei**ne Limon**a**de, und W**o**lfgang (er) trinkt ④ ein Bier.

10 – G**u**ten **A**bend, Frau H**e**rder!
11 – G**u**ten **A**bend, Herr Schmitt!
12 – Das ist Fr**äu**lein W**a**gner.
13 – Freut mich! Tr**i**nken Sie ⑤ ein Glas Wein mit mir?

***5** yah, gern içh h**ah**b<u>e</u> doorst **6** vass tr**i**ng-kst doo **7** içh tr**i**ng-k<u>e</u> … limon**ah**d<u>e</u>. oont doo **8** Içh n**eh**m<u>e</u> ine Beer **9** **a**nn<u>e</u> (zee) tring-kt **i**-n<u>e</u> limon**ah**d<u>e</u> oont v**o**lfgang (ehr)*

Notes

④ We have already seen the singular form of the present tense: **ich trinke**, *I drink*; **du trinkst**, *you drink*; **er/sie/es trinkt**, *he/she/it drinks*.

⑤ Now, here is the formal form: **Sie trinken**: *you drink*. The verb in its formal form always ends in **-en**.

***

Übung 1 – Übersetzen Sie bitte

❶ Guten Tag! Wie geht's? ❷ Ich habe Durst. ❸ Trinkst du ein Bier? ❹ Nein, danke! Ich nehme eine Limonade. ❺ Kommen Sie mit ins Café? ❻ Was trinken Sie?

5 – Yes, with pleasure. I am thirsty *(I have thirst).* **4**
6 – What are you having *(drinking)*?
7 – I'll have *(drink)* a lemonade *(f.). And you?*
8 – I'll have a beer *(n.).*
9 Anne *(she)* drinks a lemonade, and Wolfgang *(he)* drinks a beer.

10 – Good evening, Mrs. Herder!
11 – Good evening, Mr. Schmitt!
12 – This is Miss Wagner.
13 – Nice to meet you! Will you have a glass *(n.)* [of] wine *(m.)* with me *(do you drink...)*? □

tring-kt ine beer ***10*** *goot*__*e*__*n* ***ah****bent, frow h****er****d*__*e*__*r.* ***11*** *... herr shmitt.* ***12*** *dass ist fr****oy****lyne v****a****gner* ***13*** *froyt miçh. tring-ken zee ine glass vyne mit meer*

***

Answers to exercise 1

❶ Hello! How are you? ❷ I am thirsty. ❸ Will you have a beer *(do you drink a beer)*? ❹ No, thanks! I'll have a lemonade. ❺ Will you come to the café with me? ❻ What will you have *(to drink)*?

4 Übung 2 – Ergänzen Sie bitte

❶ Good evening, Miss Wagner! How are you?
Guten ..... Fräulein Wagner! ... geht's?

❷ This is Mr. Müller.
Das ... Herr Müller.

❸ What are you having *(do you drink)*?
Was .... Sie?

❹ Anne drinks a lemonade.
Anne ...... eine Limonade.

❺ Will you come *(with)* to the café [with me]?
. . . . . . du mit ins Café?

❻ I am thirsty. And you?
Ich . . . . Durst. Und . . ?

Answers to exercise 2

❶ – Abend – Wie – ❷ – ist – ❸ – trinken – ❹ – trinkt – ❺ Kommst – ❻ – habe – du

Don't worry about any words or expressions that have not yet been explained; just try to repeat and to understand them in their context. We'll have a closer look at them soon.

5 Fünfte Lektion *[fünfte lektsiohn]*

Am Telefon

1 – Guten Tag! Hier ist Peter Schmitt.
2 Ich möchte bitte Fräulein Wagner sprechen ①.
3 – Verzeihung! Wer sind Sie?
4 – Mein ② Name ist Peter Schmitt.
5 – Einen Moment, bitte. Meine Tochter kommt sofort. ②
6 – Hallo, Peter! Wo bist du?
7 – Ich bin noch im Büro; aber ich fahre jetzt nach Hause ③.
8 Gehen wir heute abend ins Kino? ④

Pronunciation Key
***1** gooten tak!* heer ist pehter shmitt **2** içh merçhte ... shpreçhen **3** fertsy-oong! vehr zinnt zee **4** myne nahme ist ... **5** i-nen mohment bitte. my-ne tocHter kommt zohfort **6** halloh pehter! voh bist doo **7** içh bin nocH im büroh; ahber*

Notes

① Have you noticed the sentence's word order? **Ich möchte**, *I'd like...* **sprechen**, *talk to*. The infinitive **sprechen** is placed at the end of the sentence.

② **der Name**, *the name*; **mein Name**, *my name*. **Mein** is the possessive pronoun of the masculine and the neuter gender. **Meine** is the feminine form (indefinite article: **ein/eine**). ▸

Fifth Lesson 5

On The Phone *(n.)*

1 – Hello! This is Peter Schmitt speaking *(here is Peter Schmitt)*.
2 I would like to speak to Miss Wagner, please.
3 – Pardon me! Who is speaking *(Who are you)*?
4 – My name *(m.)* is Peter Schmitt.
5 – One moment *(m.)*, please. My daughter *(f.)* will be here right away *(comes at once)*.
6 – Hi, Peter! Where are you?
7 – I am still at the office *(m.)*; but I'm leaving now *(driving)*.
8 Are we going to the cinema *(n.)* tonight?

*içh fa**h**re yetst nacH h**o**wze* ***8*** *ge**h**en veer h**o**yte **ah**bent ins keeno*
* The final **g** in the first sentence is pronounced **k** (except **-ig**, see lesson 3, note 6). The final **b** is pronounced **p**, and **d** is pronounced **t** (see sentence 11): **sind** *[zinnt]*.

③ **das Haus**, *the house*; **nach Hause**, *home*, **nach** indicates the direction to a place. But please note: *I am at home*, **Ich bin zu Hause**.

④ **heute**, *today*; but: **heute abend**, *tonight*, *this evening*.

5 **9** – Nein, lieber morgen; heute ⑤ abend möchte ich fernsehen.
10 – Gut! Dann bis morgen!
11 Ich bin, du bist, er/sie/es ist, Sie sind ⑥. □

***9** nyne, leeber morgen; ... fernzeh'n **10** goot! dann bis morgen*
***11** içh bin, doo bist, ehr/zee/ess ist, zee zinnt*

Notes

⑤ **das Fernsehen**, *the television*; **fernsehen**, *to watch TV* (literally, **fern**, *far*; **sehen**, *see*).

⑥ The verb **sein**, *to be*, is irregular in German as it is in English.

***

Übung 1 – Übersetzen Sie bitte

❶ Wer sind Sie? – Ich bin Anne Müller. ❷ Herr Schmitt geht nach Hause. ❸ Fräulein Wagner ist noch im Büro. ❹ Gehst du heute abend ins Restaurant? ❺ Herr und Frau Herder sind sehr müde. ❻ Kommen Sie mit ins Kino?

Übung 2 – Ergänzen Sie bitte

❶ Hello! This is Miss Wagner speaking.
Guten Tag! . . . . ist Fräulein Wagner.

❷ My name is Wolfgang.
Mein . . . . ist Wolfgang.

❸ Excuse me, who are you?
Verzeihung, . . . bist du?

❹ I'm going home now.
Ich gehe jetzt . . . . Hause.

9 – No, rather tomorrow; tonight I would like to watch the television.
10 – Fine! See you tomorrow then *(then until tomorrow)*!
11 I am, you are, he/she/it is, you are *(formal)*. □

***

Answers to exercise 1

❶ Who is speaking *(who are you)*? — I am Anne Müller. ❷ Mr. Schmitt goes home. ❸ Miss Wagner is still at the office. ❹ Are you going to the restaurant tonight? ❺ Mr. and Mrs. Herder are very tired. ❻ Will you come *(with)* to the cinema with me?

❺ Where is Peter? — He is at home.
.. ist Peter? – Er ist .. Hause.

❻ My daughter is still small.
Meine .... ist noch klein.

Answers to exercise 2

❶ – Hier – ❷ – Name – ❸ – wer – ❹ – nach – ❺ Wo – zu –
❻ – Tochter –

6 Sechste Lektion *[zekste lektsiohn]*

Immer dasselbe...

1 – Komm schnell! Der Zug fährt ① in zehn Minuten.

2 – Hast du die Fahrkarten ②?

3 – Ich habe meine Fahrkarte ③, aber nicht deine.

4 – Vielleicht hast du meine und nicht deine?

5 – Also gut, ich habe nur eine Karte. Wer hat die andere?

6 – Ich habe sie nicht. Du mußt zwei Karten haben ④.

7 – Oh Gott, das ist immer dasselbe Theater! Ich fahre allein!

8 – Warte! Hier ist meine Karte - in meiner Manteltasche ⑤!

Pronunciation Key
*immer dasselbe **1** komm shnell! dehr tsook fehrt in tsehn Minooten **2** hast doo dee fahrkarten **3** içh hahbe my-ne ... ahber night dy-ne **4** feelyçht ... **5** allzoh goot içh hahbe*

Notes

① **fahren**, *to go (by car, train...), to leave*. **Gehen** means *to go on foot*. Please note that we say: **ich fahre**, but: **du fährst**, **er/sie/es fährt** (the a becomes ä).
The plural is regular: **wir fahren**, *we go/leave*; **Sie fahren**, *you go/leave* (formal), and **sie fahren**, *they go/leave*.

② The plural has only one gender; its definite article is **die**. The plural forms of the nouns are not regular: **die Karte - die Karten**, *the ticket - the tickets*; **der Zug - die Züge**, *the train - the trains*; **das Theater - die Theater**, *the theater - the theaters...* ▶

Sixth Lesson 6

Always The Same...

1 – Hurry up *(come quickly)*! The train *(m.)* is leaving in ten minutes *(f.)*.
2 – Have you [got] the tickets *(f.)?*
3 – I have my ticket, but not yours.
4 – Maybe, you have [got] mine and not yours?
5 – Well then, I have only [got] one ticket. Who has [got] the other one?
6 – I have not got it. You must have two tickets.
7 – Oh dear *(God)*, it's always the same old story *(theater) (n.)!* I'll go on my own!
8 – Wait! Here is my ticket - in my coat pocket *(f.)*.

*noor **i**-ne karte. vehr hat dee **an**dere? **6** içh h**ah**be zee niçht. Doo moosst tsvy **kar**ten h**ah**ben **7** oh gott, dass ist **im**mer dass**el**be te**ah**ter! içh **fah**re all**y**ne **8** **var**te! Heer ... in **my**ner **man**teltashe*

③ **die Fahrkarte** is feminine. **Meine/deine Karte**, *my/your ticket.*

④ Pay attention to the position of **haben**. You can go back to note **1** in the previous lesson.

⑤ **die Manteltasche**, *the coat pocket.* One of the peculiarities of the German language is the compound words. Their gender is determined by the gender of the second word: **der Mantel**, *the coat*; **die Tasche**, *the pocket*; **die Manteltasche**. You see why it is important to learn the nouns with their article.

6 **9** – Endlich…! Wir haben nur noch zwei Minuten Zeit.

10 – Ich habe, du hast, er/sie/es hat, wir haben, Sie haben. □

__9__ entliçh! veer hahben noor nocH tsvy minooten tsyte __10__ içh hahbe, doo hast, ehr/zee/ess hat, veer hahben, zee hahben

***

Übung 1 – Übersetzen Sie bitte

❶ Wer hat die Fahrkarten? ❷ Endlich kommst du! ❸ Ich warte schon zehn Minuten. ❹ Mein Mantel hat zwei Taschen. ❺ Sie haben (formal form) nur noch eine Minute Zeit. ❻ Das ist mein Glas.

Übung 2 – Ergänzen Sie bitte

❶ The train leaves at six o'clock.
Der Zug . . . . . um sechs Uhr.

❷ Where is my ticket?
Wo ist . . . . . Fahrkarte?

❸ Wait! I am coming immediately!
. . . . . ! Ich komme . . . . . . !

❹ We have only ten minutes [left].
Wir . . . . . nur . . . . Minuten Zeit.

❺ My name is Anne Müller.
. . . . Name ist Anne Müller.

❻ It's always the same!
Das ist immer . . . . !

9 – At last…! We only have two minutes [left]. 6
10 – I have, you have, he/she/it has, we have, you have (formal). □

***

Answers to exercise 1

❶ Who has the tickets? ❷ There you are, finally *(finally you are coming)*! ❸ I have already been waiting [for] ten minutes *(I wait already ten minutes)*. ❹ My coat has two pockets. ❺ You have only one minute [left]. ❻ That is my glass.

Answers to exercise 2

❶ – fährt – ❷ – meine – ❸ Warte – sofort ❹ – haben – zehn – ❺ Mein – ❻ – dasselbe

We have covered quite a lot already in this first week. We will finish each week with a review lesson, which will explain the most important points of the preceding lessons. Don't learn the rules by heart; try to assimilate them in the given context.

7 Siebte Lektion *[zeep-te lektsi**oh**n]*

Wiederholung und Erklärungen

(Revision and Explanations)

1 German Pronunciation

During this first week we have learnt short sentences, and have gradually familiarized ourselves with German Pronunciation. Below, you will find the whole alphabet with the Pronunciation of each letter:

a *[ah]*, **b** *[beh]*, **c** *[tseh]*, **d** *[deh]*, **e** *[eh]*, **f** *[eff]*, **g** *[geh]*, **h** *[hah]*, **i** *[ee]*, **j** *[yot]*, **k** *[kah]*, **l** *[ell]*, **m** *[em]*, **n** *[en]*, **o** *[oh]*, **p** *[peh]*, **q** *[koo]*, **r** *[err]*, **s** *[ess]*, **t** *[teh]*, **u** *[oo]*, **v** *[fow]*, **w** *[veh]*, **x** *[iks]*, **y** *[eepsilon]*, **z** *[tsett]*, **ä**, *[ai]*, **ö** *[er]*, **ü** *[ü]*.

2 Genders in German

We have seen that there are three genders in German: masculine, feminine, neuter.
The definite articles are: **der** *(m.)*, **die** *(f.)*, **das** *(n.)*; the indefinite articles: **ein** *(m./n.)*, **eine** *(f.)*; the demonstrative pronouns *this*, **dieser** *(m.)*, **diese** *(f.)*, **dieses** *(n.)*.
The plural has only one gender, so there is only one definite article: **die**, *the*; and one demonstrative pronoun: **diese**, *these*.

3 Verbs

We have already learnt the present tense of:
trinken, *to drink*:
ich trinke, *I drink*
du trinkst, *you drink*
er/sie/es trinkt, *he/she/it drinks*
wir trinken, *we drink*
sie trinken, *they drink*
Sie trinken, *you drink* (formal)

Seventh lesson 7

The formal way of addressing a person **Sie trinken** and the third person of the plural are identical in Pronunciation Key. The difference is only apparent in the written language: the formal form takes an initial capital **S**. The second person of the plural will be considered a little later.

Do you remember the two irregular verbs we saw?
ich bin Amerikaner, *I am American*
du bist müde, *you are tired*
er/sie /es ist groß, *he/she/it is tall*
Sie sind Amerikanerin, *you are American* (formal, feminine)

ich habe die Fahrkarte, *I have the ticket*
du hast, *you have*
er/sie/es hat, *he/she/it has*
wir haben, *we have*
Sie haben, *you have* (formal)

The advantage of German is that the present tense translates the simple and the progressive (-ing) forms in English.

Remember: Don't spend too much time on the explanations. Listen regulary to the recordings of the lessons, read the sentences aloud – sentence by sentence – without asking yourself too many questions.

8 Achte Lektion *[acHte lektsi**oh**n]*

Ein Fest

1 Viele ① Leute sind heute abend bei Fischers.
2 Fischers geben eine Party.
3 Man trinkt, tanzt und lacht viel.
4 Alle amüsieren sich gut. Alle?
5 Wer ist die Frau dort? Sie ist ganz allein.
6 Ich möchte wissen ②, wer sie ist.
7 – Anne, wer ist die blonde ③ Frau dort?
8 – Ich weiß nicht. Ich kenne sie nicht.
9 Aber ich glaube, sie ist eine Freundin ④ von Frau Fischer.
10 – Gut! Ich frage sie…(**Fo**rtsetzung folgt) □

Pronunciation Key
*ine Fest **1 fee**le **loy**te … by **fish**ers **2 fish**ers **ge**ben … **3** mann tring'kt, tanntst oont lacHt feel **4 a**lle amü**see**ren siçh goot … **5** … gannts all**yne 6** … **vi**ssen, … **7** … **blo**nnde … **8** … vise niçht … **9 ah**ber içh **glow**be … **froyn**-din fonn … **10 frah**ge …*

Notes

① **viel**, *many/a lot*, when it is used as an adjective it has to agree with the noun it qualifies. **Viele Freunde**, *many friends*.

② **wissen**, *to know*. The first person singular does not end in **-e**: **ich weiß**, *I know*. **ß** stands for **ss** at word endings, preceding a consonant and between two vowels when the first one is long. Please note: **wissen**, *to know something*; **kennen**, *to know someone*.

③ Adjectives before the noun are always declined (see note 1); preceded by a definite article the singular form ends in **-e**: **die** ▸

Eighth Lesson 8

A Party *(n.)*

1 There are many people at [the] Fischers' tonight.
2 [The] Fischers are giving a party.
3 Everybody is drinking and dancing and laughing a lot.
4 All [of them] are enjoying [themselves] a lot *(well)*. All [of them]?
5 Who is the woman *(f.)* [over] there? She is all alone.
6 I would like to know who she is.
7 – Anne, who is the fair-haired *(blonde)* woman [over] there?
8 – I don't know. I don't know her.
9 But I think *(believe)* she is a friend *(f.)* of Mrs. Fischer's.
10 – Well! I'll ask her… (Continuation follows) □

MAN TRINKT TANZT UND LACHT VIEL

▸ **blonde Frau**; **der blonde Mann**; **das blonde Kind**. But: **das Kind ist blond**.

④ **der Freund**, *the friend* (m.); **die Freundin**, *the friend* (f.). **Der Student**, *the student* (m.); **die Studentin**, *the student* (f.).

Übung 1 – Übersetzen Sie bitte

❶ Wer ist die Freundin von Frau Fischer? ❷ Die Leute trinken und lachen. ❸ Das Kind ist ganz allein. ❹ Kennen Sie Fräulein Wagner? ❺ Der kleine Mann dort ist mein Freund.

Übung 2 – Ergänzen Sie bitte

❶ Who is it? – I don't know.
. . . ist das? – Ich . . . . nicht.

❷ All of them are enjoying themselves and dancing.
. . . . amüsieren sich und . . . .

❸ I think *(believe)* he is a friend of Miss Schmitt's.
Ich . . . . . . er ist ein . . . . . . von Fräulein Schmitt.

9 Neunte Lektion *[noynte lektsiohn]*

Ein Fest (Fortsetzung)

1 – Guten Abend! Tanzen Sie nicht gern ①?
2 – Doch, sehr gern. Aber ich kenne niemand hier.
3 – Ach so. Darf ich mich vorstellen? Mein Name ist Klaus Frisch.

Pronunciation Key
... fortsetsoong ***1*** *... tanntsen ... gern* ***2*** *... kenne neemannt heer* ***3*** *acH zoh. darf ... for'shtellen? ...*

Answers to exercise 1

❶ Who is the friend of Mrs Fischer? ❷ The people are drinking and laughing. ❸ The child is all alone. ❹ Do you know Miss Wagner? ❺ The small man over there is my friend.

④ He doesn't know her/them.
Er ..... sie nicht.

⑤ Do you know why he is laughing?
Wissen Sie, ... er lacht?

⑥ The small woman [over] there is my mother.
Die ...... Frau dort ist meine Mutter.

Answers to exercise 2

❶ Wer – weiß – ❷ Alle – tanzen ❸ – glaube – Freund – ❹ – kennt – ❺ – warum – ❻ – kleine –

Ninth Lesson 9

A Party (continued)

1 – Good evening! Don't you like dancing?
2 – On the contrary, I do *(very much)*. But I [don't] know anybody here. *(I know nobody here)*.
3 – Oh, I see! May I introduce myself? My name is Klaus Frisch.

Note

① **Ich tanze gern**, *I like dancing/to dance.* **Er trinkt gern Wein**, *He likes drinking wine.*

9 **4** Ich bin ein Kollege von Herrn Fischer.
5 – Ich heiße ② Elisabeth. Frau Fischer ist meine Schwester.
6 – Ihre ③ Schwester? Das ist nicht möglich!
7 – Warum nicht?
8 – Sie sind groß ④, blond und schlank und
9 Ihre Schwester ist klein, dunkel und … mh… nicht so schlank.
10 – Das ist ganz einfach. Mein Vater ist groß, dick und dunkel, und meine Mutter klein, blond und dünn. □

4 … kollege … 5 ich hyse elizabett … shvester 6 eere shvester? … merglich 7 varoom … 8 … gross, blonnt oont

Notes

② **heißen**, *to be called*. **Ich heiße**, *I am called*, *my name is…* This is how we introduce ourselves.

③ We have already seen **mein/e**, *my*, and **dein/e**, *your*. **Ihr/e** is the formal way of addressing someone. Have you already noticed the use of the capital **I**.

④ Don't forget that the attributive adjective never agrees with the noun it refers to. **Der Mann ist dick**, *The man is fat*. However, **der dicke Mann**, *the fat man*.

***

Übung 1 – Übersetzen Sie bitte

❶ Trinken Sie gern Kaffee? ❷ Wie heißen Sie? – Ich heiße Klaus. ❸ Kennst du meine Schwester? ❹ Er hat eine große Schwester und eine kleine Schwester. ❺ Haben Sie Ihre Fahrkarte?

4 I am a colleague *(m.)* of Mr. Fischer's.
5 – My name is Elisabeth. Mrs. Fischer is my sister *(f.)*.
6 – Your sister? That is impossible! *(not possible)*
7 – Why *(not)*?
8 – You are tall, fair-haired *(blond)* and slim, and
9 your sister is small, dark-[haired] and… mm… not very *(so)* slim.
10 – It's very *(all)* simple. My father *(m.)* is tall, fat and dark-[haired], and my mother *(f.)* [is] small, fair-haired and thin.

9** … **doo**ng'k<u>e</u>l … shlang-k* ***10 *… **i**ne-facH … **Fah**t<u>e</u>r … dikk … dünn*

ER HAT EINE GROßE SCHWESTER
UND EINE KLEINE SCHWESTER

***

Answers to exercise 1

❶ Do you like drinking coffee? ❷ What is your name? — My name is Klaus. ❸ Do you know my sister? ❹ He has a big sister and a little sister. ❺ Do you have your ticket?

10 Übung 2 – Ergänzen Sie bitte

❶ My brother is tall and slim.
Mein Bruder ist . . . . und . . . .

❷ What is your sister's name?
Wie heißt . . . . Schwester?

❸ May I introduce myself?
. . . . ich mich vorstellen?

❹ We know nobody here.
Wir kennen . . . . hier.

---

10 Zehnte Lektion *[tsehnte lektsiohn]*

Eine Überraschung

1 – Was machst du **heu**te **a**bend, P**e**ter?
2 – Ich weiß noch nicht ①. Ich h**a**be Zeit.
3 M**ei**ne Fr**eu**ndin kommt nicht. **I**hre M**u**tter ist krank.
4 – Gehen wir ins K**i**no! M**ei**ne Fr**eu**ndin kommt auch nicht ②.

Pronunciation Key
*i-ne überrashoong ... **2** ... nocH ... tsyte **3** ... mootter ist krang'k*

Notes

① **noch**, *yet/still*. **Sie ist noch zu Hause**, *She is still at home*. But: **noch nicht**, *not yet*.

② **auch**, *also/too*, **auch nicht**, *either*.

❺ They like going to the cinema.
Sie .... ins Kino.

❻ What is this woman's name? — I don't know.
Wie ..... diese Frau? – Ich .... nicht.

Answers to exercise 2

❶ – groß – schlank ❷ – Ihre – ❸ Darf – ❹ – niemand – ❺ – gehen gern – ❻ – heißt – weiß –

10th Lesson 10

A Surprise

1 – What are you doing tonight, Peter?
2 – I don't know yet *(yet not)*. I am free *(I have time [f.])*.
3 My girlfriend is not coming. Her mother is ill.
4 – Let's go *(go we)* to the cinema *(n.)*! My girlfriend isn't coming either *(also not)*.

5 Sie hat zuviel Arbeit.
6 – Vielleicht hat Helmut auch Zeit.
7 Seine ③ Frau ist nicht da.
8 – Prima! Wir sind alle frei.
9 Treffen wir uns ④ um acht Uhr!
(Um acht Uhr im Kino)
10 – Schau ’mal ⑤, Peter! Ist das nicht deine Freundin dort?
11 – Mensch ⑥, ja! Und deine Freundin und Helmuts Frau auch!
12 – Na sowas! Das ist ja ⑦ eine Überraschung! □

5 *… tsoo-feel arbyte* **6** *feelyçht …* **7** *Zyne…* **8** *preema! …* **9** *treffen veer oons oomm acHt oohr!* **10** *show* mal …* **11** *… helmoots frow …*

* **au** is pronounced like **-ow** in *how*!

Notes

③ **sein(e)/ihr(e)**, *his/her*. The possessive pronoun ends in **-e** if it is followed by a feminine singular or a plural noun: **seine Mutter**, *his mother*; but: **sein Vater**, *his father*.

④ **sich treffen**, *to meet*, is a reflexive verb in German. Notice: **wir treffen uns**, *we meet (us)*. ▸

***

Übung 1 – Übersetzen Sie bitte

❶ Schauen Sie ’mal! Ist das nicht Ihre Mutter? ❷ Seine Freundin ist sehr schön, nicht wahr? ❸ Treffen wir uns um 10 Uhr im Café! ❹ Meine Frau hat zuviel Arbeit. ❺ Ihr Bruder ist sehr groß und dick.

5 She has too much work *(f.)*.
6 – Maybe Helmut is free too *(has also time)*.
7 His wife is not there.
8 – Super! We are all free.
9 Let's meet *(meet us)* at eight o'clock! (At eight o'clock at the cinema)
10 – Look *(once)*, Peter! isn't that your girlfriend [over] there?
11 – Dear me, yes! And your girlfriend and Helmut's wife, too!
12 – Think of that! That's a nice surprise, indeed! □

⑤ **mal**: its usage is very common in spoken language. The entire form is: **einmal** which means *once*. **Schau mal**, *Look!* is the imperative form for the second person singular. To address someone in the formal way, you need to add the third person pronoun: **Schauen Sie!** *Look!* In the same way, the pronoun is added for the first person plural: **Schauen wir!** *Let's look!*

⑥ **mensch**, *man, human being*. Here: **Mensch** is used to express surprise, because you meet someone or come across something unexpectedly.

⑦ **ja** is used in an emphatic way.

***

Answers to exercise 1

❶ Look *(once)*! Isn't that your mother? ❷ His girlfriend is very beautiful, isn't she? ❸ Let's meet at ten o'clock at the café! ❹ My wife has too much work. ❺ Her brother is very tall and fat.

11 Übung 2 – Ergänzen Sie bitte

❶ Are you free today *(have you time today)*?
Hast du . . . . heute?

❷ His mother is ill.
. . . . . Mutter *(Helmuts Mutter)* ist krank.

❸ Her sister [will] come tomorrow.
. . . . Schwester *(Annes Schwester)* kommt morgen.

---

11 Elfte Lektion *[elfte lektsiohn]*

Eine Begegnung ①

1 – Was machen Sie denn ② hier? Sind Sie verrückt?
2 – Warum? Ich möchte ③ nur schlafen!
3 – Ja, aber das ist meine Garage. Woher kommen Sie?
4 – Ich komme aus Frankreich, aus England, aus Indien und aus Südamerika.
5 – Ja, aber wo wohnen Sie?
6 – Ich wohne in Frankreich, in England, in Indien und manchmal in Australien.
7 – Ja, aber Sie sind hier in Deutschland, und das ist meine Garage.

Pronunciation Key
i-ne be-gegnoong **1** *… ferrückt* **2** *… noor shlahfen* **3** *… my-ne garashe … * **4** *… ows frangkryçhe … englannt … indyen … südamerika* **5** *… vohnen …* **6** *… mannçh-mahl in ows-tralien* **7** *… doytshlannt …*

❹ His friend likes drinking much.
. . . . Freund *(Peters Freund)* trinkt gern viel.

❺ Her brother likes dancing.
. . . Bruder *(Annes Bruder)* tanzt gern.

❻ Maybe her husband *(man)* is also free *(has also time)*?
. . . . hat ihr Mann auch Zeit?

Answers to exercise 2
❶ – Zeit – ❷ Seine – ❸ Ihre – ❹ Sein – ❺ Ihr – ❻ Vielleicht –

Eleventh Lesson 11

An Encounter *(f.)*

1 – What are you doing here? Are you out of your mind?
2 – Why? I only want to sleep.
3 – Yes, but this is my garage *(f.)*. *(From)* where do you come from?
4 – I come from France *(m.)*, England *(n.)*, India *(n.)* and South America *(n.)*.
5 – Yes, but where do you live?
6 – I live in France, in England, in India and sometimes in Australia *(n.)*.
7 – Yes, but here you are in Germany *(n.)*, and this is my garage.

Notes

① All nouns with an **-ung** ending have a feminine gender.

② You will often come across words like **denn**, **doch**, **ja** in German. It is impossible to give a single translation for them; we'll use them in different contexts so that you'll be able to understand their meaning. In this context, **denn** underlines disapproval of something.

③ **Ich möchte**, *I want to...* or *I would like to...*

11

8 – Oh, das ist **I**hre Gar**a**ge! Das tut mir leid. Dann s**u**che ich ein Hot**e**l [N.1] ④

9 – H**a**ben Sie denn Geld?

10 – Ja, ich h**a**be viel Geld - in Fr**a**nkreich, in **E**ngland und in Sp**a**nien.

11 – Ja, **a**ber verst**e**hen Sie nicht? Sie sind in der B**u**ndesrepubl**i**k D**eu**tschland ⑤, und das ist m**ei**ne Gar**a**ge.

12 – Ach ja, das ist r**i**chtig; in D**eu**tschland h**a**be ich l**ei**der kein B**a**nkk**o**nto ⑥. Wo ist der B**a**hnhof, b**i**tte? □

Notes

④ [N] refers to a paragraph in the next revision lesson.

⑤ **BRD = Bundesrepublik Deutschland**, *Federal Republic of Germany* or *the former "West Germany"*.

⑥ Word for word: "In Germany have I got unfortunately any bank account". **Ich habe kein Geld**, *I haven't got any money/ I have no money.*

***

Übung 1 – Übersetzen Sie bitte

❶ Woher kommt Peter? ❷ Er kommt aus Deutschland. ❸ Sie hat nicht viel Geld. ❹ Ich wohne in München. ❺ Ich habe leider kein Auto. ❻ Hier möchte ich nicht schlafen. ❼ Wo möchten Sie schlafen?

8 – Oh, this is your garage! I am sorry. Then I[’ll] look for a hotel *(n.)*.
9 – Have you got any money then?
10 – Yes, I have a lot of money – in France, in England and in Spain.
11 – Yes, but don’t you understand? You are in Germany and this is my garage.
12 – Oh yes, that’s right. Unfortunately I don’t have a bank account *(n.)* in Germany. Where is the train station *(m.)*, please? □

***

Answers to exercise 1
❶ Where does Peter come from? ❷ He comes from Germany. ❸ She doesn’t have much money. ❹ I live in Munich. ❺ Unfortunately I don’t have a car. ❻ I wouldn’t like to sleep here. ❼ Where would you like to sleep?

Übung 2 – Ergänzen Sie bitte

❶ Where do you come from? – I come from Berlin.
..... kommst du? – Ich komme ... Berlin.

❷ Where do you live? – I live in Frankfurt.
Wo ...... Sie? – Ich .... Frankfurt.

❸ Do you drink a lot [of] beer? – No, I only drink wine.
Trinken Sie .... Bier? – Nein, ich trinke ... Wein.

❹ Is this your child? – No, I don't have a child.
Ist das ... Kind? – Nein, ich habe .... Kind.

---

12 Zwölfte Lektion *[tsverlfte lektsiohn]*

Wenn das Wetter schön ist…

1 – Wohin ① fahren Sie in Urlaub, Frau Herder?
2 – Ich fahre ② nach ③ Hamburg und an die Ostsee…, wenn das Wetter schön ist…
3 – Kennen Sie Hamburg?
4 – Ja, ich kenne die Stadt gut. Meine Schwester wohnt dort.

Pronunciation Key
*... vetter ... **1** voheen ... oorlowb ... **2** ... Hammboork oont ... ostzay ... **3** kennen ... **4** ... dee shtatt ...*

Notes

① **wo**, *where*, determines the place you are in. **Wohin**, *where*, determines the place you go to. **Wo wohnt Peter?**, *Where does Peter live?*; **Wohin geht Peter?**, *Where does Peter go?* ▸

❺ Mrs. Pivot lives in France, and Mr. Johnson lives in England.
Frau Pivot ..... in .... und Herr Johnson ..... in ....

❻ Sorry? I do not understand.
Wie bitte? Ich .... nicht.

Answers to exercise 2

❶ Woher – aus – ❷ – wohnen – wohne in – ❸ – viel – nur – ❹ – Ihr – kein – ❺ – wohnt – Frankreich – wohnt – England ❻ – verstehe –

Twelfth Lesson 12

If The Weather Is Fine…

1 – Where are you going on holiday *(m.)*, Mrs. Herder?
2 – I am going to Hamburg and to the Baltic Sea *(f.)*... if the weather *(n.)* is fine…
3 – Do you know Hamburg?
4 – Yes, I know the town *(f.)* well. My sister *(f.)* lives there.

② German is more precise than English:
Ich gehe, *I go (on foot).*
Ich fahre, *I go/leave (by car, train…).*
Ich fliege, *I go (by plane).*

③ The preposition **nach** indicates the direction; it is used before the names of towns and countries. **Ich gehe nach Paris**, *I go to Paris.*

5 – Und Sie, Herr H**u**ber, wohi**n** f**a**hren Sie?
6 – Wir f**a**hren nach **Ö**sterreich in die **A**lpen und nach S**a**lzburg…, wenn das W**e**tter schön ist…
7 – K**e**nnen Sie schon S**a**lzburg?
8 – Ja, ich k**e**nne es gut, **a**ber m**ei**ne Frau kennt es noch nicht.
9 – Die **A**ltstadt ist w**i**rklich sehr schön und die Umg**e**bung auch.
10 Und Sie, Fr**äu**lein W**a**gner, wohi**n** f**a**hren Sie?
11 – Ach wissen ④ Sie, ich fl**ie**ge ② nach Mallorca, denn ⑤ hier ist das W**e**tter **i**mmer so schlecht. □

*6 … er**st**e̲r-rygh … **al**pe̲n … zaltsboork … 9 … **al**t'shtatt … **vir**kliçh … oomg**ay**boong … 11 … **flee**ge̲ … mall**o**rca … shleçht*

Notes

④ **wissen**, *to know*; we've already seen **ich weiß**, *I know*. Here we come across the first and third person of the plural and the formal way of addressing someone: **wir wissen**, *we know*; **sie wissen**, *they know*; **Sie wissen**, *you know*. ▸

***

Übung 1 – Übersetzen Sie bitte

❶ Wohin fährst du in Urlaub? ❷ Ich fahre nach Italien. Und du? ❸ Ich fliege nach Südamerika. ❹ Kennen Sie Berlin gut? ❺ Die Umgebung von München ist sehr schön. ❻ Herr Wagner kennt Österreich wirklich gut.

5 – And you Mr. Huber, where are you going?
6 – We are going to Austria *(n.),* to the Alps *(plur.)* and to Salzburg..., if the weather is fine…
7 – Do you already know Salzburg?
8 – Yes, I know it well, but my wife does not know it yet.
9 – The old part of the town *(old town)* is really very nice and the surroundings too.
10 And you, Miss Wagner, where will you go?
11 – Oh, you know, I'll go to Majorca, because the weather is always so bad here. □

▸ ⑤ **Denn**: here is used as a conjunction, which means *because*.

***

Answers to exercise 1

❶ Where are you going on holiday? ❷ I go to Italy. And you? ❸ I go to South America. ❹ Do you know Berlin well? ❺ The surroundings of Munich are very nice. ❻ Mr. Wagner really knows Austria well.

Übung 2 – Ergänzen Sie bitte

❶ Ich komme aus Deutschland. *(I come from Germany.)*
. . . . ? *(Where do you come from?)*

❷ Ich wohne in Frankfurt. *(I live in Frankfort.)*
. . . . ? *(Where do you live?).*

❸ Ich gehe nach Hause. *(I'm going home).*
. . . . ? *(Where are you going?).*

❹ Mein Name ist Gisela Weber. *(My name is Gisela Weber.)*
. . . . ? *(What (how) is your name?)*

---

13 Dreizehnte Lektion *[dry-tsehnte lektsiohn]*

Ich kann es versuchen…

1 – Was machen Sie da, Herr Samson?
2 – Ich lerne Deutsch.
3 – Warum lernen Sie Deutsch?
4 – Ich will in Deutschland arbeiten ①. Meine Firma hat eine Filiale in Frankfurt.
5 – Und wann wollen Sie nach Frankfurt gehen ①?
6 – Meine Arbeit beginnt in vier Monaten ②.

Pronunciation Key
*… fer-zoocHen **2** … lerne doytsh **4** … vill … arby-ten … firma … filyahle … **5** … vollen **6** … beginnt … monaten*

❺ Das ist Herr Huber. *(This is Mr. Huber.)*
. . . . ? *(Who is this?)*

❻ Das ist ein Hotel. *(This is a hotel.)*
. . . . ? *(What is this?)*

Answers to exercise 2

❶ Woher kommen Sie ❷ Wo wohnen Sie ❸ Wohin gehen Sie ❹ Wie ist Ihr Name ❺ Wer ist das ❻ Was ist das

Thirteenth Lesson 13

I Can Try (It)…

1 – What are you doing there, Mr. Samson?
2 – I am learning German.
3 – Why are you learning German?
4 – I want to work in Germany. My company *(f.)* has a subsidiary *(f.)* in Frankfurt.
5 – And when do you want to go to Frankfurt?
6 – My job *(work)* starts in four months *(m.)*.

Notes

① Pay attention to where the infinitive is placed: **Ich will in Berlin arbeiten**, *I want to work in Berlin.* **Wann wollen Sie nach Berlin gehen?**, *When do you want to go to Berlin?* It is always at the end of the sentence.

② **der Monat**, *the month.*

7 – Aber das ist nicht möglich. Sie können ③
nicht in vier Monaten Deutsch lernen.

8 – Ich kann ③ es versuchen. Aller Anfang ist
schwer.

9 – Sie sprechen doch Englisch, oder?

10 – Natürlich spreche ich Englisch. Aber hören
Sie, ich spreche auch schon ein bißchen
Deutsch:

11 „Ich möchte bitte ein Bier und ein Steak!
– Wo ist das Hotel Ritz? – Kommen
Sie mit? – Wann fährt der nächste Zug nach
Frankreich?"

12 Das ist doch schon ganz gut, nicht wahr? ☐

7 ... mergliçh ... lernn__e__n ... **8** ... anfang ... shver
9 ... shpreçh__e__n docH english **10** natürliçh ... her-r__e__n ...
biss-çh__e__n ... **11** ... fairt ... nekst__e__ tsook ...

Note

③ **können**, *can*; **ich kann**, *I can*; **Sie können**, *you can*. **Wollen**,
to want; **ich will**, *I want*; **Sie wollen**, *you want*. The first person of the singular does not end in **-e**.

Übung 1 – Übersetzen Sie bitte

❶ Sprechen Sie Französisch? ❷ Ja, ich spreche
ganz gut Französisch. ❸ Warum wollen Sie nach
Frankfurt fahren? ❹ Ich will dort arbeiten. ❺ Wann
beginnt Ihr Urlaub? ❻ Mein Urlaub beginnt
morgen. ❼ Ja, das ist schon ganz gut!

7 – But that is impossible *(not possible)*. You can't learn German in four months.

8 – I can try. The first step is always the hardest *(every beginning [m.] is hard)*.

9 – But you speak English, don't you *(or)*?

10 – Of course I speak English. But listen, I already speak a little German too:

11 "I would like a beer and a steak *(n.)* please. — Where is the Ritz hotel? — Will *(do you)* you come with [me]? — When is the next train leaving for *(going to)* France?"

12 That's not bad at all, is it? *(That's already quite good, not true?)* □

***

Answers to exercise 1

❶ Do you speak French? ❷ Yes, I speak French quite well. ❸ Why do you want to go to Frankfurt? ❹ I want to work there. ❺ When do your holidays begin? ❻ My holidays begin tomorrow. ❼ Yes, that's not bad at all.

14 **Übung 2 – Ergänzen Sie bitte**

1. Was lernt Herr Samson?
   Er . . . . . Deutsch.
2. Wo will er arbeiten?
   . . . . Deutschland . . . .
3. Wann beginnt die Arbeit?
   . . . . vier . . . .

14 Vierzehnte Lektion

Wiederholung und Erklärungen (Revision and Explanations)

1 Constructing Sentences in German

Let's have a closer look at the construction of sentences in German:

Herr Wagner kommt aus Deutschland, *Mr. Wagner comes from Germany.*
Sie sprechen Deutsch, *You speak German.*
There is nothing exceptional about these sentences. The word order is the same as in English: subject – verb – object.
We have already mentioned that questions are formed by inverting subject and verb:
Kommt Herr Wagner aus Deutschland?, *Does Mr. Wagner come from Germany?*
Sprechen Sie Deutsch?, *Do you speak German?*

In German you can start a sentence with the subject, the object or an adverb, but the verb does not change its position, namely it remains in the second position:

❹ Spricht Herr Samson Englisch? [N.3]
Ja, ...

❺ Sprechen Sie Deutsch?
Ja, ich . . . . ein . . . .

Answers to exercise 2

❶ – lernt – ❷ Er will in – arbeiten ❸ Die Arbeit beginnt in – Monaten ❹ – er spricht Englisch ❺ – spreche – bißchen Deutsch

14th Lesson 14

Natürlich kommt er morgen, *Of course he is coming tomorrow.*
Vielleicht kommt Herr Wagner aus Österreich, *Maybe Mr. Wagner comes from Austria.*
In vier Monaten beginnt meine Arbeit, *My job starts in four months.*

2 The Indefinite Negative Article: *kein*

Ich habe kein Geld, *I have no money/I haven't got any money.*
Wir trinken kein Bier, *We don't drink beer.*
Ich habe keine Freunde, *I have no friends.*

Kein always belongs to a noun; in English you use either *not* + *any* or *no*. **Kein** must agree with the noun it precedes: **keine Freunde**.

3 Infinitives End and Irregularity

All verb infinitives end in **-en** (or **-n**). Nevertheless there are regular and irregular verbs. The irregularity occurs in the second and third person singular of the present tense, the simple past and the present perfect.
The radical vowel of the present tense **e** becomes **i** or **ie**:

sprechen, *to speak*
ich spreche, *I speak*
du sprichst, *you speak*
er, sie, es spricht, *he, she, it speaks*
wir sprechen, *we speak*
sie sprechen, *they speak*
Sie sprechen, *you speak*

15 Fünfzehnte Lektion

Ich habe einen ① Freund…

1 – Ich bin so deprimiert.
2 Komm, gehen wir einen trinken!
3 – Nein, ich gehe lieber nach Hause.
4 Ich muß morgen früh arbeiten.
5 – Ach, komm! Es ist noch nicht spät.
6 Wir bleiben nicht lange.
7 – Das kenne ich. Das sagst du immer,
8 und dann bleibst du 3 oder 4 Stunden.
9 – Das ist nicht wahr; heute sicher nicht.
10 Ich trinke nur einen ① kleinen ① Whisky. Komm!

(Fortsetzung folgt) □

Pronunciation Key
… i-nen froynt ***1*** *… deprimeert* ***3*** *… leeber … **4** … mooss … früh … **5** … shpait **6** … bly-ben … lange **7** … kenne … zakst … **8** … shtoondenn **9** … vahr … ziçher … **10** … fort-zetsoong folkt*

Some other examples: **geben**, *to give:* **ich gebe**, **du gibst**...; **nehmen**, *to take:* **ich nehme**, **du nimmst**; **lesen**, *to read:* **ich lese**, **du liest**...

Remember that the first person of the singular and the plural forms of the present tense are always regular.
You will meet new irregular verbs in the "Notes" of the next lessons.
Now, let's come back to our lessons: that's where you really practice the grammar rules you have learnt.

Fifteenth Lesson 15

I have A Friend...

1 – I feel so depressed.
2 Come [on], let's go and have a drink *(drink one)*!
3 – No, I'd rather go home *(n.)*.
4 I have to work tomorrow.
5 – Oh, come [on]! It's not late yet.
6 We [won't] stay [for a] long [time].
7 – I know that. You always say that,
8 and then you stay [for] three or four hours.
9 – That's not true; today I won't, sure *(sure not)*.
10 I will only have a small whisky *(m.)*. Come on!

(to be continued) □

Note

① **ein Freund**, *a friend*, is a masculine noun. When a masculine noun is the object, or the accusative, of the sentence, the indefinite article **ein** becomes **einen**. In order to indentify the object of a sentence, you need to ask the question whom or what.
E. g.: **Wir haben einen Hund**, *We have got a dog.* What have we got? – *a dog,* **einen Hund.**
You not only have to decline the article but also the adjective preceding the noun (qualifying adjective). You add **-en**. **Ich treffe einen alten Freund**, *I'm meeting an old friend* (m.).

15 **Übung 1 – Übersetzen Sie bitte**

❶ Möchten Sie einen Kaffee? ❷ Nein, danke. Ich trinke keinen Kaffee. ❸ Anne und Elisabeth bleiben lange im Café. ❹ Peter muß heute nicht arbeiten. ❺ Ich bleibe nur eine Stunde. ❻ Das ist nicht wahr.

Übung 2 – Ergänzen Sie bitte

❶ She drinks a lemonade and he drinks a whisky.
Sie trinkt .... Limonade, und er trinkt ..... Whisky.

❷ Come on, let's go home.
Komm, gehen wir ....

❸ I'd rather stay here.
Ich bleibe ...... hier.

❹ We have to work tomorrow.
Wir müssen ...... arbeiten.

❺ Why are you depressed?
Warum sind Sie .... ?

❻ He always stays [for] one or two hours.
Er ...... immer zwei oder drei ....

Answers to exercise 1

❶ Would you like some *(a)* coffee? ❷ No, thank you. I drink no coffee. ❸ Anne and Elisabeth are staying in the café [for a] long [time]. ❹ Peter does not have to work today. ❺ I'[ll] only stay [for] an hour. ❻ That is not true.

Answers to exercise 2

❶ – eine – einen – ❷ – nach Hause ❸ – lieber – ❹ – morgen – ❺ – deprimiert ❻ – bleibt – Stunden

Don't forget to read each lesson aloud, it's the best way to familiarize yourself with the pronunciation.

16 Sechzehnte Lektion

Drei Stunden später...

1 – Siehst du, jetzt trinkst du schon den ① f**ü**nften Wh**i**sky!
2 – Und du das **a**chte Bier!
3 Das ist auch nicht b**e**sser!
4 – Komm, wir n**e**hmen ein T**a**xi und f**a**hren nach H**au**se!
5 – Oh nein. Es geht mir ② so gut hier!
6 – W**ie**viel Uhr ist es?
7 – Es ist zwölf (Uhr).
8 – Was? Schon so spät?
9 – Ja, es ist M**i**tternacht ③, G**ei**sterst**u**nde ③!
10 – **A**lso komm **e**ndlich! Ich bringe dich ④ nach H**au**se.
11 – W**a**rte!... Ich br**au**che noch **ei**nen kl**ei**nen Wh**i**sky...
12 g**e**gen die G**ei**ster! □

Pronunciation Key
*... **1** zeest ... yetst ... **3** ... besser **6** vee-feel oohr ... **9** ... mitternacht, **guy**ster-sht**oo**nde **10** ... **e**nntliçh **11** ... browcHe ... **12** gegen ...*

Notes

① **der**, the definite article of the masculine gender becomes **den** when the following noun is the object of the verb (accusative). **Der Mann arbeitet**, *The man works.* (**Der Mann** is the subject of the sentence, the nominative). You ask: Who works? **Ich sehe den Mann**, *I see the man.* (Whom do I see?) ▸

Three Hours Later…

1 – You see, *(now)* you are already drinking your *(the)* fifth whisky!
2 – And that's your eighth beer *(and you the eighth beer)*!
3 That's not better either.
4 – Come on, we'll take a taxi *(n.)* and go *(drive)* home.
5 – Oh, no. I feel so good here! *(It goes me so good here)*.
6 – What time is it?
7 – It is twelve (o'clock).
8 – What? Already so late!
9 – Yes, it's midnight *(f.)*, witching hour *(ghost hour)*!
10 – Come on, then! I will take *(bring)* you home.
11 – Wait!… I need another *(a small)* whisky…
12 against the ghosts *(plur.)*! □

② **Es geht mir gut**, *I am fine*, is an impersonal expression in German. The question is: **Wie geht es dir?/Ihnen?**, *How are you?*

③ **mitternacht**, *midnight*; **die Nacht**, *the night*; **die Mitte**, *the middle*. **Der Geist** means *the ghost* or *the spirit/mind*. Plural: **die Geister**.

④ **dich**, *you*, accusative: **Ich sehe dich morgen**, *I'll see you tomorrow*. **Mich**, *me*, accusative: **Er bringt mich nach Hause**, *He takes me home*. **Bringen** means *to bring* and *to take*.

16 **Übung 1 – Übersetzen Sie bitte**

❶ Sie nehmen ein Taxi und fahren nach Hause. ❷ Wie geht es Ihnen? ❸ Es geht mir gut. Danke. Und Ihnen? ❹ Wieviel Uhr ist es? – Es ist elf Uhr. ❺ Er braucht einen Cognac. ❻ Es ist kalt. Sie nimmt den Mantel.

Übung 2 – Ergänzen Sie bitte

❶ What time is it?
. . . . Uhr ist es?

❷ How are you? – Very well, thanks.
. . . geht es dir? – Danke, ... gut.

❸ Peter is taking *(bringing)* me home.
Peter bringt . . . . nach Hause.

❹ We'll take the car. That's better.
Wir nehmen . . . Wagen *(m.)*.
Das ist . . . .

❺ Everybody needs money.
Alle Leute . . . . Geld.

❻ It is midnight. The ghosts are coming.
Es ist . . . .
Die Geister . . . .

Answers to exercise 1

❶ They/you take a taxi and go home. ❷ How are you? ❸ I am fine, thanks. And you? ❹ What time is it? – It is eleven o'clock. ❺ He needs a cognac. ❻ It is cold. She takes her *(the)* coat.

Answers to exercise 2

❶ Wieviel – ❷ Wie – sehr – ❸ – mich – ❹ – den – besser ❺ – brauchen – ❻ – Mitternacht – kommen

DREI STUNDEN SPÄTER
U-BAHN

17 Siebzehnte Lektion

Der Zahnarzt

1 – Ich h**a**be seit drei T**a**gen Z**a**hnschmerzen ①.
2 K**e**nnen Sie **ei**nen g**u**ten Z**a**hnarzt ②?
3 – M**ei**ne T**a**nte kennt **ei**nen. Sie f**i**ndet ihn ③ sehr nett.
4 – K**ö**nnen Sie mir b**i**tte s**ei**nen ④ N**a**men und s**ei**ne Adr**e**sse g**e**ben?
5 – Ja, w**a**rten Sie! Er heißt Dr. Knorr und wohnt W**a**gnerstr**a**ße 13.
6 S**ei**ne Telef**o**nn**u**mmer ist 26 35 16 (s**e**chsundzw**a**nzig f**ü**nfunddr**ei**ßig s**e**chzehn). [N.4]
7 – V**ie**len Dank. S**a**gen Sie mir, kennt **I**hre T**a**nte ihn schon l**a**nge?
8 – Oh ja, seit **u**ngefähr zehn J**a**hren.

Pronunciation Key

... tsahn'artst ***1*** *... zyte ... tsahnshmertsen* ***3*** *... tannte ... een zehr nett ...* ***4*** *... sy-nen nahmen ... adresse* ***5*** *knorr ... vahgnershtrasse dry-tsehn* ***7*** *... zagen zee ...* ***8*** *... oongefair ... yahren*

Notes

① **der Schmerz**, **die Schmerzen**, *the ache*, *the aches*; **der Zahn**, **die Zähne**, *the tooth*, *the teeth*. **Die Zahnschmerzen**, *the toothache*; **die Kopfschmerzen**, *the headache*; (**der Kopf**, *the head*).

② **der Arzt** or **der Doktor**, *the doctor*; **die Ärztin** (f.).

③ **ihn**, *him*, is the accusative of **er**, *he*. **Ich sehe ihn**, *I see him*. ▸

The Dentist

1 – I have [had] a toothache *(toothaches [plur.])* for three days now.
2 Do you know a good dentist?
3 – My aunt knows one. She finds him very kind.
4 – Can you give me his name *(m.)* and *(his)* address *(f.)*, please?
5 – Hang on! His name is Dr. Knorr and he lives at Wagnerstreet 13.
6 His telephone number *(f.)* is 26 35 16.
7 – Thank you very much *(many thanks)*. Tell me, has your aunt known him for a long time? *(Does your aunt know him…)*
8 – Oh yes, for about ten years *(plur.)*.

▸ ④ The possessive pronouns have the same endings as the indefinite article: **ein/einen**; **sein/seinen**. **Sein Name ist Wolfgang**, *His name is Wolfgang*. But: **Ich kenne seinen Namen nicht**, *I don't know his name*. **Namen** also ends in **-n**, but this is an exception.

17 **9** – Und sie sieht ihn oft?
10 – Oh ja, sehr oft. Wissen Sie, sie hat viele Probleme mit ihren Zähnen.
11 – Ah ja? Was für Probleme ⑤?
12 – Sie verliert ihre Plomben, hat Abszesse usw ⑥.
13 Aber ich sage Ihnen, der Zahnarzt ist wirklich phantastisch! □

***10** … tsaihnen **12** … ferleert eere plommben, … aps'tsesse … vy-ter **13** … fanntastish*

***

Übung 1 – Übersetzen Sie bitte

❶ Meine Schwester kennt einen netten Zahnarzt. ❷ Können Sie mir bitte Ihre Adresse geben? ❸ Was für ein Buch ist das? ❹ Haben Sie Probleme mit Ihren Zähnen? ❺ Ich kenne ihn seit ungefähr drei Jahren.

Übung 2 – Ergänzen Sie bitte

❶ Do you have a headache?
Haben Sie . . . . ?

❷ My doctor is very nice.
Mein Arzt ist sehr . . . . . .

❸ I have known him for five years.
Ich kenne . . . seit . . . . Jahren.

❹ Do you know my husband?
Kennen Sie . . . . . . Mann?

9 – And she often [goes to] see him?
10 – Oh yes, very often. She has a lot of problems *(plur.)* with her teeth *(plur.)*, you know.
11 – Oh, does she? What kind *(for)* of problems?
12 – She loses her fillings *(plur.)*, has abscesses *(plur.)* and so on.
13 But I assure *(tell)* you, the dentist is really fantastic! □

Notes

⑤ **Was für Probleme?**, *What kind of problems (What for...)?*; **Was für ein Auto hast du?**, *What kind of car have you got?*

⑥ **usw.** is the abbreviation for **und so weiter**, *and so on.*

***

Answers to exercise 1

❶ My sister knows a nice dentist. ❷ Can you give me your address, please? ❸ What kind of book is that? ❹ Do you have [any] problems with your teeth? ❺ I have known him for about three years.

❺ Unfortunately I do not know your brother.
Leider kenne ich ..... Bruder nicht.

❻ Can you give me your telephone number, please?
...... Sie ... bitte Ihre Telefonnummer geben?

Answers to exercise 2

❶ – Kopfschmerzen ❷ – nett ❸ – ihn – fünf – ❹ – meinen – ❺ – Ihren – ❻ Können – mir –

18 Achtzehnte Lektion

Das Verbot

1 – Halt! Hier d**ü**rfen ① Sie nicht p**a**rken! (N.2)
2 – Oh, das tut mir leid; **a**ber ich bin in fünf Min**u**ten zur**ü**ck.
3 – Nein! Hier ist P**a**rkverb**o**t, auch für fünf Min**u**ten.
4 – Ich weiß. **A**ber es gibt nun 'mal ② k**ei**nen **a**nderen ② P**a**rkplatz hier.
5 – H**ö**ren ③ Sie, ich diskut**ie**re nicht mit **I**hnen.
6 – S**ei**en Sie ④ doch nicht so! Ich muß nur schnell auf die Bank,
7 und die ist nur bis s**e**chzehn Uhr ge**ö**ffnet.
8 – W**ie**viel Uhr ist es jetzt?
9 – Es ist s**ie**ben Min**u**ten vor vier. (N.3)
10 – Oh, dann h**a**ben Sie nicht mehr viel Zeit.
11 M**a**chen Sie schnell!
12 – Oh, v**ie**len Dank! Sie sind w**i**rklich süß!
13 Ich k**o**mme sof**o**rt zur**ü**ck. □

Pronunciation Key
*dass ferb**oh**t **1** halt ... d**ü**rfen ... p**a**rken **2** ... tsoo-r**ü**kk **4** ... ess gipt ... p**a**rkplats ... **5** ... disskoot**ee**re ... **7** ... ge-**e**rffnett **10** ... mehr ... **11** ... shnell **12** züss*

Notes

① Please note that **dürfen** is used to convey an interdiction here. When used in an affirmative sentence, it expresses the permission to do something: **Ich darf bis um 10 Uhr fernsehen**, *I may watch TV until 10 o'clock.* ▸

The Prohibition

1 – Stop! You must not park here!
2 – Oh, I am sorry; but I will be back in five minutes.
3 – No! No parking here *(here is park prohibition)*, even *(also)* for five minutes.
4 – I know. But there is no other parking space *(m.)*.
5 – Listen, I am not going to argue with you.
6 – Don't be like that! I just have to go *(quickly)* to the bank *(f.)*,
7 and it is only open until 4 p.m. *(sixteen hours)*.
8 – What time is it now?
9 – It is seven minutes to four.
10 – Oh, then you don't have much time *(f.)* [left].
11 Hurry up!
12 – Oh, thank you very much! You are really sweet!
13 I will be back immediatly.

▸ ② **nun 'mal** is used when the speaker knows that he is wrong, but he can't or doesn't want to act in another way: **Ich darf das Auto meiner Schwester nicht benutzen; aber ich muß nun 'mal um 4 Uhr in Frankfurt sein**, *I must not use my sister's car; but I have to be in Frankfurt at 4 o'clock*. **Der**, **die**, **das andere**, *the other* (m., f., n.) is declined like an adjective.

③ **Hören** means *to hear* and *to listen to*. **Ich höre Radio**, *I listen to the radio*. **Er hört nichts**, *He does not hear anything*.

④ **Seien Sie**… (from the verb **sein**, *to be*) is the imperative form of the formal way of addressing somebody. The imperative of the second person singular is: **sei**…, *be*.

18 **Übung 1 – Übersetzen Sie bitte**

❶ Sie dürfen hier nicht rauchen! ❷ Hier ist Rauchen verboten. ❸ Es gibt hier viele Parkplätze. ❹ Ich muß schnell machen. ❺ Ich habe nicht mehr viel Zeit. ❻ Die Post ist bis achtzehn Uhr geöffnet.

Übung 2 – Ergänzen Sie bitte

❶ You must not telephone here!
Hier . . . . . . Sie nicht telefonieren!

❷ The bank closes in three minutes. Hurry up!
Die Bank schließt . . . . . . Minuten. Mach . . . .

❸ It is ten to eight.
Es ist . . . . acht.

❹ She is really very nice.
Sie ist . . . . sehr nett.

❺ My mother will be back immediately.
Meine Mutter kommt sofort . . . .

❻ The supermarket is open from 9 a.m. to 6 p.m.
Der Supermarkt ist . . . neun Uhr . . . achtzehn Uhr geöffnet.

Answers to exercise 1

❶ You must not smoke here! ❷ No smoking here *(smoking is forbidden here)*. ❸ There are many parking spaces here. ❹ I must hurry up *(to make quickly)*. ❺ I don't have much time [left]. ❻ The post-office is open until 6 p.m.

Answers to exercise 2

❶ – dürfen – ❷ – in drei – schnell ❸ – zehn vor – ❹ – wirklich – ❺ – zurück ❻ – von – bis –

19 Neunzehnte Lektion

Mögen Sie Würstchen ①?

1 – Hallo, Mutti! Ich habe einen Bärenhunger ②.
2 Was essen wir heute mittag?
3 – Es gibt Frankfurter ③ Würstchen und Kartoffelsalat.
4 – Och, schon wieder! Ich mag keinen Kartoffelsalat. (N.2)
5 – Dann ißt ④ du deine Würstchen eben ohne Kartoffelsalat.
6 – Aber mit Senf!
7 – Wie du willst, mit oder ohne Senf.
8 – Kann ich vielleicht Reis haben?
9 – Ja, aber du mußt ihn dir selbst ⑤ kochen.
10 – Gut, ich mache ihn selbst. Willst du auch Reis?
11 – Ja, gern. Das ist eine gute ⑥ Idee.
12 Und wir essen den Kartoffelsalat morgen.
13 – Oh nein, nur das nicht!

Pronunciation Key

mergen...vürst-çhen ***1****...bairen-hoonger* ***2****...mittak* ***3****...kartoffel-zalat* ***4*** *... mak ...* ***5*** *... isst ... ohne ...* ***6*** *... zennf* ***8*** *... rice ...* ***9*** *... zelpst kocHen...*

Notes

① **die Wurst**, **die Würste**, *the sausage*, *the sausages.* **Das Würstchen**, *small sausage*, **-chen** is a diminutive ending. Nouns ending in **-chen** or **-lein** (another diminutive) always have a neuter gender. That's why we say **das Mädchen**, *the girl*; **das Fräulein**, *Miss* (an unmarried lady).

Nineteenth Lesson 19

Do You Like Small Sausages?

1 – Hello, Mummy! I could eat a horse *(I have a hunger [m.] of a bear)*.
2 What are we having for lunch today? *(What do we eat today noon?)*
3 – We are having frankfurters and potato salad *(m.)*.
4 – Oh, again! I don't like potato salad.
5 – Then you just eat your sausages without potato salad.
6 – But with mustard *(m.)*!
7 – As you like *(want to)*, with or without mustard.
8 – May I have some rice *(m.)*, then *(perhaps)*?
9 – Yes but you must do *(cook)* it yourself.
10 – Well, I will do it myself. Do you also want [some] rice?
11 – Yes, I'd love some. That is a good idea.
12 And we will eat the potato salad tomorrow.
13 – Oh no, certainly not *(only not that)*! □

② **der Bär**, **die Bären**, *the bear, the bears.*

③ Names of towns used as adjectives end in **-er**. **Die Frankfurter Würstchen**; **die Frankfurter Universität**, *Frankfurt University*, **das Berliner Theater**, *the Berlin Theater.*

④ **essen**, *to eat*, is an irregular verb: **ich esse**, **du ißt**, **er ißt**.

⑤ **selbst** or **selber**, *self*, is used to mean the fact of doing something oneself. **Er kann das selbst machen**, *He can do it himself.* Please note that we do not repeat the personal pronoun (himself) in German.

⑥ Remember that qualifying adjectives (adjectives which precede a noun) are declined: **Eine Idee ist gut**, *An idea is good*; but: **Das ist eine gute Idee**, *That's a good idea.*

20 **Übung 1 – Übersetzen Sie bitte**

❶ Ich mag keinen Tee. ❷ Was gibt es heute mittag zu essen? ❸ Es gibt Omelett und Salat. ❹ Viele Leute gehen in die Hamburger Oper. ❺ Das kannst du selbst machen.

Übung 2 – Ergänzen Sie bitte

❶ He eats his sausages without mustard.
Er . . . seine Würstchen ohne Senf.

❷ Do you like your boss?
. . . . . du deinen Chef gern?

❸ This lunchtime *(today at noon)* I will go to the canteen.
Heute . . . . . . gehe ich in die Kantine.

❹ Do you drink coffee with sugar?
. . . . du den Kaffee . . . Zucker?

❺ That is a good idea.
Das ist eine . . . . Idee.

❻ Don't you want any potato salad?
. . . . . . du . . . . . . Kartoffelsalat?

20 Zwanzigste Lektion

Wo ist der Bahnhof?

1 – Weißt du, wo der Bahnhof ist?
2 – Keine Ahnung ①. Wir müssen fragen.
3 Entschuldigen Sie bitte, wo…

Pronunciation Key
*Voh ist der bahn-hohf **2** … ahnoong … **3** ennt'shooldigen …*

Answers to exercise 1
❶ I don't like tea. ❷ What are we having for lunch today? ❸ We're having omelet and salad. ❹ Many people go to the Hamburg Opera. ❺ You can do it by yourself.

Answers to exercise 2
❶ – ißt – ❷ Magst – ❸ – mittag – ❹ Trinkst – mit – ❺ – gute – ❻ Willst – keinen –

20th Lesson 20

Where is The Station *(m.)*?

1 – Do you know where the station is?
2 – No idea *(f.)*. We must ask.
3 Excuse [me], please, where…

Note

① **die Ahnung**, *the idea* (remember that nouns ending in **-ung** are always feminine): **Ich habe keine Ahnung**, *I have no idea.*

4 – Die L**eu**te h**a**ben **a**lle k**ei**ne Zeit.
5 – W**a**rte, ich h**a**be **ei**ne Id**ee**. Dort ist ein Hot**e**l. Ich bin gleich zur**ü**ck.

6 – G**u**ten **A**bend! H**a**ben Sie ein Z**i**mmer ② frei?
7 – S**i**cherlich, mein Herr. M**ö**chten Sie ein D**o**ppelz**i**mmer **o**der ein **Ei**nzelz**i**mmer?
8 – Ein Z**i**mmer für sechs Pers**o**nen, b**i**tte.
9 – Wie b**i**tte? Wie v**ie**le ③ Pers**o**nen? Sechs Pers**o**nen?
10 Dann n**e**hmen Sie doch gleich **ei**nen L**ie**gew**a**gen ④. Dort h**a**ben Sie sechs Pl**ä**tze.
11 – Ah, ja. Das ist **ei**ne g**u**te Id**ee**. K**ö**nnen Sie mir b**i**tte s**a**gen, wo der B**a**hnhof ist?
12 – Sie f**a**hren die **e**rste Str**a**ße links ⑤ und dann die zw**ei**te rechts ⑤, und Sie s**e**hen den B**a**hnhof gleich gegen**ü**ber.
13 – D**a**nke schön! Auf W**ie**ders**e**hen! □

5 *… gliçhe …* **6** *… tsimmer fry* **7** *ziçherliçh … ine-tsel'tsimmer*
10 *… leegevahgen …* **12** *lingkss … reçhts … gegenübeer…*

Notes

② **das Zimmer**, *the room*. Plural: **die Zimmer**. Nouns ending in **-er** do not change in the plural form.

③ **Wieviel**, *how much*, is declined in the plural like **viele**, *many* (see lesson 8) and is written in two words: **Wie viele Brüder hast du?**, *How many brothers do you have?* ▸

4 – *(The)* people *(all)* have no time.
5 – Wait, I have an idea. There is a hotel. I'll be back at once.

6 – Good evening! Do you have a room *(n.) (free)*?
7 – Certainly, sir. Would you like a double room or a single room?
8 – A room for six persons *(f.)*, please.
9 – What *(How please)?* How many persons? Six persons?
10 Take a couchette *(m.)* in that case; there are six places.
11 – Oh, yes. That is a good idea. Can you tell me where the station is, please?
12 – You take *(go)* the first street [on the] left and the second [on the] right, and you'll see the station just across the street.
13 – Thank you very much! Goodbye! □

DIE LEUTE HABEN ALLE KEINE ZEIT

▸ ④ **der Wagen**, *the car*; **liegen**, *to lie*; **der Speisewagen**, *the dining car.*

⑤ **links**, *on the left*; **rechts**, *on the right*. There is no preposition in German: **Das Hotel ist rechts und die Post links**, *The hotel is on the right and the post-office on the left.*

Übung 1 – Übersetzen Sie bitte

❶ Wollen Sie ein Doppelzimmer oder ein Einzelzimmer? ❷ Ein Zimmer für zwei Personen, bitte. ❸ Ich weiß nicht, wo meine Tante wohnt. ❹ Sie weiß nicht, wo ihre Tante wohnt. ❺ Wie viele Leute wohnen hier? ❻ Wir müssen fragen, wieviel Uhr es ist.

Übung 2 – Ergänzen Sie bitte

❶ Excuse [me], do you know what time it is?
. . . . Sie, wissen Sie . . . . Uhr es ist?

❷ I would like a double room for one night, please.
Ich möchte bitte ein . . . . für eine Nacht.

❸ Can you tell me where there is a hotel?
. . . . . . Sie mir sagen, . . ein Hotel ist?

❹ The first street on the left and then always straight on.
Die erste Straße . . . . . und dann . . . . . geradeaus.

21 Einundzwanzigste Lektion

Wiederholung und Erklärungen

1 Declension in German

Little by little we have made you familiar with German **declensions**. Remember that the article, the ending of the qualifying adjective and sometimes the ending of the noun itself depend on the case of the noun. Up to now we have seen the **nominative** (subject) and the **accusative** (object) cases of the noun.

Answers to exercise 1

❶ Do you want a double room or a single room? ❷ A room for two persons please. ❸ I don't know where my aunt lives. ❹ She doesn't know where her aunt lives. ❺ How many people live here? ❻ We must ask what time it is.

❺ Good evening! Do you have a room *(free)*?
Guten . . . . . ! Haben Sie ein Zimmer . . . . ?

❻ Wait! We will come immediately!
. . . . . . Sie! Wir kommen . . . . . . !

Answers to exercise 2

❶ Entschuldigen – wieviel – ❷ – Doppelzimmer – ❸ Können – wo – ❹ – links – immer – ❺ – Abend – frei ❻ Warten – gleich (sofort)

21st Lesson 21

Der Mann dort ist mein Bruder, *The man over there is my brother.*
Der Mann is the subject/nominative of the sentence.
Ich trinke den Tee mit Zucker, *I drink tea with sugar.*
Den Tee is the object/accusative of the sentence.
The accusative singular of the masculine article is: **der** → **den**; **ein** → **einen**.
The feminine, the neuter and the plural of all genders do not change in the accusative: feminine: **die/eine**; neuter: **das/ein**; plural: **die**.

21 The accusative of the indefinite negative article **kein**:
Ich habe keinen Hunger (m.), *I am not hungry.*
Ich habe keine Zeit (f.), *I have no time.*
Ich habe kein Geld (n.), *I have no money.*
Ich mag keine Tomaten, *I don't like tomatoes.*
You will find a complete list of the declension in the next revision section.

2 Auxiliary Verbs

The following verbs are called auxiliary verbs: **müssen**, *must, to have to*; **sollen**, *to be to, shall*; **wollen**, *to want*; **können**, *can*; **dürfen**, *may.*
They all belong to the same group and have some features in common: (I.) The third person of the present tense singular does not end in **-t**. (II.) The infinitive following one of these verbs is placed at the end of the sentence.

Here are the conjugations and some examples:

2.1 *Müssen*

ich muß, du mußt, er/sie/es muß, wir müssen, ihr müßt, sie/Sie müssen.
sollen: ich soll, du sollst, er/sie/es soll, wir sollen, ihr sollt, sie/Sie sollen.
Müssen and **sollen** express obligation or necessity; **sollen** is used when the obligation is imposed by someone else, as in *to have to* in English. Incidentally you might recognize our word *shall* in **sollen**.
Er soll um acht Uhr zurückkommen, *He has to be back at eight o'clock.* Or: *He is to be back…*
Müssen implies necessity or obligation imposed by circumstances or the person itself, like our *must* (which derives from **müssen**).
Ich muß morgen arbeiten, *I must work tomorrow.*

2.2 *Können, dürfen*

ich kann, du kannst, er/sie/es kann, wir können, ihr könnt, sie/Sie können.

dürfen: ich darf, du darfst, er/sie/es darf, wir dürfen, ihr dürft, sie/Sie dürfen.

Whereas **können** depends on our own capacity to do something, **dürfen** depends on the authorization of someone else.
Ich kann heute abend nicht kommen, *I cannot come tonight*, (i.e. I have something else to do).
Sie darf heute abend nicht kommen, *She cannot* (is not allowed to) *come tonight*.

2.3 *Wollen, mögen*

ich will, du willst, er/sie/es will, wir wollen, ihr wollt, sie/Sie wollen.

mögen: ich mag, du magst, er/sie/es mag, wir mögen, ihr mögt, sie/Sie mögen.
Willst du nach Deutschland fahren?, *Do you want to go to Germany?*
Magst du Kartoffelsalat?, *Do you like potato salad?*
Ich möchte, du möchtest, er/sie/es möchte, wir möchten,... are the forms of the subjunctive of **mögen**.
Möchtest du nach Deutschland fahren?, *Would you like to go to Germany?* When English uses the conditional (would + infinitive), German uses the subjunctive. You are not supposed to know all this by heart, we just try to answer the questions you may ask yourself.

3 Time

Wieviel Uhr ist es? or **Wie spät ist es?**, *What time is it?*
Example:
Es ist fünf Minuten nach drei, *It is five (minutes) past three.*
Es ist zehn Minuten vor acht, *It is ten (minutes) to eight.*
Es ist vier (Uhr) or **Es ist sechzehn Uhr**.
Es ist fünfzehn Minuten nach sechs or **Es ist viertel nach sechs**. (It's not necessary to add **Uhr**).
Es ist zwanzig Minuten vor drei (Uhr) or **Es ist zwei Uhr vierzig**.
Es ist fünfzehn Minuten vor eins (ein Uhr) or **Es ist viertel vor eins**. (Notice: **eins** with **-s**; we say **eins**, but **ein Uhr**).
Es ist acht Uhr dreißig or **Es ist halb (half) neun**.

Say the following in German (the answers are at the end of the lesson):
6.30 a.m.; 9.45 a.m.; 5.10 p.m.; 8.50 a.m.; 1.20 a.m.; 1.45 p.m.; 4.30 a.m.

21 4 Die Zahlen

0 null *nooll*
1 eins *ine-ss*
2 zwei *tsvy*
3 drei *dry*
4 vier *feer*
5 fünf *fünf*
6 sechs *zeks*
7 sieben *zeeben*
8 acht *acHt*
9 neun *noyn*
10 zehn *tsehn*
11 elf *ellf*
12 zwölf *tsverlf*
13 dreizehn
14 vierzehn
15 fünfzehn
16 sechzehn
17 siebzehn
18 achtzehn
19 neunzehn
20 zwanzig *tsvanntsich*

21 einundzwanzig
22 zweiundzwanzig
23 dreiundzwanzig
24 vierundzwanzig
25 fünfundzwanzig
26 sechsundzwanzig
27 siebenundzwanzig
28 achtundzwanzig
29 neunundzwanzig
30 dreißig *draïssiçh*
40 vierzig *fîrtsiçh*
50 fünfzig *funnftsiçh*
60 sechzig *zeçh'tsiçh*
70 siebzig
80 achtzig
90 neunzig
100 hundert
101 hunderteins
102 hundertzwei
1.000 tausend *taouzënnt*
1.001 tausendeins

2.244 zweitausendzweihundertvierundvierzig
1.000.000 eine Million

Answer Key to Paragraph 3

6.30 a.m.	**Es ist halb sieben.**
	Es ist sechs Uhr dreißig.
9.45 a.m.	**Es ist viertel vor zehn.**
	Es ist neun Uhr fünfundvierzig.
5.10 p.m.	**Es ist zehn (Minuten) nach fünf.**
	Es ist siebzehn Uhr zehn.
8.50 a.m.	**Es ist zehn (Minuten) vor neun.**
	Es ist acht Uhr fünfzig.
1.20 a.m.	**Es ist zwanzig (Minuten) nach eins.**
	Es ist ein Uhr zwanzig.
1.45 p.m.	**Es ist viertel vor zwei.**
	Es ist dreizehn Uhr fünfundvierzig.
4.30 a.m.	**Es ist halb fünf.**
	Es ist vier Uhr dreißig.

22 Zweiundzwanzigste Lektion

Eine schöne Wohnung

1 – Doch, doch ich s**a**ge **I**hnen, die W**o**hnung ist sehr schön und groß: vier Z**i**mmer, K**ü**che und Bad.
2 – Und r**u**hig? Ist sie auch w**i**rklich r**u**hig?
3 – Ja, **au**ßergew**ö**hnlich r**u**hig. K**ei**ne K**i**nder ①, k**ei**ne H**u**nde ①...
4 – Gut! Wann k**ö**nnen Sie mir ② die W**o**hnung z**ei**gen?
5 – Paßt **I**hnen ③ m**o**rgen um halb elf?
6 – Ja, das paßt mir.

7 – Gef**ä**llt ④ **I**hnen die W**o**hnung?
8 – Oh, ja. Sie gef**ä**llt mir sehr gut.

Pronunciation Key
i-ne sherne Vohnoong ***1*** *... küçhe ... baht* ***2*** *... roohiçh ...* ***3*** *... owsser-gevernliçh ... hoonde* ***4*** *... tsygen* ***5*** *passt ...* ***7*** *gefaillt ...*

Notes

① **das Kind**, **die Kinder**, *the child, children*; **der Hund**, **die Hunde**, *the dog, dogs*. Remember that there are different plural endings in German. Learn each noun with its article and its plural.

② **mir**, *(to) me*. This is the indirect object or the dative of the sentence. To identify the indirect object in a sentence, you need to ask the question "to whom". ▸

A Nice Flat *(f.)*

1 – Of course, I assure you, the flat is very nice and big: four rooms, kitchen *(f.)* and bath[room] *(n.)*.
2 – And calm? Is it really calm?
3 – Yes, extraordinarily calm. No children, no dogs…
4 – Fine! When can you show me the flat *(to me)*?
5 – Does half past ten tomorrow suit you?
6 – Yes, that suits me.

7 – Do you like the flat?
8 – Oh, yes, I like it very much *(she pleases to me very much)*.

③ **Ihnen**, *(to) you*, is the dative of the personal pronoun **Sie**, *you*. Remember that it is only the capital **S** which differs from the third person plural. Therefore **ihnen** means *(to) them*. **Das paßt ihnen**, *That suits them*. But: **Das paßt Ihnen?**, *That suits you?*

④ **gefallen**, *to like, to please*. **Gefallen** is always followed by the dative. **Ich gefalle, du gefällst, er/sie/es gefällt**.

9 – Gut! Dann gehen wir in mein Büro und erledigen sofort die Formalitäten.
10 – Warten Sie! Ich muß die Wohnung zuerst meinem Mann ⑤ zeigen.
11 – Ach so? Sie sind verheiratet?
12 Sagen Sie, haben Sie auch Kinder?
13 – Ja, sieben kleine Kinder. Aber wissen Sie, meine Kinder sind sehr musikalisch und hassen Lärm.

*9 … erledigen … formalitaiten **10** … tsoo-erst … **11** … fer-hy-ratet **13** … moozikalish … hassen Lairm*

***

Übung 1 – Übersetzen Sie bitte

❶ Ihre Wohnung gefällt mir sehr. ❷ Zeigen Sie mir bitte Ihre Fotos! ❸ Sie gibt dem Mann ihre Telefonnummer. ❹ Er ist verheiratet und hat zwei Kinder. ❺ Gefallen Ihnen meine Hunde?

Übung 2 – Ergänzen Sie bitte

❶ Do you like my car?
Gefällt . . . . . mein Wagen?

❷ He shows his brother his camera *(… to his brother)*.
Er zeigt . . . . . . Bruder . . . . . . Fotoapparat.

❸ Give me a kilo of tomatoes, please.
Geben Sie . . . bitte ein Kilo Tomaten!

❹ No, that does not suit me.
Nein, das . . . . nicht.

9 – Fine! Then let's go to my office to *(and)* settle the formalities at once.
10 – Wait! I must show the flat to my husband first.
11 – Oh, I see! You are married?
12 Tell me, do you also have children?
13 – Yes, seven little children. But you know, my children have a talent for music and they hate noise *(m.)*. □

Note

⑤ **meinem Mann**, *to my husband*, is the dative of **mein Mann**, *my husband*. Whereas the accusative of the masculine gender ends in **-n** or **-en**, the **dative** ends in **-m** or **-em**: **Sie zeigt dem Freund ihre Wohnung**, *She shows her flat to her friend*. **Er zeigt seinem Vater seine Wohnung**, *He shows his flat to his father*.

***

Answers to exercise 1

❶ I like your flat very much. ❷ Show me your photos, please! ❸ She gives the man her telephone number *(... to the man)*. ❹ He is married and has two children. ❺ Do you like my dogs?

❺ I hate noise and dogs.
Ich . . . . . Lärm und Hunde.

❻ They like your photos very much.
Deine Fotos . . . . sehr gut.

Answers to exercise 2

❶ – Ihnen – ❷ – seinem – seinen – ❸ – mir – ❹ – paßt mir – ❺ – hasse – ❻ – gefallen ihnen –

23 Dreiundzwanzigste Lektion

Schwierige Gäste ①

1 T**a**nte Math**i**lde und ihr Mann verbr**i**ngen **ei**ne W**o**che bei ② **i**hrer N**i**chte **A**nne.
2 Sie sind schon **e**twas alt und h**a**ben **i**hre Gew**o**hnheiten ③.
3 – **A**nne, der K**a**ffee ist zu stark für ④ mich.
4 – Oh, das tut mir leid. Nimm viell**ei**cht etwas Milch!
5 – Nein, ich tr**i**nke K**a**ffee n**ie**mals mit Milch.
6 Was m**a**chen wir h**eu**te n**a**chmittag?
7 – Wollt ihr ⑤ die Stadt **a**nsehen?
8 Ich kann euch ⑥ die **A**ltstadt z**ei**gen.

Pronunciation Key
shveerige Gaiste ***1*** *… ferbringen … vocHe … niçhte …* ***2*** *… etvass … ge-vohn-hy-ten* ***3*** *… shtark … miçh* ***4*** *… milçh* ***5*** *… nee-mals …* ***6*** *… nacHmittak* ***7*** *… ann-zehen* ***8*** *… oyçh …*

Notes

① **der Gast, die Gäste**, *the guest, guests.*

② The proposition **bei** is always followed by the dative: **bei meinem Vater**, *at my father's, with my father.*
The dative of the feminine gender ends in **-r** or **-er**: **Ich zeige der Frau das Hotel**, *I show the woman the hotel (... to the woman).* **Gehört das Buch ihrer Frau?**, *Does the book belong to your wife?*

③ **die Gewohnheit**, *the habit*; nouns ending in **-heit**, **-keit** or **-ung** are always feminine. Plural: **-en**. But: **Ich habe meine Gewohnheiten**, *I am set in my ways.* ▸

Difficult Guests *(m.)*

1 Aunt Mathilde and her husband are spending one week *(f.)* with their niece *(f.)* Anne.
2 They are already quite old and set in their ways *(have their habits)*.
3 – Anne, the coffee *(m.)* is too strong for me.
4 – Oh, I am sorry. Maybe you [should] take some *(a bit)* milk *(f.)*.
5 – No, I never drink coffee with milk.
6 What are we doing *(today)* this afternoon?
7 – Do you want to visit *(to look at)* the town?
8 I can show you the old part of the town *(old town)*.

SIE SIND SCHON ETWAS ALT UND HABEN IHRE GEWOHNHEITEN

④ The preposition **für**, *for*, is always followed by the accusative: **Das Buch ist für meinen Bruder**, *The book is for my brother.* **Die Schokolade ist nicht für dich**, *The chocolate is not for you*.

⑤ **ihr**, *you*, is the plural of **du**, *you*. The ending of the verb is **-t**: **ihr kommt**, *you come*; **ihr habt**, *you have;* exception: **ihr seid**, *you are*.

⑥ **euch**, *you*, is both dative/accusative of the personal pronoun **ihr**. **Ich sehe euch morgen** (acc.), *I'll see you tomorrow.* **Er zeigt euch Paris** (dat.), *He shows you Paris.*

23

9 – Nein, h**eu**te ist D**o**nnerstag. Wir g**e**hen nur s**o**nntags ⑦ in die Stadt.

10 – Ja, **a**ber ihr seid in **U**rlaub.

11 – Das **ä**ndert nichts. Ich g**e**he mit Math**i**lde nur s**o**nntags in die Stadt, denn s**o**nntags sind die Gesch**ä**fte ⑧ geschl**o**ssen. □

9 *... donners-tak ... sonntaks ...* ***10*** *... zyte ...* ***11*** *... geshaifte ...*

Notes

⑦ **der Sonntag**, *Sunday*; **sonntags**, *on Sundays*, i.e. every Sunday. **Sonntags gehe ich tanzen**, *On Sundays I go dancing.* ▸

***

Übung 1 – Übersetzen Sie bitte

❶ Anne geht mit ihrer Schwester ins Kino. ❷ Ihr Freund Klaus kommt auch mit. ❸ Sie zeigt ihnen die Altstadt. ❹ Gefällt euch die neue Wohnung? ❺ Habt ihr nur sonntags Zeit? ❻ Warum kommt ihr nicht Donnerstagabend?

Übung 2 – Ergänzen Sie bitte

❶ Anne shows *(to)* her aunt and her uncle the old part of the town.
Anne zeigt ..... Tante und ..... Onkel die Altstadt.

❷ The coffee is for me, and the tea is for you.
Der Kaffee ist für .... und der Tee ist für ..... .

❸ On Thursday, I will go to *(in the)* town with them.
Am .... gehe ich mit ..... in die Stadt.

9 – No, today is Thursday. We only go to town [on] Sundays. **23**

10 – Yes, but you are on *(in)* holiday.

11 – That doesn't change anything. With Mathilde I only go to town [on] Sundays, because [on] Sundays the shops are closed. □

▸ As well: **morgens**, **abends**, **mittags**..., *every morning, every evening, every noon...*

⑧ **das Geschäft, die Geschäfte**, *the shop, shops* or *the business*: **der Geschäftsmann**, *the businessman.*

***

Answers to exercise 1

❶ Anne goes to the cinema with her sister. ❷ Her friend Klaus also comes *(with)*. ❸ She shows them the old part of the town. ❹ Do you like the new flat? ❺ Are you only free on Sundays? ❻ Why don't you come on Thursday evening?

❹ Tell me, do you like my new car?

Sagen Sie, gefällt ..... mein neuer Wagen?

❺ Are you free tomorrow *(have you time)*? I can meet you tomorrow.

.... ihr morgen Zeit? Ich kann .... morgen treffen.

❻ The shops are closed on Sundays.

Die Geschäfte sind ....

Answers to exercise 2

❶ – ihrer – ihrem – ❷ – mich – dich ❸ – Donnerstag – ihnen – ❹ – Ihnen – ❺ Habt – euch – ❻ – sonntags geschlossen

24 Vierundzwanzigste Lektion

Verstehen Sie das?

1 – Wann fährt der n**ä**chste Zug nach M**ü**nchen, b**i**tte?
2 – In zehn Min**u**ten, Gleis f**ü**nfzehn.
3 – Das ist zu früh. Ich muß noch m**ei**nem ① H**ü**ndchen W**a**sser g**e**ben.
4 – Das k**ö**nnen Sie doch im ② Zug m**a**chen.
5 – Unm**ö**glich! Das ist kein Tr**i**nkwasser!
6 – Dann k**ö**nnen Sie **ei**ne St**u**nde sp**ä**ter **a**bfahren, um 14 Uhr 27; **a**ber da m**ü**ssen Sie in St**u**ttgart **u**msteigen.
7 – Nein, ich will nicht **u**msteigen. P**u**tzi vertr**ä**gt das nicht.
8 – G**e**ben Sie dem H**ü**ndchen doch **ei**ne Schl**a**ftabl**e**tte!
9 – Was hat **I**hnen denn mein Hund get**a**n ③?
10 – Schon gut, schon gut. Dann n**e**hmen Sie den Interc**i**ty…
11 Der fährt ④ um 15 Uhr 20 ab ④ und kommt um 20 Uhr 45 in M**ü**nchen an.

Pronunciation Key
1 *... münçh<u>e</u>n ... **2** ... glise ... **3** ... my-n<u>e</u>m hünt-çh<u>e</u>n vass<u>e</u>r ... **5** oon-merkliçh! **6** ... shtoott-gart **oo**mm-shty-g<u>e</u>n **7** ... fertraikt ... **9** ... ge-tahn*

Notes

① The dative of the neuter is the same as the masculine: **Die Mutter gibt ihrem Kind ein Glas Milch**, *The mother gives* ▸

Do You Understand That?

1 – When is the next train leaving for Munich, please?
2 – In ten minutes, platform *(n.)* 15.
3 – That is too early. I must give some water *(n.)* to my little dog *(n.)*.
4 – You can do that in the train, can't you?
5 – Impossible! That's not drinking water!
6 – You can leave an hour later, then, at 2.27 p.m.; but in that case you must change at Stuttgart.
7 – No, I don't want to change. Putzi can't *(doesn't)* bear that.
8 – Why don't you give a sleeping pill *(f.)* to the little dog? *(So, give this little dog a sleeping pill)*.
9 – What [on earth] has my dog done to you?
10 – It's alright, it's alright *(already well)*. Take the inter-city then.
11 It leaves at 3.20 p.m. and arrives in Munich at 8.45 p.m.

▸ *her child a glass of milk*. **Der Ball gehört dem Kind**, *The ball belongs to the child.*

② **im** is the contraction of **in dem**.

③ **getan** is the past participle of **tun**, *to do*.

④ **abfahren**, *to leave*; **ankommen**, *to arrive*. **Ab** and **an** are prefixes which are placed at the end of the sentence when the verb is conjugated: **Ich fahre ab**, *I leave*. **Er kommt um fünf Uhr an**, *He arrives at five o'clock*. In the infinitive the stress is on the prefix.

24 **12** – Oh nein. Das ist zu spät.
13 – Wissen Sie 'was ⑤, ich gehe jetzt mittagessen. Kommen ⑥ Sie, wenn Sie wollen, in einer Stunde wieder ⑥!
14 – Das haben wir gut gemacht, was Putzi? Und der Schaffner weiß nicht einmal, daß ⑦ wir eigentlich nach Hamburg fahren! □

***14** ... ge-macHt ... shaffner ... **i**-gentliçh ...*

Notes

⑤ **was** stands for **etwas**. When used as an adverb, it means: *a bit*. **Er ist etwas müde**, *He is a bit tired.*

⑥ **wiederkommen**, *to come back*. **Wieder** is another **separable prefix**: **Ich komme sofort wieder**, *I come back at once.*

⑦ **daß**, *that*, is a conjunction. Please note the spelling! In subordinate clauses with **daß** the verb is **always** placed at the **end** of the sentence: **Er sagt, daß er morgen kommt**, *He says that he'll come tomorrow.* Principal clause and subordinate clause are separated by a comma.

***

Übung 1 – Übersetzen Sie bitte

❶ Mein Zug fährt um sechzehn Uhr ab. ❷ Ich muß in Frankfurt umsteigen. ❸ Der Zug aus Frankfurt kommt um zwölf Uhr sechs an. ❹ Sie sagt, daß sie nach München fährt. ❺ Wohin wollen Sie eigentlich fahren? ❻ Um wieviel Uhr kommen Sie wieder?

12 – Oh no. That is too late.
13 – I tell you what *(you know something)*, I'll have lunch now. Come back in an hour, if you want to!
14 – We did a good job, didn't we Putzi? And the conductor *(m.)* doesn't even know that actually we are going to Hamburg! □

***

Answers to exercise 1

❶ My train leaves at 4 p.m. ❷ I must change at Frankfurt. ❸ The train from Frankfurt arrives at 12.06. ❹ She says that she is going to Munich. ❺ Where do you actually want to go? ❻ What time do you come back?

25 Übung 2 – Stellen Sie bitte die Fragen
Exercise 2 – Ask the questions please

❶ . . . . Berlin . . ? Der Zug nach Berlin fährt um 15 Uhr 35 ab.

❷ . . . . Berlin . . ? Er kommt um 22 Uhr 15 in Berlin an.

❸ . . . . ? Nein, Sie müssen nicht umsteigen.

❹ . . . . ? Ich will nach Stuttgart fahren.

---

25 Fünfundzwanzigste Lektion

Ein wahrer ① Schatz

1 – Guten **A**bend, Li**e**bling! Warum bist du noch im Bett?
2 Bist du krank?
3 – Nein! Es geht mir ② sehr gut. **A**ber mein Krimi ist so spannend!
4 Hol dir 'was zum **E**ssen aus dem ③ K**ü**hlschrank, ja?

Pronunciation Key
... vahrer shats ***1*** *... leebling ... imm bett* ***2*** *... krang'k*
3 *... shpannent* ***4*** *... kühl-shrang'k ...*

Notes

① You remember: definite article plus qualifying adjective: **der große Mann**, *the tall man*; **die große Frau**, *the tall woman*; ▸

❺ . . . . ? Ich will morgen früh fahren.

❻ . . . . ? Nein, ich fahre mit meinem Sohn.

❼ . . . . Uhr . . . . ? Ich komme um acht Uhr zurück.

Answers to exercise 2

❶ Wann fährt der Zug nach – ab ❷ Wann kommt er in – an ❸ Muß ich umsteigen ❹ Wohin wollen Sie fahren ❺ Wann wollen Sie fahren ❻ Fahren Sie allein ❼ Um wieviel – kommen Sie zurück

25th Lesson 25

A Real Darling

1 – Good evening, dear! Why are you still in bed *(n.)*?
2 Are you ill?
3 – No! I am very well. But my detective story is so exciting!
4 Fetch yourself something to eat from the refrigerator *(m.)*, will you?

▸ **das kleine Kind**, *the little child.* When the indefinite article precedes the noun, the endings are: **ein großer Mann**; **eine große Frau**; **ein kleines Kind**.

② See lesson 16 note 2.

③ **aus**, *from*; this preposition is always followed by the dative: **Ich komme aus der BRD**, *I come from West Germany.*

5 – Sag mal, weißt du, wie spät es ist? ④

6 – Nein, war**u**m?… Hör 'mal, der M**ö**rder ist nicht der G**ä**rtner, s**o**ndern ⑤…

7 – Was erz**ä**hlst du da?

stell **8** – Ja,… und stel**l** dir vor, der Br**u**der **i**hres ⑥ M**a**nnes ⑥ liebt sie auch…

9 – Du, es ist halb acht, und wir erw**a**rten 10 Pers**o**nen zum **A**bendessen!

10 – Was sagst du da? Um G**o**tteswillen, ist heute der dr**ei**zehnte?

11 – Ja, Fr**ei**tag, der dr**ei**zehnte J**a**nuar.

12 – Mein Gott, was s**o**llen wir bloß m**a**chen?

13 – Das, was wir **i**mmer m**a**chen, mein Schatz. Ich reserv**ie**re **ei**nen Tisch im Rest**au**rant und du ziehst ⑦ dich inzw**i**schen an ⑦, nicht wahr?

□

5 _zak mal … **6** … mer**d**e**r** … gairtner, zonn**d**e**r**n **7** … ertsailst … **8** … eeh**r**es mann**e**s leebt … **9** … tsehn perz**oh**nen …_

Notes

④ **Wie spät ist es?**, **Wieviel Uhr ist es?**, _What time is it?_

⑤ **sondern**, _but_; it is only used after a negative sentence.

⑥ The genitive, the fourth case of the declension. It corresponds to the English possessive. In English you say: _the child's father_ or _the father of the child_. In German: **der Vater des Kindes**; _the dog of my brother_, **der Hund meines Bruders**. The noun which follows "of" is in the genitive form. The masculine and the neuter end in **-es** or **-s** and the feminine in **-r** or **-er**. **Die Tasche meiner Tante**, _my aunt's bag_.

⑦ **sich anziehen**, _to get dressed_, is a reflexive verb: **ich ziehe mich an**, _I get dress_; **du ziehst dich an**, _you get dress…_
Please note that the prefix **an** is separable, like **sich vor/stellen**, _to imagine_.

5 – Tell me, do you know what time it is?
6 – No, why? Listen, the killer is not the gardener, but…
7 – What are you telling [me]?
8 – Yes… and imagine *(you)*, the brother of her husband is in love with her, too… *(loves her…)*
9 – You know that it's half past seven and we are expecting 10 persons for dinner *(n.)!*
10 – What are you telling [me]? For Heaven's sake, is it the 13th today?
11 – Yes, Friday 13th January.
12 – Good God! What on earth shall we do?
13 – What we always do, my darling. I'll book a table in a restaurant and you'll get dressed in the meantime, won't you? □

***10** … oomm **go**ttes**vi**llen … **11** … **fry**-tak … **ya**noo-ar*
***13** … ray-zer**vee**re … tseehst … diçh in-ts**vi**shen ann …*

25 **Übung 1 – Übersetzen Sie bitte**

❶ Stellen Sie sich vor, mein Bruder liebt Ihre Schwester. ❷ Anne bleibt heute im Bett, denn sie ist krank. ❸ Ich hole mir 'was zum Trinken aus dem Kühlschrank. ❹ Heute ist Donnerstag, der elfte September. ❺ Sie erwarten heute abend viele Gäste.

Übung 2 – Ergänzen Sie bitte

❶ Today is Sunday 10th October.
Heute ist . . . . der . . . . . . Oktober.

❷ My brother's wife is a real darling.
Die Frau . . . . . . Bruders ist ein wahrer Schatz.

❸ My sister's husband is my dentist.
Der Mann . . . . . . Schwester ist . . . . Zahnarzt.

❹ Your father is a handsome man.
. . . . Vater ist ein . . . . Mann.

Answers to exercise 1

❶ Imagine *(you)*, my brother loves your sister. ❷ Today Anne is staying in bed because she is ill. ❸ I'll fetch something to drink from the refrigerator. ❹ Today is Thursday 11th September. ❺ They are expecting many guests tonight.

❺ We book a table in the restaurant.
Wir reservieren . . . . . Tisch . . Restaurant.

❻ My dear, dress quickly; I've already been waiting for an hour.
Mein . . . . , zieh . . . . schnell an; ich warte schon eine . . . .

Answers to exercise 2

❶ – Sonntag, – zehnte – ❷ – meines – ❸ – meiner – mein – ❹ Dein – schöner – ❺ – einen – im – ❻ – Schatz – dich – Stunde

26 Sechsundzwanzigste Lektion

Der Hausmeister

1 – Sieh 'mal! Dort **o**ben sitzt **ei**ne kl**ei**ne K**a**tze auf dem Gar**a**gendach.
2 Die kann all**ei**n ① nicht mehr r**u**nter ②.
3 – Komm, wir h**e**lfen ihr ③!
4 – Hast du sie?
5 – Ja, sie z**i**ttert am g**a**nzen Leib und ist ganz m**a**ger.
6 – Wem ④ kann die wohl geh**ö**ren?
7 – Wahrsch**ei**nlich n**ie**mandem.
8 – Weißt du was, wir n**e**hmen sie mit nach H**au**se!
9 – W**a**rte! Paß auf! Dort steht ⑤ der H**au**smeister vor der Tür; der mag k**ei**ne K**a**tzen.

Pronunciation Key
*... h**o**wss-my-ster* ***1*** *zitst ... gar**a**shendacH* ***3*** *... h**e**lfen eehr* ***5*** *... tsi**tt**ert ... g**a**nntsen lipe ...* ***7*** *vahrsh**i**ne-liçh ...* ***9*** *... shteht ...*

Notes

① **allein**, *alone*, here it has the meaning without anybody's help.

② **runter = herunter**, *down*, it implies a verb of movement like *to go*.

③ **ihr** is the dative of **sie**, *she*. The verb **helfen**, *to help*, is always followed by the dative.

④ The interrogative pronouns are declined like the masculine article: **wem**, *to whom* = dative; **Wem zeigst du die** ▸

The Caretaker *(m.)*

1 – Look! There is a little cat *(f.)* sitting on the garage roof *(n.)*. *(Up there sits a little cat)*.
2 She cannot get down on her own *(alone)*.
3 – Come on, let's help her!
4 – Have you got her?
5 – Yes, she is trembling all over and she is all skinny.
6 – Whom can she possibly belong to?
7 – Probably to nobody.
8 – You know what? We'll take her home!
9 – Wait! Be careful! *(There)* the caretaker is standing in front of the door *(f.)*; he doesn't like cats.

▸ **Wohnung?**, *(to) Whom do you show the flat?* **Wen**, *whom/who* = accusative; **Wen liebt sie?**, *Who does she love?*

⑤ In German we specify the position of objects and persons: **stehen**, *to stand*; **liegen**, *to lie*; **sitzen**, *to sit*. **Das Glas steht auf dem Tisch**, *The glass is (stands) on the table.* **Die Zeitung liegt auf dem Stuhl**, *The newspaper is (lies) on the chair.*

26 **10** – Ach, der sieht uns nicht. Der ist mit den ⑥ Mülleimern ⑥ beschäftigt.
11 – Warte lieber! Ich gehe zu ihm ⑦ und frage ihn ⑦ etwas, und du gehst inzwischen schnell rein.
12 – Zu spät! Er hat uns schon gesehen…
13 – Jungens ⑧, denkt bloß nicht, daß das Vieh ⑨ ins Haus kommt… □

***10** … beshaiftikt **11** … inn-tsvishen … **13** yoongens … deng'kt bloss … feeh …*

Notes

⑥ **den Mülleimern** is the dative plural. The definite article is **den** and the nouns end in **-n**, or **-en**, this is true for all genders!

⑦ **ihm**, *(to) him*, is the dative of the pronoun **er**, *he*; **ihn**, *him* is the **accusative**: **Ich gebe ihm meine Telefonnummer**, *I give him my phone number*. **Sie liebt ihn**, *she loves him*.

⑧ **der Junge**, **die Jungen**, *the boy*, *boys*. **Jungens** is a colloquial way of addressing several boys.

⑨ **das Vieh**, *the cattle*; but it is also a pejorative word for *animal*.

***

Übung 1 – Übersetzen Sie bitte

❶ Er geht zu ihm und fragt ihn, wie er heißt. ❷ Wo ist dein Schlüssel? – Ich habe ihn in meiner Tasche. ❸ Der Hausmeister mag keine Katzen. ❹ Die kleine Katze sitzt auf dem Mülleimer. ❺ Gehört die Tasche Frau Meier? – Ja, sie gehört ihr.

10 – Oh, he [won't] see us. He is busy with the dustbins.

11 – You'd better wait! I'll go and see him *(I go to him)* and ask him something, and you go in there quickly in the meantime.

12 – Too late! He's already seen us.

13 – Boys, don't imagine *(believe)* that this beast *(n.)* is going to enter the house *(comes in the house)*… □

DER HAUSMEISTER MAG
KEINE KATZEN

***

Answers to exercise 1

❶ He goes towards him and asks his name. ❷ Where is your key? – It's in my pocket *(I have it in my pocket)*. ❸ The caretaker does not like cats. ❹ The little cat is sitting on the dustbin. ❺ This bag belongs to Mrs. Meier. – Yes, it belongs to her.

Übung 2 – Ergänzen Sie bitte

❶ Whom do these books belong to? – They belong to the children.
... gehören diese Bücher? – Sie gehören ... .

❷ There is *(stands)* the caretaker. We'll ask him.
Dort ..... der Hausmeister. Wir fragen .... .

❸ My mother has a lot of work. We'll help her.
Meine Mutter hat .... Arbeit. Wir helfen .... .

27 Siebenundzwanzigste Lektion

Wer soll das bezahlen ①?

1 – Trink ② dein Glas aus ②! Wir m**ü**ssen gehen!
2 – Du, Peter, ich h**a**be **i**mmer noch H**u**nger...
3 – Das gibt's doch nicht! ③ Gem**ü**sesuppe, W**ie**ner Schn**i**tzel mit Pommes Fr**i**tes und Sal**a**t und, als N**a**chtisch, Eis mit Schl**a**gsahne, und du bist **i**mmer noch nicht satt?
4 Sag 'mal, hast du viell**ei**cht einen B**a**ndwurm?

Pronunciation Key
... betsahlen ***3*** *... gemüze-zooppe, veener shnitsel ... ice ... shlakzahne ... zatt* ***4*** *... banntvoorm*

Notes

① **bezahlen** or **zahlen**, *to pay*. **Bezahlen** is used with a direct object: **Ich bezahle das Eis**, *I pay for the ice-cream.* ▸

❹ The old man sits on the bench and sleeps.
Der alte Mann ..... auf der Bank und ....

❺ Where are the bottles of wine? – In the kitchen.
.... die Weinflaschen? – In ... Küche.

❻ Where are the newspapers? – On the table.
.... die Zeitungen? – Auf ... Tisch.

Answers to exercise 2

❶ Wem – den Kindern ❷ – steht – ihn ❸ – viel – ihr ❹ – sitzt – schläft ❺ Wo stehen – der – ❻ Wo liegen – dem –

27th Lesson 27

Who Will Pay for That?

1 – Drink up *(your glass)*! We must leave *(go)*!
2 – You know, Peter, I'm still hungry *(I have hunger)...*
3 – That's not possible! Vegetable soup *(f.)*, breaded veal cutlet *(n.)* with French fries and salad, and, for dessert *(m.)*, ice-cream *(n.)* with whipped cream *(f.)* [on top], and you are not full up yet?
4 Tell me, maybe you have a tapeworm *(m.)?*

② **austrinken**, *to drink up*; **aus** as an adverb means: *finished* or *over.*

③ **es gibt** generally means *there is*. Here it is used idiomatically: **Das gibt's nicht**, *That does not exist, that's impossible.*

5 – Re**d**e k**ei**nen **U**nsinn! Best**e**ll für mich noch ein Stück **A**pfelk**u**chen, ja?
6 Ich g**e**he inzw**i**schen auf die Toil**e**tte.
7 – Fr**äu**lein, br**i**ngen Sie uns ④ b**i**tte noch ein Stück **A**pfelk**u**chen
8 und die R**e**chnung!
9 – Z**a**hlen ① Sie zus**a**mmen oder getr**e**nnt ⑤?
10 – Zus**a**mmen, b**i**tte!
11 – Das macht 63,10 DM.
12 – Hier b**i**tte 65 DM. Stimmt so, d**a**nke!
13 Mein Gott, ist das t**eu**er. Ich gl**au**be, ich s**u**che mir **ei**ne Fr**eu**ndin, die auf Kalor**i**en **a**chtet ⑥!

***5** … **oo**nnzinn … shtükk apfel-koocHen … **9** … tsoo-z**a**mmen … getrennt **13** … Kalor**i-en a**cHtet*

Notes

④ **uns**, *us*, dative and accusative of **wir**, *we*. **Sie bringt uns die Rechnung**, *She brings us the bill.* **Ihr trefft uns**, *You meet us.*

⑤ **getrennt** is the past participle of the verb **trennen**, *to separate*. **Getrennt**, *separated* or the adverb: *separately.*

⑥ **achten auf**, *to mind, to pay attention to.*

***

Übung 1 – Übersetzen Sie bitte

❶ Er bestellt einen Apfelkuchen mit Schlagsahne. ❷ Redet nicht soviel Unsinn ! ❸ Wo sind bitte die Toiletten? – Die erste Tür rechts. ❹ Der Ober bringt ihnen ein Schnitzel und einen Salat. ❺ Achten Sie auf Ihre ~~Pronunciation~~? ~~Aussprache~~ Aussprache

5 – Stop *(don't)* talk nonsense! Order me a slice *(n.)* of apple pie *(m.)*, won't you? **27**
6 I'll go to the toilet in the meantime.
7 – Waitress *(Miss)* bring us a piece of apple pie, please
8 and the bill *(f.)*!
9 – Are you paying together or separately?
10 – Together please!
11 – That's 63.10 DM.
12 – Here you are, 65 DM. That's all right, [keep the change], thank you!
13 Oh my God, that's expensive! I think I'll look for a girlfriend who minds her weight *(calories)*! □

***

Answers to exercise 1

❶ He orders an apple pie with whipped cream. ❷ Don't talk such *(so much)* nonsense! ❸ Where are the toilets, please? – The first door on the right. ❹ The waiter brings them a breaded veal cutlet and a salad. ❺ Are you paying attention to your pronunciation?

Übung 2 – Ergänzen Sie bitte

1. Bring me the bill, please.
   Bringen Sie . . . bitte die . . . . !
2. He has no car? But that's impossible!
   Er hat . . . . Auto? Das . . . . . . doch nicht!
3. I would like champagne! – Impossible! Who will pay [for] that?
   Ich . . . . . . Champagner! – . . . .! Wer . . . . denn das . . . . ?
4. That is 18.60 DM. – Here are 20 DM. That's all right, keep the change, thank you!
   Das . . . . . 18,60 DM. – Hier 20 DM. . . . . . . so, danke!

28 Achtundzwanzigste Lektion

Wiederholung und Erklärungen

1 Cases in German

Here is a complete list of all the different cases we have seen:

SINGULAR

Masculine	Feminine	Neuter
Nominative **der/ein Mann**	**die/eine Frau**	**das/ein Kind**
Accusative **den/einen Mann**	**die/eine Frau**	**das/ein Kind**
Dative **dem/einem Mann**	**der/einer Frau**	**dem/einem Kind**
Genitive **des/eines Mannes**	**der/einer Frau**	**des/eines Kindes**

❺ Are you paying together?

. . . . . . Sie alles . . . . ?

❻ May I eat another *(still one)* piece [of] pie?

. . . . ich noch ein . . . . . Kuchen essen?

Answers to exercise 2

❶ – mir – Rechnung ❷ – kein – gibt's – ❸ – möchte – Unmöglich – soll – bezahlen ❹ – macht – Stimmt – ❺ Zahlen – zusammen ❻ Darf – Stück –

Time for another revision section. Don't spend too much time on it if you have assimilated the previous lessons. This lesson gives you a list of the personal pronouns, the declensions and some explanations of the verbs with prefix.

28th Lesson 28

Read the following story to practice your newly acquired knowledge: **die Reise**, *the journey*.

Das Kind gibt der Mutter den Koffer. Aber die Mutter gibt dem Vater den Koffer, denn der Koffer ist schwer. Der Vater trägt aber schon die kleine Tochter. Er gibt also die kleine Tochter der Mutter, und die Mutter gibt der kleinen Tochter einen Kuß.

1.1 Now Answer The Following Questions

Was gibt das Kind der Mutter? . . . .
Wer gibt der Mutter den Koffer? . . . .
Wen gibt der Vater der Mutter? . . . .
Wem gibt die Mutter einen Kuß? . . . .
Wem gibt die Mutter den Koffer? . . . .
(The answer is at the end of the lesson.)

PLURAL

Nominative	**die Männer/Frauen/Kinder**
Accusative	**die Männer/Frauen/Kinder**
Dative	**den Männern/Frauen/Kindem**
Genitive	**der Männer/Frauen/Kinder**

1.2 Now Answer The Following Questions

Die Bücher gehören . . . . , *The books belong to the children.*
Aber die Mütter . . . . **mögen sie nicht**. *But the children's mothers don't like them.*
Die Kinder erzählen . . . . **die Geschichte**. *The children tell the fathers the story.*
Aber die Geschichte interessiert . . . . **nicht**. *But the story does not interest the fathers.*

2 The Personal Pronouns

Nominative					
ich	**du**	**er/sie/es**	**wir**	**ihr**	**sie/ Sie**
Accusative					
mich	**dich**	**ihn/sie/es**	**uns**	**euch**	**sie/Sie**
Dative					
mir	**dir**	**ihm/ihr/ihm**	**uns**	**euch**	**ihnen/ Ihnen**

Ich zeige dir mein Haus. *I show you my house.*
Wir zeigen euch unser Haus. *We show you our house.*
Zeigt ihr uns euer Haus? *Do you show us your house?*
Der Ober bringt ihnen das Bier. *The waiter brings them the beer.*
Ich bringe Ihnen sofort den Wein. *I bring you the wine at once.*
Sie sagt ihm „gute Nacht". *She says "Goodnight" [to] him.*
Er antwortet ihr nicht. *He does not answer her.*

Magst du mich, dann mag ich dich. *[If] you like me, I like you.*
Einfach, nicht wahr? *Easy, isn't it?*

3 Verbs with Separable Prefixes

When these verbs are conjugated the prefixes are placed at the end of the sentence:

- example: **ausgehen**, *to go out* ; but: **Ich gehe aus**, *I go out.*
- **aufmachen**, *to open:* **Machen Sie bitte die Tür auf!**, *Open the door please!*

weggehen, *to go away/to leave:* **Er geht am Morgen weg und kommt am Abend zurück**, *He leaves in the morning and comes back in the evening* (*to come back*, **zurückkommen**).
There are, however, also prefixes which are never separated from the verb. Example: **bezahlen**, *to pay*: **ich bezahle**…; **erzählen**, *to tell*: **ich erzähle**…; **verbringen**, *to spend*: **ich verbringe**…

The stress is only on the separable prefix!

4 Prepositions Followed by Dative or Accusative

4.1 Prepositions Followed by The Dative

bei, *at*; **zu**, *to* (+ movement); **nach**, *after*; **mit**, *with*…: **Ich bleibe heute abend bei meinem Freund**, *Tonight I'm staying at my friend's.* **Ich gehe zu ihm**, *I go [to see] him.* **Nach dem Essen gehe ich ins Bett**, *After the meal I go to bed.*

4.2 Prepositions Followed by The Accusative

für, *for*; **ohne**: *without*; **gegen**, *against*…:
Das Buch ist für meinen Bruder, *The book is for my brother.*
Ohne dich kann ich nicht leben, *I can't live without you.*

But there are also prepositions which are followed by the dative when there is **no movement** (question: **wo?**) and by the accusative when there is movement (question: **wohin?**).
Er liegt im (in dem) Bett, *He is in bed.*
But: **Er geht ins (in das) Bett**, *He goes to bed.*

Wir essen in der Küche, *We eat in the kitchen.*
But: **Ich gehe in die Küche**, *I go into the kitchen.*

29 **Sie wohnen im Wald** (m.), *They live in the wood.*
But: **Sie fahren in den Wald**, *They go into the wood.*

Enough for today!

---

29 Neunundzwanzigste Lektion

Ein Brief

Berlin, den 23. Januar

Sehr geehrte Damen und Herren! ①

1 Ihre Anzeige in der „Berliner Morgenpost" vom ② 18. Januar interessiert mich sehr.
2 Ich glaube, ich bin genau das, was Sie suchen: ein Zirkusprofi!
3 Ich bin 30 Jahre alt, groß und sportlich.
4 Ich bin ledig und habe keine Kinder.
5 Ich bin also frei und unabhängig und kann soviel reisen wie es nötig ist.

Pronunciation Key
1 berlinn dehn dry-oont-tsvanntsiçhstenn yanoo-ar zehr geehrte … anntsy-ge … innteresseert … 3 … yahre … 5 … oonnap'haingiçh …

5 Answer Key
1.1 – den Koffer – das Kind – die Tochter – der kleinen Tochter – dem Vater
1.2 – den Kindern – der Kinder – den Vätern – die Väter

29th Lesson 29

A Letter

Berlin, 23rd January

Dear Sirs,
(Very honoured Ladies and Gentlemen)

1 I am very interested in your advertisement *(f.)* in the "Berliner Morgenpost" of 18th January. *(Your advertisement... interests me very much)*.
2 I think I am exactly what you are looking for: a professional *(m.)* of the circus!
3 I am thirty years old, tall and athletic.
4 I am single and have no children.
5 So, I am free and independent and can travel as much as necessary.

Notes

① This is the expression we use when we don't know whether we are writing to a man or a woman. When we address a woman we write: **Sehr geehrte Frau X**, when we address a man: **sehr geehrter Herr X**.

② **von**, *of*, with dative. **Vom** is the contraction of **von dem**.

6 Ich kann **ei**ne St**u**nde lang auf dem Kopf st**e**hen und G**oe**thes „Faust“ **au**swendig **au**fsagen.
7 (Man kann mich dab**ei** sog**ar** an den F**u**ßsohlen ③ k**i**tzeln.)
8 Das ist m**ei**ne beste N**u**mmer.
9 Noch **ei**nige kl**ei**ne Fr**a**gen:
10 Was für ein Geh**a**lt b**ie**ten Sie? (Ich verd**ie**ne zur Zeit 1.780 DM m**o**natlich.)
11 Und ab ④ wann ist die St**e**lle frei?
12 Ich h**o**ffe auf eine b**a**ldige **A**ntwort und verbl**ei**be

mit fr**eu**ndlichen Gr**ü**ßen
P**e**ter Frisch □

*6 ... **ger**th**e**ss Fowst ... 7 ... **kit**s**e**ln 10 ferd**ee**n**e** ... **tow**ss**e**nt-zeeb**e**n-hoond**e**rt-**a**chtsiçh mark ...*

Notes

③ **die Sohle**, *the sole*; **der Fuß**, *the foot*: **die Fußsohle**. Feminine nouns ending in **-e** often take **-n** in the plural: **Die Dame, die** ▸

***

Übung 1 – Übersetzen Sie bitte

❶ Sie glauben*, ich bin genau das, was sie brauchen. ❷ Meine Tochter ist drei Jahre alt. ❸ Deine Arbeit interessiert mich sehr. ❹ Er kann soviel reden, wie er will. ❺ Ich glaube ihm nicht. ❻ In dieser Firma hat sie ein sehr gutes Gehalt. ❼ Mein Bruder kann essen und dabei sprechen.

* **daß** may be left out, but the main clause and subordinate clause must be separated by a comma.

6 I can stand upside down *(on the head [m.])* [for] an hour *(long)* and can recite Goethe's "Faust" by heart.
7 (Doing that, you can even tickle the soles of my feet.)
8 That is my best act *(number) (f.)*.
9 Some more *(little)* questions:
10 What salary *(n.)* are you offering? (At the moment I earn 1,780 DM a month).
11 And from when is the job *(position)* vacant?
12 I hope to hear from you soon *(for an answer soon)* and remain
Yours Faithfully *(with kind regards)*

Peter Frisch □

▸ **Damen**, *the lady, the ladies*; **die Frage, die Fragen**, *the question, the questions.*

④ **ab**, *from… onwards.* **Ab Montag**, *from Monday on(wards).*

***

Answers to exercise 1

❶ They think *(that)* I am exactly what they need. ❷ My daughter is three years old. ❸ I am very interested in your work. ❹ He can talk as much as he wants. ❺ I don't believe him. ❻ She earns *(has)* a very good salary in this company. ❼ My brother can eat and *(doing that)* speak at the same time.

Übung 2 – Ergänzen Sie bitte

❶ He is very interested in the newspaper advertisement.
Die Anzeigen in ... Zeitung interessieren .../... sehr.

❷ She is single and independent.
Sie ist ..... und ....

❸ He earns 1,500 Marks a month.
Er .... 1.500 DM ....

❹ You can eat as much as you want!
Sie können ...... essen ... Sie wollen!

❺ My brother is 18 years old and I am 14.
Mein Bruder ist 18 .... und ich ... 14.

❻ I hope that I will receive an *(quick)* answer soon.
Ich ....., daß* ich .... bekomme.

30 Dreissigste Lektion

Ein ruhiger Nachmittag im Hotel

1 – Ich habe keine Lust, länger im Hotel zu bleiben ①.

2 Es gibt hier soviel zu sehen, und wir bleiben nur drei Tage.

Pronunciation Key
1 ... lainger ...

* **daß** may be left out, but the main clause and subordinate clause must be separated by a comma.

Answers to exercise 2

❶ – der – ihn – sie – ❷ – ledig – unabhängig ❸ – verdient – monatlich ❹ – soviel – wie – ❺ – Jahre alt – bin – ❻ – hoffe – eine schnelle Antwort –

Thirtieth Lesson 30

A Quiet Afternoon at The Hotel

1 – I don't feel like staying at the hotel [any] longer.

2 There is so much to be seen *(to see)* here and we are only staying 3 days.

Note

① **Lust zu haben**, *to feel like.* **Sie hat Lust zu gehen**, *She feels like going.* The verb in the infinitive sentence is placed at the end; a comma is put before the infinitive sentence if it consists of more than **zu** + infinitive.

30 **3** Warum siehst du den ganzen Nachmittag ② fern?

4 – Erstens ist es ③ gut für mein Deutsch, und zweitens bezahle ich ③ nicht umsonst ein Zimmer mit Fernsehapparat.

5 – Wir können das Zimmer wechseln.

6 – Kommt nicht in Frage! Ich ziehe nicht alle fünf Minuten um ④!

7 – Laß ⑤ uns nur ein Stündchen ⑥ in die Stadt gehen! Wir können an der Alster* spazierengehen.

8 – Bei dem Wetter? Es regnet in Strömen.

9 – Dann laß uns in ein Café am ⑦ Hafen gehen und die Schiffe beobachten!

10 – Schiffe kann ich zu Hause jeden ⑧ Tag sehen.

11 – Fernsehen auch! Warum hast du die Reise nach Hamburg bezahlt, wenn du die ganze Zeit im Hotelzimmer sitzt?

12 – Das weißt du doch genau..., um dir eine Freude zu machen ⑨! □

***4** erstens ... tsvytenns ... oomm-zonnst ... **5** ... vekseln*
***6** ... tseehe ... **7** ... shtüntçhen ... shpatseerengehen ...*

Notes

② Dates expressing the duration are in the accusative: **Er arbeitet den ganzen Abend**, *He works all evening*.

③ Remember to pay attention to the inversion! **Erstens ist es, zweitens bezahle ich...** After **und**, *and*; **aber**, *but*; **denn**, *for, because*, the word order is regular; **Ich gehe nicht spazieren, denn es regnet**, *I'm not going for a walk, because it is raining*.

④ **umziehen**, *to move*; **um** is a separable prefix: **Ich ziehe um**, *I move*.

3 Why are you watching the TV *(m.)* all afternoon?
4 – Firstly, it is good for my German, and secondly, I'm not paying for a room with a TV for nothing.
5 – We can change the room.
6 – That's out of the question *(does not come in...)*! I'm not moving every 5 minutes!
7 – Let's go to town just for an *(little)* hour *(n.)*! We can go for a walk along (at) the Alster.
8 – In this weather? It is pouring.
9 – Then, let's go to a cafe at the port and watch the ships!
10 – I can see ships every day at home.
11 – Watch the TV also! Why did you pay for the trip *(f.)* to Hamburg if you sit in the hotel room all the time?
12 – You know exactly why... to please you! □

▸ ⑤ The imperative forms of the first person plural are: **gehen wir!** or **wir wollen gehen!** or **laßt uns gehen!** (it is the same as in English).

⑥ **-chen** and **-lein** are diminutive endings: **die Stunde, das Stündchen**. Notice that: 1. **-e** of **Stunde** is left out 2. When there is **a**, **o**, **u**, or **au** you have to add the **Umlaut = Der Hut, das Hütchen**; **das Haus, das Häuschen** diminutives are always neuter.

⑦ **am** is the contraction of **an dem**. **An** means *to, at, along.* **Wir verbringen unsere Ferien am Meer**, *We spend our holidays at the seaside.* **Wir fahren ans Meer**, *We go to the seaside.*

⑧ **jeder/jede/jedes**, *every*, is declined like the definite article.

⑨ *(in order) to* + verb is translated by **um...zu**; **zu** is always placed before the infinitive and **um** at the beginning of the subordinate clause; **Wir lernen Deutsch, um in Deutschland zu arbeiten**, *We learn German (in order) to work in Germany.* **Er kommt, um mit dir zu sprechen**, *He comes to speak with you.*

30 **Übung 1 – Übersetzen Sie bitte**

❶ Haben Sie Lust, mit mir zu essen? ❷ Er arbeitet den ganzen Tag und die ganze Nacht. ❸ Ich möchte gern länger bleiben. ❹ Bei dem Wetter gehe ich nicht auf die Straße. ❺ Er sitzt die ganze Zeit zu Hause in seinem Zimmer und sieht fern. ❻ Laß uns ein wenig spazierengehen!

Übung 2 – Ergänzen Sie bitte

❶ Would you like to go *(do you feel like...)* to Germany with me?

. . . . du Lust, mit . . . nach Deutschland . . fahren?

❷ Come on! the weather is so fine. We go to the Alster.

. . . . ! Das . . . . . . ist so schön. Wir gehen . . die Alster.

❸ That is out of the question! Firstly, I don't have the time, and secondly, I don't feel like it!

Kommt nicht in . . . . . ! . . . . habe ich keine . . . . und . . . . keine . . . . !

❹ He is a musician. He often moves.

Er ist Musiker. Er . . . . . oft . . .

❺ I would like to please you. What can I do for you?

Ich möchte . . . eine . . . . . . machen. . . . kann ich für . . . . tun?

❻ We need a lot of money to live well.

Wir brauchen . . . . Geld, . . gut . . leben.

Answers to exercise 1

❶ Would you like to eat with me? ❷ He works all day and all night. ❸ I would like to stay *(I feel like...)* longer. ❹ In this weather I don't go out into the street. ❺ He sits at home all the time and watches the TV. ❻ Let's go for a walk *(walk a bit)*!

Answers to exercise 2

❶ Hast – mir – zu – ❷ Komm – Wetter – an – ❸ – Frage – Erstens – Zeit – zweitens – Lust ❹ – zieht – um ❺ – dir – Freude – Was – dich – ❻ – viel – um – zu –

31 Einunddreissigste Lektion

Ein Gespräch *(n.)* **mit dem Chef** *(m.)*

1 – Entschuldigen Sie, Herr Direktor, darf ich Sie **ei**nen **Au**genblick st**ö**ren?
2 – Aber nat**ü**rlich, mein l**ie**ber Schmitt, was gibt's? ①
3 – **A**lso, da ist zu**e**rst das Probl**e**m mit m**ei**nem Geh**a**lt. Ich h**a**tte seit zwei J**a**hren k**ei**ne Erh**ö**hung.
4 – D**a**mit g**e**hen Sie b**e**sser zum Person**a**lchef!
5 – Beim Person**a**lchef war ② ich schon.
6 – Dann g**e**hen Sie noch **ei**nmal zu ihm und s**a**gen ihm, ich w**ü**nsche, daß man **I**hren Fall überpr**ü**ft ③.
7 – Ja, und dann sind da die n**eu**en Comp**u**ter und die b**ei**den Koll**e**gen, die man entl**a**ssen will!…
8 – Mit d**ie**sen Fr**a**gen w**e**nden Sie sich an den ④ Betr**ie**bsrat.

Pronunciation Key
… geshpraiçh … ***1*** *… shter-ren* ***8*** *… betreeps-rat*

Notes

① **was gibt's**, *what is the matter.*

② **ich war**, *I was*, the simple past of **ich bin**. **Ich hatte**, *I had*, the simple past of **ich habe**. ▸

A Conversation with The Boss

1 – Excuse [me], sir *(Mr. director)*, may I disturb you for a moment *(m.)*?
2 – But certainly, *(my)* dear Schmitt, what is the matter?
3 – Well, firstly, there is the problem *(n.)* of my salary. I haven't had an increase for two years *(I had no)*.
4 – You'd better see the personnel manager about that *(with that you better go to the...)*!
5 – I've already seen the personnel manager.
6 – Then go and see him again *(go once more to him)* and tell him that I wish him to examine your case *(m.) (that one examines your case)*.
7 – Yes, and secondly, there are the new computers and the two colleagues who are to be dismissed *(one wants to dismiss)*…
8 – Consult the works committee *(m.)* about these questions.

③ Remember, in subordinate clauses introduced by **daß**, the verb is at the end of the sentence. **Ich weiß, daß er morgen kommt**, *I know that he is coming tomorrow.*

④ **sich wenden an**, *to consult, to apply to, to address*; with accusative.

9 – Mmm, und dann war ich krank und soll eine Kur machen…

10 – Für diese Fragen ist Fräulein Dickmann zuständig ⑤. Noch etwas?

11 – Ja, und außerdem möchte ich einen Baum vor meinem Fenster. An wen soll ich mich damit wenden? Haben Sie vielleicht eine Idee? □

***10** … tsoo-shtaindiçh …*

Note

⑤ **zuständig**, *responsible*; **Herr Schmitt ist zuständig für Fragen der Sicherheit**, *Mr. Schmitt is responsible for security matters*; **Herr Schmitt ist dafür zuständig**, *Mr. Schmitt is responsible for that*; **Dafür, damit**… see lesson 35 paragraph 4.

***

Übung 1 – Übersetzen Sie bitte

❶ Er will, daß man seinen Fall überprüft. ❷ Für die Fragen der Sicherheit ist Herr Dünne zuständig. ❸ Er soll sich an den Betriebsrat wenden. ❹ Darf ich Sie einen Augenblick stören, Frau Kroger? ❺ Sie war drei Jahre lang in Deutschland und hatte dort eine gute Stelle. ❻ Außerdem ist sie mit einem Deutschen verheiratet.

9 – Mm, and then, I was ill and had to take a cure *(f.)*.
10 – [It's] Miss Dickmann [who] is responsible for these questions. Something else?
11 – Yes, and moreover, I would like a tree *(m.)* in front of my window *(n.)*. Who am I to consult about that? Maybe you have an idea? □

***

Answers to exercise 1

❶ He wants his case to be examined *(He wants that one...)* ❷ Mr. Dünne is responsible for security matters. ❸ He has to consult the works committee. ❹ May I disturb you for a moment, Mrs. Kroger? ❺ She was in Germany for three years and had a good job there. ❻ Moreover, she is married to a German.

32 Übung 2 – Beantworten Sie bitte die folgenden Fragen
Exercise 2 – Please answer the following questions

❶ Warum hat Herr Schmitt Probleme mit seinem Gehalt? Er hatte . . . . zwei . . . . . . keine . . . .

❷ Zu wem soll er gehen? . . . .

❸ War er schon beim Personalchef? Ja, er war . . . . . bei . . . .

❹ Wie viele Kollegen will man entlassen? . . . . Kollegen.

---

32 Zweiunddreissigste Lektion

Ein Interview

1 – Guten Tag! Wir machen eine Umfrage für das Institut „Zivilisation".
2 Die Umfrage steht unter dem Motto: „In Zukunft besser und intensiver ① leben".
3 – Würden Sie mir bitte dazu ② einige Fragen beantworten?
4 – Ja, gern, wenn es nicht zu lange dauert…

Pronunciation Key
... interview **1** *... tsivilisatsiohn* **2** *... inntennzeever ...* **4** *... dow-ert*

Notes

① **intensiver** is the comparative of **intensiv**. In German, the comparative is formed by adding **-er** to the adjective (this is the ▸

❺ Wer ist für diese Frage zuständig? Der 32

❻ An wen soll sich Herr Schmitt für seine Kur wenden? .. Fräulein ....

Answers to exercise 2

❶ – seit – Jahren – Erhöhung ❷ Zum Personalchef ❸ – schon – ihm ❹ Zwei – ❺ – Betriebsrat ❻ An – Dickmann

32nd Lesson 32

An Interview *(n.)*

1 – Hello! We are making an inquiry *(f.)* for the "Civilization" institute *(n.)*.

2 The inquiry is on the subject *(under the motto)*: "living better and more intensely in the future *(f.)*".

3 – Would you answer *(me)* some questions [on this subject] please?

4 – Yes, with pleasure, if it doesn't last too long…

▸ way we form the comparative of short adjectives in English): **schnell - schneller**, *faster*. Irregular forms: **gut - besser**, *better*; **viel - mehr**, *more*.

② **dazu** replaces **zu diesem Thema**, *on this subject*. We say: **Ich habe eine Frage zu diesem Thema**, *I have a question on this subject*.

5 – Nein, nur ein paar ③ Min**u**ten! Gut, die **e**rste Fr**a**ge ist:

6 L**e**ben Sie l**ie**ber ④ in der Stadt in **ei**ner Et**a**genw**o**hnung **o**der auf dem Land ⑤ in **ei**nem Haus mit G**a**rten?

7 – Nat**ü**rlich l**ie**ber auf dem Land, **a**ber…

8 – Gut, „auf dem Land". Die zw**ei**te Fr**a**ge: **E**ssen Sie l**ie**ber Schw**ei**nefleisch ⑥ **o**der R**i**ndfleisch?

9 – Nat**ü**rlich l**ie**ber R**i**ndfleisch, **a**ber…

10 – Gut, „R**i**ndfleisch". Die dr**i**tte Fr**a**ge: **A**rbeiten Sie schn**e**ller als ⑦ **I**hre Koll**e**gen?

11 – Äh… ich gl**au**be, gen**au**so schnell wie ⑧ sie!

12 – Das ist k**ei**ne **A**ntwort, d**a**für gibt es kein K**ä**stchen. Schn**e**ller **o**der l**a**ngsamer?

13 – Ich weiß nicht! Ich muß jetzt **ü**brigens nach H**au**se. M**ei**ne fünf K**i**nder w**a**rten in der sechsten Et**a**ge auf ⑨ **i**hre Schw**ei**nekoteletts… □

6 *… etashen-v**o**hnoong …*

Notes

③ **ein paar** (with a small **p**) or **einige**, *a few, some* ; **ein Paar** (with capital **P**), *a pair, a couple.*

④ **lieber**, *to prefer*, is the comparative of **gern**, *I like…* **Ich trinke gern Limonade, aber ich trinke lieber Bier**, *I like to drink lemonade, but I prefer beer.*

⑤ **das Land**, *the country.* **Ich wohne auf dem Land**, *I live in the country.* **Wir fahren auf das Land**, *We go into the country.* **Auf** is followed by the accusative when the preceding verb indicates movement (in a direction). Otherwise it is followed by the dative! Remember lesson 28, paragraph 4. ▸

5 – No, only a few minutes! Fine, the first question is:
6 Do you prefer living in a flat *(f.)* in the town or in a house with garden *(m.)* in the country?
7 – I prefer *(in)* the country of course, but…
8 – Good, "in the country". The second question: Do you prefer *(eating)* pork *(pork meat)* or beef *(beef meat)?*
9 – Beef of course, but…
10 – Good, "beef". The third question: Do you work faster than your colleagues?
11 – Eh… I think as fast as them.
12 – That's no answer *(f.),* there is no blank for that. Faster or more slowly?
13 – I don't know! By the way, I have to go home now. My five children are on the sixth floor, waiting for their pork chops… □

⑥ **das Fleisch**, *the meat*; **das Schweinefleisch**, *pork*; **das Rindfleisch**, *beef*; **das Kalbfleisch**, *veal*.

⑦ **als**, *than*. **Er ist kleiner als ich**, *He is smaller than me*. **Ihr seid älter als wir**, *You are older than us*. Monosyllabic adjectives take the **Umlaut** in the comparative: **alt - älter**; **groß - größer**.

⑧ **so… wie**, *as… as*. **Er ist so klein wie sie**, *He is as small as her.*

⑨ **warten**, *to wait*, is always followed by the preposition **auf**: **Ich warte auf meinen Bruder**, *I am waiting for my brother.*

32 **Übung 1 – Übersetzen Sie bitte**

❶ Lesen Sie lieber Krimis oder Liebesromane? ❷ Ich esse lieber Salzkartoffeln als Pommes Frites. Und Sie? ❸ Mein Freund wohnt in der dritten Etage. ❹ Würden Sie mir bitte sagen, wo der Bahnhof ist? ❺ Meine Freundin spricht so gut Deutsch wie du. ❻ Aber sie spricht besser als ich.

Übung 2 – Ergänzen Sie bitte

❶ I can watch the film if it does not last too long.
Ich kann den Film ansehen . . . . er nicht zu lange . . . .

❷ Is your father older than my father?
Ist Ihr Vater . . . . mein Vater?

❸ I think he is as old as me.
Ich glaube, er ist . . . . ich.

❹ Do you prefer sausages or pork chops?
Mögen Sie . . . . . . Würstchen oder Schweinekoteletts?

Answers to exercise 1

❶ Do you prefer reading detective stories or love stories? ❷ I prefer *(eating) (salt)* potatoes to French fries. And you? ❸ My friend lives on the third floor. ❹ Could *(would)* you tell me where the station is? ❺ My friend speaks German as well as you. ❻ But she speaks better than me.

❺ My new car goes more slowly than my old one, but it brakes as well as the old one.
Mein neues Auto fährt .... mein altes; aber es bremst genau .. .. mein altes.

❻ Do you prefer living in the country or on the 28th floor in the town centre?
Wohnen Sie ...... auf ... Land oder in ... . Etage im Stadtzentrum?

Answers to exercise 2

❶ – wenn – dauert ❷ – älter als – ❸ – so alt wie – ❹ – lieber – ❺ – langsamer als – so gut wie – ❻ – lieber – dem – der achtundzwanzigsten –

33 Dreiunddreissigste Lektion

Ein sympathischer Besuch

1 – Es kl**i**ngelt. Das sind best**i**mmt schon die F**i**schers.
2 Die sind **i**mmer **ü**berp**ü**nktlich ①.
3 – Geh b**i**tte an die Tür, W**e**rner! Ich bin noch nicht ganz f**e**rtig ②.
4 – Ah, g**u**ten Tag! Wir fr**eu**en uns ③ sehr, daß Sie gek**o**mmen sind!
5 – Wir auch! V**ie**len Dank für **I**hre **Ei**nladung!
6 – **A**ber ich b**i**tte Sie ④... K**o**mmen Sie doch b**i**tte her**ei**n!
7 – Oh, was für **ei**ne sch**ö**ne, h**e**lle W**o**hnung!
8 – Ja, es ist die h**e**llste ⑤ W**o**hnung, die ich k**e**nne!
9 – Oh, und was für **ei**ne h**e**rrliche **Au**ssicht **ü**ber die Stadt und die W**ä**lder ⑥!

Pronunciation Key
*... zümmp**a**tisher bes**oo**cH* **2** *... **ü**berp**ü**ng'ktliçh ...*

Notes

① **pünktlich**, *punctual*; **über**, *over*, but when added to an adjective or adverb it means more than, over: **übergroß**, *oversized*.

② **fertig**, *ready*; *finished*. **Das Essen ist fertig**, *The meal is ready*. **Ich bin mit meiner Arbeit fertig**, *I have finished my work*.

③ **sich freuen**, *to be pleased*; **ich freue mich**, **du freust dich**, **er freut sich**...

④ **ich bitte Sie**, *you are welcome, don't mention it*. **Hereinkommen** or **eintreten**, *to come in*; *to enter*. **Ein** and **herein** are separable prefixes, **Er kommt herein**, *He comes in*, – **Tritt ein!**, ▸

A Nice Visit *(m.)*

1 – Someone's at the door *(it rings)*. That must be the Fischers already *(are certainly...)*.
2 They are always too early.
3 – Go and open the door *(f.)* please, Werner! I am not ready yet *(not quite...)*.
4 – Oh, hello! We are pleased that you [have managed] to come!
5 – So are we *(we, too)*! Thank you *(many thanks)* for your invitation *(f.)*!
6 – You are welcome *(But I beg you)*... Come in, please!
7 – Oh, what a nice *(and)* bright flat!
8 – Yes, it's the brightest flat I know!
9 – Oh, and what a splendid view *(f.) of (over)* the town and the woods!

EIN SYMPATHISCHER BESUCH

▸ *Enter!* **Eintreten** is irregular: **ich trete ein**, **du trittst ein**, **er tritt ein**.

⑤ The superlative is formed by adding **-ste** to the adjective, **der Tisch ist teuer** – **das ist der teuerste Tisch**, *This is the most expensive table.*

⑥ **der Wald**, *the wood*; **die Wälder**, *the woods.*

33 **10** – Ja, es ist die schönste **Au**ssicht, die ⑦ wir jemals **ha**tten.

11 W**o**llen wir jetzt viell**ei**cht K**a**ffee tr**i**nken?

12 M**ei**ne Frau macht **ü**brigens den b**e**sten ⑧ K**a**ffee, den ich j**e**mals getr**u**nken habe. □

Notes

⑦ The relative pronoun refers to **Aussicht**, a feminine noun; that's why you must say: **die**. It is declined like the definite article, and always agrees with the noun it refers to. ▸

***

Übung 1 – Übersetzen Sie bitte

❶ Sie freuen sich sehr, uns zu sehen. ❷ Bist du mit deiner Arbeit fertig? ❸ Das ist die schönste Stadt, die ich kenne. ❹ Wer macht die besten Kuchen in der Stadt? ❺ Mein Bruder ist der stärkste Mann, den es gibt. ❻ Freust du dich, nach Deutschland zu fahren? ❼ Fischers haben die teuerste Wohnung von allen.

Übung 2 – Ergänzen Sie bitte

❶ The most handsome man *(who)* I know is my father.
Der . . . . Mann, . . . ich kenne, ist . . . . Vater.

❷ The cakes at the Müllers' are the best.
Die . . . . . . bei Müllers sind die . . . .

❸ The most intelligent woman in town is my friend.
Die . . . . Frau in der Stadt ist . . . . . Freundin.

10 – Yes, it's the nicest view we've ever had.
11 Let's have coffee now *(perhaps)*?
12 By the way, my wife makes the best coffee I've ever had. □

▸ ⑧ **beste**, *best*; the superlative of **gut**. Accusative masculine: **den besten Kaffee**; do you remember lesson 21, paragraph 1?

***

Answers to exercise 1

❶ They are very pleased to see us. ❷ Have you finished your work? ❸ That is the nicest town *(that)* I know. ❹ Who makes the best cakes in *(the)* town? ❺ My brother is the strongest man there is *(that exists)*. ❻ Are you pleased to go to Germany? ❼ The Fischers have the most expensive flat of all.

❹ I am very pleased to see you. Come in please!
Ich . . . . sehr, Sie zu sehen. Kommen Sie doch bitte . . . . . . !

❺ What is your most beautiful memory?
Was ist Ihr . . . . Souvenir?

❻ Are you always punctual or are you often *(too)* late?
Sind Sie immer . . . . oder kommen Sie oft zu . . . . ?

Answers to exercise 2

❶ – schönste – den – mein – ❷ – Kuchen – besten ❸ – intelligenteste – meine – ❹ – freue mich – herein ❺ – schönstes – ❻ – pünktlich – spät

34 Vierunddreissigste Lektion

Beim „Fondue"-Essen ①

1 – Mm, am b**e**sten ② schmeckt die S**o**ße mit dem gr**ü**nen Pf**e**ffer!
2 – Die P**a**prikasoße schmeckt auch **au**sgez**ei**chnet! Prob**ier**' sie mal!
3 – Oh, ja, w**i**rklich gut! Die ist noch sch**ä**rfer ③ als die Pf**e**ffers**o**ße!
4 – Ich **e**sse am l**ie**bsten ④ die S**e**nfsoße. Die ist **e**twas ganz Bes**o**nderes!
5 – Und wie schmeckt euch der Wein?
6 – Auch **au**sgez**ei**chnet! Das ist der b**e**ste Wein, den ich seit zwei T**a**gen getr**u**nken habe.
7 – Was willst du denn d**a**mit s**a**gen?
8 – Ach, das war ein Scherz! Das ist w**i**rklich ein sehr g**u**ter Wein, und er paßt pr**i**ma zum ⑤ Fond**ue**.
9 – **A**chtung, es riecht **a**ngebrannt! Paßt auf **eu**er Fleisch auf!

Pronunciation Key
1 *... zosse ... **3** ... shairfer ... **4** zennf'zosse*

Notes

① **beim** is the contraction of **bei dem**. Each verb can be used as a noun, you simply need to add the neuter article before it and a capital letter: **essen**, **das Essen**, *the meal*; **leben**, **das Leben**, *the life*; **lesen**, *to read*, **das Lesen**, *the reading*.

Having *(at)* a "Fondue" *(n.)*

1 – Mmm, the sauce *(f.)* with the green pepper *(m.)* tastes best.
2 – The red pepper sauce tastes very good too! Try it!
3 – Oh, yes, really good! It is even *(still)* hotter than the pepper sauce!
4 – It's mustard sauce I like best. It's something special!
5 – And how do you like the wine *(m.)* *(how tastes the wine to you)*?
6 – Excellent, too! That is the best wine I have had for two days.
7 – What do you mean by that *(What do you want to say with that)*?
8 – Oh, it was [only] a joke! That really is a very good wine, and it goes excellently with the fondue *(n.)*.
9 – Be careful! I can smell burning! *(It smells burnt!)* Watch out for your meat *(f.)*!

▸ ② This is the superlative form : **am** + adjective + the ending **-sten**: **am schönsten, am kleinsten, am besten**...

③ **scharf**, *hot; sharp*. **Schärfer, am schärfsten**. Please note the use of the **Umlaut** on the letter "a"!

④ **am liebsten** is the superlative of **gern**: **Ich esse gern Brot**, *I like to eat bread*. **Ich esse lieber Brot mit Butter**, *I prefer eating bread with butter*. **Am liebsten esse ich Brot mit Wurst und Käse**, *I like (to eat) bread with sausage and cheese best*.

⑤ **zum** is the contraction of **zu dem**: it is always followed by the dative declension.

34 **10** – Wessen ⑥ G**a**bel ist das denn? Was? Das Wißt ihr nicht mehr?

11 Ich gl**au**be, ihr seid ⑦ schon **a**lle Seicht betr**u**nken!

12 – Das macht nichts! K**i**nder, was für ein herrliches **E**ssen! Reicht mir noch 'mal die So**ß**en und schenkt ⑧ mir **e**twas Wein nach ⑧, und ich bin der gl**ü**cklichste Mensch auf der **E**rde! □

Notes

⑥ **wessen**, *whose*, is the interrogative pronoun of the genitive: **Wessen Buch ist das?**, *Whose book is it?*

⑦ **ihr seid**, *you are*, the plural of **du bist**.

⑧ **einschenken**, *to pour, to help a person to…* **nachschenken**, *to help a person to some more…* **Darf ich Ihnen Wein nachschenken?**, *May I help you to some more wine?* **Schenken** without a prefix means *to give* (as a present).

***

Übung 1 – Übersetzen Sie bitte

❶ Dieser Rotwein schmeckt mir am besten. ❷ Er trinkt am liebsten Whisky mit Eis. ❸ Das ist der größte Mann, den ich jemals gesehen habe. ❹ Wessen Mantel ist das? ❺ Reichen Sie mir bitte den Zucker! ❻ Es riecht nicht gut hier! Ist vielleicht etwas angebrannt?

10 – Whose fork *(f.)* is this? What? You don't remember *(you don't know it any more)*?
11 I think you are already *(all)* slightly drunk!
12 – That doesn't matter! Oh boys, what a delicious meal *(n.)*! Pass me the sauces again *(still once)* and help me to some more wine *(and pour me a bit wine after)*, and I am the happiest man *(m.)* on *(the)* earth *(f.)*! □

***

Answers to exercise 1

❶ I like this red wine best. ❷ He likes whisky on the rocks best *(with ice)*. ❸ He *(that)* is the tallest man I have ever seen. ❹ Whose coat is it? ❺ Pass me the sugar please! ❻ It does not smell nice here! Perhaps something has burnt?

35 Übung 2 – Ergänzen Sie bitte

1. What do you like *(to eat)* best?
   Was essen Sie am . . . . ?

2. I find the article in the *Süddeutschen Zeitung* best.
   It is the most interesting.
   Ich finde den Artikel in der *Süddeutschen Zeitung* . . . .
   Er ist . . . .

3. During the meal you *(one)* must not speak.
   . . . . Essen soll . . . nicht . . . .

35 Fünfunddreissigste Lektion

Wiederholung und Erklärungen

1 Declension of The Adjective

You know that you have to decline the qualifying adjective. Another slight complication is that there are three different declensions according to the article which precedes it:

1.1 The Adjective Is Preceded by The Definite Article

	Masculine	Feminine
nom.	**der grüne Tisch**	**die kleine Tasse**
acc.	**den grünen Tisch**	**die kleine Tasse**
dat.	**dem grünen Tisch**	**der kleinen Tasse**
gen.	**des grünen Tischs**	**der kleinen Tasse**

4 Do you need spectacles to read?
Brauchen Sie eine Brille . . . . ?

5 Which *(what kind of books)* books do you like *(to read)* best?
. . . . liest du . . . . ?

6 Help me to some more wine please!
. . . . Sie mir bitte . . . . etwas Wein . . . . !

Answers to exercise 2

1 – liebsten 2 – am besten – am interessantesten 3 Beim – man – sprechen 4 – zum Lesen 5 Was für Bücher – am liebsten 6 Schenken – noch – nach

35th Lesson 35

	Neuter	Plural
nom.	**das liebe Kind**	**die alten Freunde**
acc.	**das liebe Kind**	**die alten Freunde**
dat.	**dem lieben Kind**	**den alten Freunden**
gen.	**des lieben Kinds**	**der alten Freunde**

1.2 The Adjective Is Preceded by The Indefinite Article

	Masculine	Feminine
nom.	**ein neuer Hut**	**eine blaue Tasche**
acc.	**einen neuen Hut**	**eine blaue Tasche**

35

dat.	**einem neuen Hut**	**einer blauen Tasche**
gen.	**eines neuen Huts**	**einer blauen Tasche**

	Neuter
nom.	**ein großes Haus**
acc.	**ein großes Haus**
dat.	**einem großen Haus**
gen.	**eines großen Hauses**

There is no indefinite article in the plural. After the possessive pronoun and the negative article, **kein**, the endings of the adjective are the same as after the indefinite article (**ein**). In the plural the adjective always ends in **-en** when preceded by an article.

1.3 The Adjective Is Without Article

	Masculine	Feminine
nom.	**guter Wein**	**deutsche Küche**
acc.	**guten Wein**	**deutsche Küche**
dat.	**gutem Wein**	**deutscher Küche**
gen.	**guten Weins**	**deutscher Küche**

	Neuter	Plural
nom.	**kaltes Wasser**	**schöne Ferien**

acc.	**kaltes Wasser**	**schöne Ferien**
dat.	**kaltem Wasser**	**schönen Ferien**
gen.	**kalten Wassers**	**schöner Ferien**

We don't want you to learn this list by heart. Just have a look at it whenever you want to check something.

2 The Comparative and The Superlative

• The comparative: **-er** is added to the adjective: **schön -schöner**. When the adjective is monosyllabic with the vowels **a**, **o**, or **u** you must add the **Umlaut** on the vowel: **alt - älter**; **groß - größer**.

• The superlative: **-ste** is added to the adjective: **schöne -schönste**; **groß - größte**; **jung -jüngste**. The superlative of the adverb: **am** + adjective with the ending: **-sten**: **am kleinsten**; **am größten**; **am dicksten**.

• The comparison:
Mein Bruder ist kleiner als ich, *My brother is smaller than me.*
Als, *than.*
Mein Bruder ist so groß wie ich, *My brother is as tall as me.*
So... wie, *as... as.*
The qualifying adjective is declined (see paragraph 1):
Ich möchte gern einen größeren und schnelleren Wagen, *I'd like a bigger and faster car.*
Ich gehe mit meinem schönsten Kleid ins Theater, *I go to the theatre in my most beautiful dress.*

3 The Months and The Days of The Week

Januar, **Februar**, **März**, **April**, **Mai**, **Juni**, **Juli**, **August**, **September**, **Oktober**, **November**, **Dezember**.
Montag, **Dienstag**, **Mittwoch**, **Donnerstag**, **Freitag**, **Samstag**, **Sonntag**.
Heute ist Montag, der dritte März, *Today is Monday 3rd March.*
Welches Datum haben wir morgen?*
* Solution is at the end of the lesson!

Er interessiert sich für Sport, *He is interested in sports (He interests himself in...)*
Für den Sport can be replaced by **dafür**; when you want to avoid repetition: **Ich interessiere mich auch dafür**, *I am also interested in that.* **Sie denkt an ihre Ferien**, *She thinks of her holidays.* **An ihre Ferien** can be replaced by **daran. Ich denke auch daran**, *I think of them too.*
This adverbial pronoun is formed by **da** + the corresponding preposition.
When the preposition begins with a vowel we add **r**: **da** + **r** + preposition.
Sie sprechen über ihre Arbeit, Sie sprechen darüber, *They speak about their work, they speak about it.*

36 Sechsunddreissigste Lektion

Das liebe Geld!

1 – Der W**ie**vielte ist h**eu**te?
2 – Der f**ü**nfzehnte.
3 – Was? Erst ① der f**ü**nfzehnte und schon w**ie**der kein Geld mehr auf dem K**o**nto!
4 – Das ist nicht m**ei**ne Schuld! Ich h**a**be nichts Bes**o**nderes gek**au**ft ②.
5 – Ich auch nicht! Die h**a**ben s**i**cher bei der Bank **ei**nen F**e**hler gem**a**cht!

Notes

① **erst**, *only*, is used when it refers to time: **Er arbeitet erst seit drei Stunden**, *He has only been working for three hours**. Otherwise we use **nur, er arbeitet nur drei Stunden pro Tag**, *He only works three hours a day.*

* We don't know yet how long he'll be working.

Er beschäftigt sich mit seinen Briefmarken, Er beschäftigt sich damit, *He is busy with his stamps, he is busy with them.*
Was machst du mit deinem Assimil-Buch?, *What are you doing with your Assimil book?* **Was soll ich damit machen? Ich lese es natürlich**, *What do you want me to do with it?*
What do you think I'm doing with it? I read it, of course!
Sehr gut! Machen Sie so weiter!, *Very good, go on (like that!).*

5 Answer Key

* Answer to paragraph 3:
Morgen haben wir Dienstag den vierten März, *Tomorrow it will be Tuesday 4th March.*
Und morgen erwartet uns eine neue Lektion, *And tomorrow another lesson will be waiting for us.*

36th Lesson 36

This Dear Money *(n.)*!

1 – What is today's date?
2 – The 15th.
3 – What? Only the 15th and again there is no money [left] in the bank *(account)*!
4 – That is not my fault *(f.)*! I haven't bought anything special.
5 – Neither have I! They've certainly made a mistake *(m.)* at the bank *(f.)*!

② **gekauft** is the past participle of **kaufen**, *to buy*. The past participle of regular verbs is formed with the prefix **ge-** and **-t** at the end of the stem: **machen - gemacht**, *done*; **suchen - gesucht**; **tanzen - getanzt**. Generally the perfect is formed with the present tense of **haben** + the past participle (exceptions see lesson 42). **Sie hat gekauft**, *she (has) bought*; **du hast gesagt**, *you (have) said.*

6 – Das glaube ich auch! Laß uns 'mal nachrechnen:
7 Also da war die Telefonrechnung; die war ziemlich hoch, weil ③ wir so oft mit Mutti in Hamburg telefoniert ④ haben.
8 – Ja, und dann die Stromrechnung; die war auch ziemlich hoch, weil es in den letzten Monaten so kalt war.
9 – Und dann haben wir dreimal in Restaurants gegessen ⑤, die nicht gerade billig waren. Erinnerst ⑥ du dich daran ⑥?
10 – Ja, ich erinnere mich an die Essen. Die waren wirklich ausgezeichnet. Etwas teuer… aber trotzdem gut!
11 – Wir haben immer mit Scheck gezahlt, nicht wahr?
12 – Ja, das ist richtig… vielleicht hat die Bank doch recht ⑦, und wir haben uns geirrt ⑧. □

Pronunciation Key
9 … er'inn<u>e</u>rst …

Notes

③ **weil**, *because*, introduces a subordinate clause. The conjugated verb is placed at the end of the sentence: **Ich bin traurig, weil ich einen Fehler gemacht habe**, *I am sad because I have made a mistake.*

④ Verbs ending in **-ieren** do not have the prefix **ge-** in the past participle: **Wir haben diskutiert**, *We discussed.*

⑤ **essen - gegessen**, *eaten*. Notice: the past participle of **essen** is irregular.

⑥ **sich erinnern an**, *to remember.* **Ich erinnere mich an meine Ferien**, *I remember my holidays.* **Erinnern Sie sich auch daran?**, *Do you remember [them] too?* ▸

6 – I think so, too! Let's check it:
7 Well, there was the telephone bill; it was rather high, because we made so many phone calls with Mummy *(we phoned)* to Hamburg.
8 – Yes, and then there was the electricity bill, it was rather high too because it has been so cold during the last months.
9 – And then we had three meals at restaurants which weren't exactly inexpensive *(we ate thrice in restaurants which...)*. Do you remember?
10 – Yes, I remember the meals. They were really excellent. A little bit expensive… but nevertheless very good!
11 – We always paid by check *(m.)*, didn't we?
12 – Yes, that's right… maybe the bank is right after all, and we are wrong *(mistaken)*. □

WIR SIND ERST EINE HALBE STUNDE HIER UND DU MÖCHTEST SCHON WIEDER GEHEN ?

⑦ **recht haben**, *to be right*: **er hat recht**, *he is right*; **unrecht haben**, *to be wrong*: **du hast unrecht**, *you are wrong.*

⑧ **sich irren**, *to be mistaken.*

36 **Übung 1 – Übersetzen Sie bitte**

❶ Wir sind erst eine halbe Stunde hier und du möchtest schon wieder gehen? ❷ Laß uns doch noch etwas hierbleiben! ❸ Ich habe heute noch nichts gegessen. Ich habe den ganzen Tag gearbeitet. ❹ Er hat gestern ein neues Auto gekauft. ❺ Müssen Sie denn immer recht haben?

Übung 2 – Ergänzen Sie bitte

❶ She bought butter, bread and cheese.
Sie . . . Butter, Brot und Käse . . . .

❷ Do you remember those good times *(the good time)* in Berlin?
. . . . Sie sich . . die schöne Zeit in Berlin?

❸ We always paid by travellers checks in Germany.
Wir . . . . . in . . . . immer mit Reiseschecks . . . .

❹ The telephone bill was very high *(in)* this month.
Die Telefonrechnung . . . in diesem Monat sehr . . . . .

Answers to exercise 1

❶ We have only been here for half an hour and you want to leave already? ❷ Let's stay a little bit longer! ❸ I haven't eaten anything, today. I've been working all day *(the whole day)*. ❹ He bought a new car yesterday. ❺ Do you always have to be right?

❺ What did you do during the week-end?
Was .... du am Wochenende .... ?

❻ I phoned my girlfriend.
Ich .... mit meiner Freundin ....

Answers to exercise 2

❶ – hat – gekauft ❷ Erinnern – an – ❸ – haben – Deutschland – gezahlt ❹ – war – hoch ❺ – hast – gemacht ❻ – habe – telefoniert

37 Siebenunddreissigste Lektion

Ein guter Tip

1 – Mensch, Sie s**e**hen ja toll aus… so br**au**ngebrannt! Wo k**o**mmen Sie denn her ①?
2 – Dir**e**kt von den Kan**a**rischen **I**nseln. Dort ist das sch**ö**nste W**e**tter, das ② man ② sich d**e**nken kann!
3 – H**e**rrlich! Ich ben**ei**de Sie w**i**rklich! W**a**ren Sie schon oft dort?
4 – Ja, schon f**ü**nfmal ③. Seit fünf J**a**hren verbr**i**ngen wir dort **u**nseren „Winter**ur**laub".
5 – M**ei**ne Frau und ich, wir w**o**llen auch schon seit l**a**ngem dorth**in** ④; **a**ber **i**mmer kommt **i**rgend **e**twas dazw**i**schen.
6 – Wenn Sie **ei**nes T**a**ges doch f**a**hren, kann ich **I**hnen **ei**nige g**u**te Tips g**e**ben.
7 – D**ie**sen S**o**mmer l**ei**der nicht, **a**ber viell**ei**cht klappt's im n**ä**chsten Fr**ü**hling.

Pronunciation Key
3 *… beny-de … **4** … ferbringen … **5** … datsvishen …*

Notes

① In spoken language you often say: **wo kommst du her?** instead of **woher kommst du?**, *where do you come from?* Here it bears the meaning of *where have you just arrived from?* Also: **wo gehst du hin?** instead of **wohin gehst du?**, *where do you go?* ▸

A Helpful *(good)* Clue *(m.)*

1 – Oh boy, you really look terrific… so tanned! Where have you been *(where do you come from)*?
2 – Straight from the Canaries. They have *(there's)* the finest weather you can imagine *(you think)*!
3 – Marvellous! I really envy you! Have you been there often?
4 – Yes, five times. We've spent our winter holidays *(m.)* there for the last five years *(since five years we spend...)*.
5 – My wife and I have wanted to go there for a long time, but something is always coming up.
6 – But if you go there one day, I can give you some helpful *(good)* tips.
7 – Unfortunately not this summer *(m.)*, but maybe it'll work out alright next spring *(m.)*.

Hin and **her** are adverbs; they denote a change in position: **her**, towards the speaker; **hin**, away from the speakers: **Komm hierher**, *Come here!* **Geh dorthin!**, *Go there!* (see note 4).

② **das** is the relative pronoun of a neuter noun (here: **das Wetter**). **Das Buch, das ich lese ist interessant**, *The book that I am reading is interesting.* **Man** is the impersonal pronoun. In English it is generally translated with a passive form or *you.*

③ **einmal**, *once*; **zweimal**, *twice…*

④ **Wir fahren dorthin**, *We go there.* **Wir kommen dorther**, *We come from there.* **Ich muß dorthin**, *I must go there*; it's not necessary to use the verb.

37

8 – Sie m**ü**ssen dann **u**nbedingt ins Hot**e**l „M**ee**resstrand ⑤“ g**e**hen.

9 Der Bes**i**tzer ist ein g**u**ter Freund von mir. Sie fr**a**gen nur nach ⑥ W**o**lfgang H**a**nsen. Und im Str**a**ndrestaur**a**nt fr**a**gen Sie nach P**e**ter Schmitt und im Cas**i**no nach W**e**rner…

10 – Sind dort denn so v**ie**le D**eu**tsche?

11 – Oh ja, das ist **ei**nes **i**hrer bel**ie**btesten Ferienz**ie**le ⑦. □

Notes

⑤ Remember that the article of a compound noun depends on the gender of the last word.

⑥ **fragen**, *to ask*, is followed by the preposition **nach** + dative: **Ich frage nach dem Weg**, *I ask the way*. **Er fragt nach Herrn Schmitt**, *He asks for Mr. Schmitt.*

⑦ **das Ziel**, **die Ziele**, *the destination(s), goal, aim.*

***

Übung 1 – Übersetzen Sie bitte

❶ Sie sieht sehr gut aus. ❷ Das ist das beste Essen, das man sich denken kann. ❸ Wir fahren jedes Jahr dorthin. ❹ Deine Schwester hat nach dir gefragt. ❺ Sie hat erst ein Kind und möchte gern ein zweites. ❻ Sein Bruder ist ein guter Freund von mir.

8 – Then you really must go to the "Seabeach" *(m.)* hotel.
9 The owner *(m.)* is a good friend of mine. You just ask for *(after)* Wolfgang Hansen. And in the beach restaurant you ask for Peter Schmitt and in the casino for Werner…
10 – Are there so many Germans?
11 – Oh yes, that's one of their most favourite holiday resorts *(destinations)*. □

***

Answers to exercise 1

❶ She is very good-looking. ❷ It is the best meal you can imagine. ❸ We go there every year. ❹ Your sister asked for you. ❺ She has only one child and would like another one *(a second)*. ❻ His brother is a good friend of mine.

Übung 2 – Ergänzen Sie bitte

1. Where are you going this summer? – We are going to Majorca.
   . . . . . fahren Sie in diesem Sommer? – Wir fahren . . . . Mallorca.
2. We are going there, too.
   Wir fahren auch . . . .
3. Where does your wife come from?
   . . . . . kommt . . . . Frau? – . . . München.
4. I come from there, too.
   Ich komme auch . . . .

38 Achtunddreissigste Lektion

Ein Ausweg?

1 – Warum hältst du an? Was ist los?
2 – Ich weiß nicht mehr, wo wir sind. Ich glaube, wir haben uns verirrt ①.
3 – Du kennst doch den Weg! Das hast du mir jedenfalls gesagt!
4 – Ja, das habe ich auch gedacht ②.

Pronunciation Key
*... **owssvayk 1** ... hailst ...*

Notes

① **sich verirren**, *to get lost*. Please note how the past participle of verbs with separable prefixes is formed: **Er hat sich verirrt**, *He got lost*. You do not add **ge-** in these instances. ▸

⑤ You really must see this film. It is marvellous.
Sie müssen . . . . diesen Film sehen. Er ist . . . .

⑥ Ask for Mr. Hansen. He is a good friend of mine.
Fragen Sie . . . . Herrn Hansen. Er ist . . . . Freund . . . mir.

Answers to exercise 2
❶ Wohin – nach – ❷ – dorthin ❸ Woher – Ihre – Aus – ❹ – dorther ❺ – unbedingt – herrlich ❻ – nach – ein guter – von –

38th Lesson 38

A Way Out?

1 – Why have you stopped *(do you stop)*? What is the matter?
2 – I don't know *(any more)* where we are. I think we've got lost.
3 – But you know the way *(m.)*! At least that's what you told me!
4 – Yes, that's what I thought, too.

② **denken**, *to think*, the past participle is irregular: **gedacht**, *thought*.

5 Aber in dieser Schneelandschaft sieht ③ alles ganz anders aus ③.
6 – Gibt es denn keine Wegweiser?
7 – Nein, nicht einen einzigen!
8 – Und weit und breit kein Mensch, den wir fragen können!
9 – Sollen wir vielleicht besser umkehren?
10 – Es wird ④ schon dunkel.
11 – Dort kommt ein Auto! Fahren wir doch einfach hinterher!
12 Es wird ⑤ uns schon irgendwohin führen.

(Fortsetzung folgt) □

5 *… shnaylanntshaft …* **6** *… vaykvizer …*

Notes

③ **aussehen**, *to look*; **Sie sehen müde aus**, *You look tired.*

④ **werden**, *to become, to get*. **Arzt werden**, *to become a doctor*; **Es wird dunkel**, *It's getting dark.*

⑤ **werden** is also used to form the future: **ich schlafe**, *I sleep*; **ich werde schlafen**, *I will sleep* (see lesson 42, paragraph 2).

***

Übung 1 – Übersetzen Sie bitte

❶ Können Sie mir den Weg zum Bahnhof sagen? ❷ Sie sehen heute so müde aus! ❸ Es wird endlich Sommer. ❹ Ich sehe weit und breit keinen Wegweiser. ❺ Die Landschaft sieht heute ganz anders aus. ❻ Das haben wir alle gedacht; aber es war nicht so.

5 But in this snow [covered] landscape *(f.)* everything looks completely different.
6 – Are there no road signs?
7 – No, not a single [one]!
8 – And no-one in sight *(far and wide)* whom we can ask!
9 – Hadn't we *(shall we)* better go back?
10 – It's already getting dark.
11 – There's a car coming! Let's follow it *(drive after)*!
12 It'll lead us somewhere.

(To be continued) □

***

Answers to exercise 1

❶ Can you tell me the way to the station? ❷ You look so tired today! ❸ Summer's coming after all *(It's getting summer...)*. ❹ There's no road sign in sight. ❺ The landscape looks completely different today. ❻ That's what we all thought; but it wasn't so.

Übung 2 – Ergänzen Sie bitte

❶ We must stop here. I don't know where we are *(any more)*.
Wir müssen hier . . . . Ich . . . . nicht mehr, . . wir sind.

❷ I can't see a road-sign. We must ask the way.
Ich sehe keinen . . . . Wir müssen nach . . . . . . fragen.

❸ What is the matter? Why is it getting so dark?
Was ist . . . ? Warum . . . . es so dunkel?

❹ But you know this town! At least, that's what you told me!
Sie . . . . . . doch diese Stadt! Das haben Sie mir . . . . gesagt!

39 Neununddreissigste Lektion

Ein Ausweg? (Fortsetzung)

1 – Du, der fährt immer ① schneller! Ich kann ihm kaum noch folgen ②.
2 – Er scheint ③ den Weg gut zu kennen.

Pronunciation Key
2 *... shaynnt ...*

Notes

① **immer**, *always*, before an adjective means more and more: **immer größer**, *bigger and bigger*; **immer besser**, *better and better.*

❺ Today everything looks completely different.
Heute ..... alles ganz anders .... .

❻ He thinks that he has got lost.
Er ......, er ... sich ....

Answers to exercise 2
❶ – anhalten – weiß – wo – ❷ – Wegweiser – dem Weg – ❸ – los – wird – ❹ – kennen – jedenfalls – ❺ – sieht – aus ❻ – glaubt – hat – verirrt

39th Lesson 39

A Way Out? (continued)

1 – Look, he is driving faster and faster! I can hardly follow him.
2 – He seems to know his *(the)* way well.

② **folgen**, *to follow* + dative (indirect object): **Wem folgen Sie?**, *Whom are you following?*

③ **scheinen**, *to seem*. **Sie scheint viel Geld zu haben**, *She seems to have a lot of money.*

3 – Wo ist er denn jetzt? K**e**ine L**i**chter ④ mehr! Das ist doch nicht m**ö**glich!
4 – Ja, das ist **u**nheimlich. Da stimmt **e**twas nicht! ⑤
5 – V**o**rsicht, ich gl**au**be, da ist j**e**mand! Mein Gott, bin ich erschr**o**cken ⑥!
6 – G**u**ten Tag, H**ä**nde hoch! War**u**m verf**o**lgen Sie mich ⑦?
7 – W**a**rten Sie, m**a**chen Sie b**i**tte k**ei**nen Quatsch ⑧! Wir sind k**ei**ne Verbr**e**cher!
8 Wir h**a**ben uns nur ver**i**rrt und ged**a**cht…
9 – Ha, ha, h**a**ben Sie k**ei**ne Angst! Das ist nur **ei**ne Schr**e**ckschußpist**o**le…
10 S**e**hen Sie, wir f**a**hren seit zehn Min**u**ten im Kreis auf m**ei**nem Priv**a**tgrundstück,
11 und h**eu**tzutage kann man nie w**i**ssen… □

***4** … **oo**nnhime-liçh. **7** … kvatsh!*
***9** … shr**e**kkshoosspist**oh**le …*

Notes

④ **das Licht**, **die Lichter**, *the light(s).*

⑤ **das stimmt**, *that's right.* Please note the expression: **Es stimmt etwas nicht**, *There is something wrong here.* ▸

***

Übung 1 – Übersetzen Sie bitte

❶ Zeigen Sie uns bitte den Weg! Wir folgen Ihnen! ❷ Es wird immer dunkler. Ich kann kaum noch die Straße sehen. ❸ Er fährt seit einer Stunde im Kreis. ❹ Sie haben sich verirrt, und sie wissen nicht mehr, wo sie sind. ❺ Sie scheint diese Person gut zu kennen.

3 – But where is he now? No more lights! That's impossible!
4 – Yes, that's frightening. Something is wrong here!
5 – Be careful! I think there is somebody there! My God! I was so frightened!
6 – Good evening *(day)*, hands up! Why do you keep following me?
7 – Wait, don't do anything silly *(any nonsense [m.])*! We are not criminals!
8 We only got lost and thought…
9 – Ha, ha don't be afraid! This is only an alarm pistol *(f.)*...
10 You see, we have been driving around in circles *(a circle [m.])* on my property *(n.)* for ten minutes,
11 and these days you can never tell *(know)*… □

⑥ **erschrecken**, *to frighten*, has two past participles: **Der Hund hat mich erschreckt**, *The dog frightened me* (transitive). But, **Ich bin erschrocken**, *I was frightened* (intransitive).

⑦ **verfolgen**, *to follow, to pursue* + accusative/direct object in German. **Die Polizei verfolgt den Verbrecher**, *The police pursue the criminal.*

⑧ **der Quatsch**: a familiar expression for **die Dummheit**, *foolishness, silliness*. **Er erzählt viel Quatsch**, *He talks a lot of nonsense.*

***

Answers to exercise 1

❶ Show us the way please! We will follow you! ❷ It's getting darker and darker. I can hardly see the road. ❸ He has been driving around in circles *(a circle)* for an hour. ❹ They've got lost and they don't know where they are any more. ❺ She seems to know this person well.

39 Übung 2 – Ergänzen Sie bitte

1. I'll show you the way. Follow me please!
   Ich . . . . . Ihnen den Weg. Folgen Sie . . . bitte!

2. He is walking more and more slowly. He seems to be tired.
   Er geht . . . . . langsamer. Er . . . . müde . . sein.

3. She was frightened but he was not afraid.
   Sie ist . . . .; aber er hat . . . . gehabt.

4. They got lost. They have been driving around in circles.
   Sie . . . . . sich . . . . Sie sind im Kreis . . . .

5. Don't do anything silly please! I can't understand you.
   Mach bitte . . . . . . Quatsch! Ich . . . . dich nicht.

6. There is something wrong here. I can't see any lights any more.
   Da . . . . . . etwas nicht. Ich sehe . . . . mehr.

Answers to exercise 2

❶ – zeige – mir – ❷ – immer – scheint – zu – ❸ – erschrocken – keine Angst – ❹ – haben – verirrt – gefahren ❺ – keinen – verstehe – ❻ – stimmt – keine Lichter –

40 Vierzigste Lektion

Endstation

1 – **E**ndstation! **A**lles **au**ssteigen ① bitte!
2 **A**lle L**eu**te st**ei**gen aus - bis auf **ei**nen ② kl**ei**nen, **a**lten Mann,
3 der **ei**ngeschlafen ③ zu sein scheint. [N. 1.3]
4 Der B**u**sfahrer geht zu ihm und spricht ④ ihn an ④:
5 – H**ö**ren Sie, Sie müssen **au**ssteigen!
6 – War**u**m? F**a**hren Sie nicht w**ei**ter ⑤?
7 – Doch, ich f**a**hre w**ei**ter.
8 – Das ist gut. Ich will auch w**ei**terfahren.
9 – Das geht nicht. Hier ist **E**ndstation.
10 – Ja, **a**ber Sie h**a**ben ger**a**de ⑥ ges**a**gt, daß Sie w**ei**terfahren ⑦.

Pronunciation Key
*enntshtatsi**oh**n **1** … **ow**s'shty-g̲en …*

Notes

① **aussteigen**, *to get off*; **einsteigen**, *to get in*. **Aus** and **ein** are separable prefixes.

② **bis**, *until*; **Er hat bis 12 Uhr gewartet**, *He waited until 12 o'clock*. But: **bis auf** + accusative: *except, but*. **Alle bis auf einen**, *all but one*.

③ **einschlafen**, *to fall asleep*: **ich schlafe ein**, *I fall asleep*. **Ich bin eingeschlafen**, *I fell (have fallen) asleep*. Please note the word order in the <u>subordinate clause where the verb is at the end!</u>

Last Stop *(End station) (f.)*

1 – Terminus! Everybody [gets] off please!
2 Everybody gets off - but *(except)* a little old man
3 who seems to have fallen asleep.
4 The bus driver *(m.)* goes towards him and talks to him:
5 – Listen. You have to get off!
6 – Why? Aren't you driving on?
7 – I am going on.
8 – That's fine. I want to go on too.
9 – That's impossible *(that does not go)*. This *(here)* is the last stop.
10 – Yes, but you just said that you drove on.

④ **sprechen**, *to speak*; **jemanden ansprechen**, *to speak/talk to someone*. **Er hat mich ohne zu zögern angesprochen**, *He spoke to me without hesitation* (**zögern**, *to hesitate*).

⑤ **weiter**: added to a verb as a prefix means *to continue, to go on*... **Sprechen Sie!**, *Speak!* **Sprechen Sie weiter!**, *Go on speaking!*

⑥ **gerade** (adverb) with a verb in the past: **Sie ist gerade eingeschlafen**, *She has just fallen asleep.*

⑦ In a subordinate clause introduced by **daß** the prefix is not separated from the verb: **Fahren Sie heute zurück?**, *Are you returning today?* But: **Er hat gesagt, daß er heute zurückfährt**.

11 – Ja… nein… gut! Ich f**a**hre nicht w**ei**ter; ich f**a**hre zur**ü**ck.

12 – Oh, das macht nichts. Dann w**e**rde ich mit **I**hnen zur**ü**ckfahren… □

***

Übung 1 – Übersetzen Sie bitte

❶ Steigen Sie bitte alle aus! ❷ Du mußt schnell einsteigen! Der Zug fährt sofort ab. ❸ Ich bin gestern angekommen und werde morgen zurückfahren. ❹ Wir bleiben heute nacht in diesem Hotel und fahren morgen früh weiter. ❺ Ich bin heute nachmittag im Büro eingeschlafen.

Übung 2 – Ergänzen Sie bitte

❶ Where do we have to get off?
Wo müssen wir . . . . ?

❷ Why are you stopping? Drive on please!
. . . . . halten Sie an? . . . . . . Sie doch bitte . . . . . .!

❸ He is returning home tomorrow.
Er . . . . . morgen . . . . . . nach Hause.

❹ That does not matter. We have a lot of time left.
Das macht . . . . Wir haben noch viel . . . . .

❺ Where did you get on?
Wo sind Sie . . . . ?

❻ You have eaten everything but this little piece of cheese?
Du . . . . alles . . . . . . dieses kleine Stück Käse . . . . ?

11 – Yes… no… well! I am not driving on. I am returning *(driving back)*.
12 – Oh, that does not matter. Then I will go back with you… □

***

Answers to exercise 1

❶ Everybody [gets] off, please! ❷ You have to get in quickly! The train is leaving immediately. ❸ I arrived yesterday and I will return tomorrow. ❹ We will stay in this hotel tonight and go on tomorrow morning. ❺ I fell asleep in the office this afternoon.

Answers to exercise 2

❶ – aussteigen ❷ Warum – Fahren – weiter ❸ – fährt – zurück – ❹ – nichts – Zeit ❺ – eingestiegen ❻ – hast – bis auf – gegessen

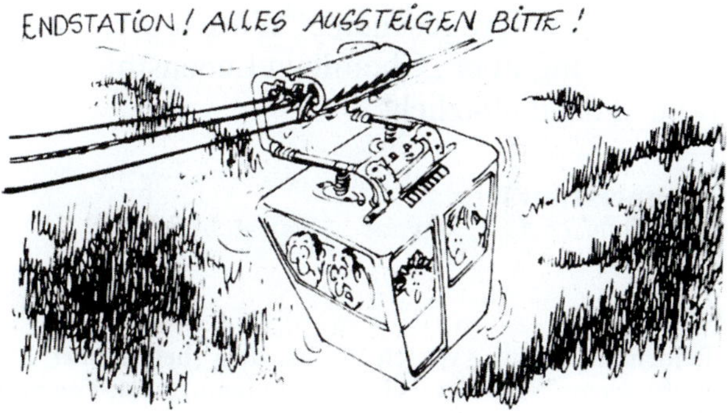
ENDSTATION! ALLES AUSSTEIGEN BITTE!

41 Einundvierzigste Lektion

Beim Arzt

1 – Sie s**e**hen **a**ber schlecht aus, Frau M**ei**er!
2 – Deshalb bin ich zu ① **I**hnen gek**o**mmen, Herr D**o**ktor.
3 – Was fehlt **I**hnen denn? ②
4 – Mir war g**e**stern **a**bend sehr schlecht. ③
5 Ich h**a**be mich den g**a**nzen **A**bend überg**e**ben.
6 – Und h**eu**te, wie geht es **I**hnen h**eu**te?
7 – B**e**sser, **a**ber ich f**ü**hle mich noch **e**twas schwach auf den B**ei**nen ④.
8 – H**a**ben Sie noch M**a**genschmerzen?
9 – Nein, mir ist nur **e**twas schw**i**ndlig. ⑤
10 – Tja, viell**ei**cht h**a**ben Sie g**e**stern **e**twas K**o**misches ⑥ geg**e**ssen?
11 – Nein, ich h**a**be das geg**e**ssen, was **a**lle geg**e**ssen h**a**ben.
12 – Mm, so. Wann ist **I**hnen denn schlecht gew**o**rden ⑦?
13 – Ich h**a**be f**e**rngesehen… W**i**ssen Sie, die S**e**ndung **ü**ber „Chem**ie** in L**e**bensmitteln ⑧“ und dann pl**ö**tzlich… □

Pronunciation Key
***9** … shvinndliçh **13** … shemee … plertsliçh*

Notes

① Remember that we say: **Ich bin bei dem (beim) Arzt**, *I am at the doctor's*. But: **Ich gehe zu dem (zum) Arzt**, *I go to the doctor's*. ▸

At the Doctor's

1 – You look really ill Mrs. Meier!
2 – That's why I've come to see you, *(Mister)* doctor!
3 – What's wrong with you?
4 – I felt very sick last night.
5 I was sick all evening.
6 – And today, how do you feel today?
7 – Better, but I still feel a little bit shaky *(weak on my legs)*.
8 – Have you still got a stomach-ache?
9 – No, I only feel a little bit dizzy.
10 – Mm, maybe you had something funny to eat?
11 – No, I ate what everybody [else] ate [too].
12 – Well, [so]. When did you begin to feel sick?
13 – I watched the TV. You know, the programme on "chemicals in food" and then all of a sudden… □

② **Was fehlt Ihnen denn?/Was haben Sie denn?**, *What's wrong with you?/what's the matter with you?* If you feel well you answer: **Es fehlt mir nichts** or **Ich habe nichts.**

③ **Es geht mir gut**, *I am fine;* (*it goes me well*). **Es ist mir heiß/kalt**; *I am hot/cold.* **Es ist mir schlecht**, *I feel/am sick*. We can leave out **es** and say, **Mir ist schlecht**.

④ **das Bein**, **die Beine**, *the leg(s).* **Den Beinen** is the dative plural.

⑤ **Es ist mir schwindlig**, *I feel dizzy.*

⑥ **etwas Schönes/Schlechtes**, *something nice/bad*; **etwas Komisches**, *something funny*; in this expression **Komisches** is a neuter noun.

⑦ **geworden** is the past participle of **werden**, *to become*, *get.*

⑧ **das Mittel**, **die Mittel**, *the stuff*; nouns ending in **-el** or **-er** do not change in the plural: **das Zimmer**, **die Zimmer**.

41 **Übung 1 – Übersetzen Sie bitte**

❶ Du siehst schlecht aus! Was hast du? ❷ Ich habe Magenschmerzen und mir ist schwindlig. ❸ Wir haben den ganzen Samstagabend ferngesehen. ❹ Ich fühle mich plötzlich ganz schwach. ❺ Ich will das essen, was du ißt. ❻ Wann sind Sie denn krank geworden?

Übung 2 – Ergänzen Sie bitte

❶ Maybe you had something bad to eat?
Hast du vielleicht . . . . gegessen?

❷ What's the matter with you?
Was . . . . . Ihnen denn?

❸ Did you watch the programme on German universities yesterday?
Haben Sie gestern . . . . über deutsche Universitäten . . . . ?

❹ When did you begin to feel dizzy?
Wann . . . Ihnen schwindlig . . . . ?

❺ Do you feel very weak?
. . . . . . Sie sich sehr . . . . ?

❻ He cannot work today. He feels very sick.
Er . . . . heute nicht . . . . Ihm ist sehr . . . .

Answers to exercise 1

❶ You look ill! What's the matter with you? ❷ I have a stomach-ache and I feel dizzy. ❸ We watched the TV all Saturday evening. ❹ I feel all dizzy suddenly. ❺ I want to eat what you eat. ❻ When did you begin to feel ill?

Answers to exercise 2

❶ – etwas Schlechtes – ❷ – fehlt – ❸ – die Sendung – gesehen ❹ – ist – geworden ❺ Fühlen – schwach ❻ – kann – arbeiten – schlecht

42 Zweiundvierzigste lektion

Wiederholung und Erklärungen

1 The Perfect Tense in German

1.1 The Perfect Tense

The perfect tense is formed with the present tense of **haben** or **sein** + the past participle of the verb. For the past participle of regular verbs you add the prefix **ge-** and **-t** at the end of the stem.
machen → gemacht, *done/made*
sagen → gesagt, *said*
fragen → gefragt, *asked*
The past participle is placed at the end of the phrase:
Er hat viel gearbeitet, *he (has) worked a lot.*

1.2 Verbs Denoting a Change in Position

Verbs denoting a change in position, form the perfect with the present tense of **sein** + the past participle: **Ich bin letzte Woche nach Berlin gefahren**, *I went to Berlin last week.*
Sie sind zu spät gekommen, *They were late (came late).*
At the end of the book you will find a list of the irregular verbs and participles.

1.3 Verbs with Separable/Inseparable Prefixes

• Verbs with separable prefixes: **ge-** is put between the prefix and the stem: **aufpassen**, *to pay attention.* **Er hat nicht aufgepaßt**, *He did not pay attention.* **Zurückfahren**, *to return.* **Wir sind sofort zurückgefahren**, *We returned immediately.*
Fernsehen, *to watch the TV.* **Hast du gestern abend ferngesehen?**, *Did you watch the TV yesterday evening?*

• Verbs with inseparable prefixes: the past participle is formed without the prefix ge-.
Bezahlen, *to pay.* **sie haben Ihre Rechnung noch nicht bezahlt**, *You have not paid your bill yet.*
Erzählen, *to tell.* **Er hat mir viele Geschichten erzählt**, *He told me a lot of stories.*
Vergessen, *to forget.* **Ich habe seine Telefonnummer vergessen**, *I forgot his telephone number.*

An exception: **sein** forms the perfect by itself: **Ich bin gewesen**, *I have been*; **du bist gewesen**, *you have been*; **er ist gewesen**…

In spoken language the perfect is generally used for the simple past (the imperfect) and the present perfect. (See examples above and on page 169).

2 The Future Tense

The future tense is formed with **werden** + the infinitive of the verb:

ich werde arbeiten	*I will work*
du wirst arbeiten	*you will work*
er, sie, es wird arbeiten	*he, she, it will work*
wir werden arbeiten	*we will work*
ihr werdet arbeiten	*you will work*
sie werden arbeiten	*they will work*

The infinitive is placed at the end of the sentence and **werden** takes the position of the verb: the second position.
Ich werde nach Hause gehen, *I will go home.* **Sie werden um 1 Uhr zu Mittag essen**, *They will have lunch at 1 o'clock.* **Was wirst du heute nachmittag machen?**, *What will you do this afternoon?*

Jetzt sind Sie dran! Übersetzen Sie bitte, *Now it's your turn! Please translate!*

Tomorrow Mr. Schmitt will go (by car) to his office at nine o'clock. But he will return (already) at eleven o'clock because he will be too tired to work. He will drink another (a second) cup of coffee and half an hour later he will go back (again) to his office. (Translation at the end of the lesson).

43 3 Adverbs and separable prefixes of position

Let's talk once more about **hin** and **her**:
Her indicates direction towards the speakers; **hin** indicates direction away from the speaker. They are **adverbs** or **separable prefixes** and can only be used with a verb denoting a change in position. They can be added to another adverb of place.
Ex.: **dahin**, **dorther**.
Woher kommt Ihre Mutter?, *Where has your mother just arrived from?* **Aus Frankreich?**, *From France?* **Mein Vater kommt auch dorther**, *My father has just arrived from there too.*
Wohin fahren Sie in Ferien? – Nach Italien? Wir fahren auch dorthin. *Where are you going on holiday? – To Italy? We are going there too.*
Komm hierhier! *Come here!*
Geh dorthin! *Go there!*

43 Dreiundvierzigste Lektion

Die guten, alten Zeiten

1 Gegen sieben Uhr ist Herr Kleinemann von der Arbeit nach Hause gekommen.
2 Er hat seiner Frau, die an der Tür auf ihn gewartet ① hat,
3 seinen Mantel und seine Aktentasche gegeben und gefragt:
4 – Ist das Abendessen fertig?

Note

① **warten**, *to wait*; **gewartet**, *waited*. When the stem of a word already ends in **-t**, we add **-et**. E.g., **antworten**, *to answer;* **ich habe geantwortet**. **Arbeiten**, *to work*; **gearbeitet**. Notice that ▸

4 The impersonal pronoun *man*

The impersonal pronoun **man** is generally translated by: *you, they* or a passive form:
Wo kann man Briefmarken kaufen?, *Where can you buy stamps?*
Man sieht sie immer zusammen, *They are always seen together.*

5 Translation (paragraph 2)

Herr Schmitt wird morgen um neun Uhr ins Büro fahren. Aber er wird schon um elf Uhr zurückfahren, denn er wird zum Arbeiten zu müde sein. Er wird mit seiner Frau eine zweite Tasse Kaffee trinken und eine halbe Stunde später wieder ins Büro fahren.

43rd Lesson 43

Good, Old Times

1 Mr. Kleinemann came home from work *(f.)* at around seven o'clock. *(Around...)*.
2 He gave his coat *(m.)* and his briefcase *(f.)* to his wife who was waiting
3 for him at the door and asked her:
4 – Is dinner ready?

▸ **warten** is followed by the preposition **auf** + accusative: **Ich habe auf meinen Freund gewartet**, *I have been waiting for my friend.*

43

5 – In fünf Minuten! Ich bin gerade ② beim Tischdecken ③.
6 – Wohin hast du das Fernsehprogramm gelegt ④?
7 – Es liegt auf dem Tisch neben dem Fenster. Ich hole ⑤ es dir sofort.
8 Dann hat sich Herr Kleinemann in den Sessel vor den Fernsehapparat gesetzt ⑥,
9 seine Beine von sich gestreckt und gerufen: ???

10 – Na? Was hat Herr Kleinemann gerufen?
11 Falls Ihnen die richtige Antwort nicht auf der Zunge liegt,
12 drehen Sie das Buch herum und Sie finden die Lösung:
13 – □ Wohin hast du meine Pantoffeln gestellt ⑦?

Pronunciation Key
7...leekt...hohle...8ge-zetst9...geshtrekt...11...tsoonge...

Notes

② **gerade**, *just*. When added to a verb in the present tense it is translated by: *to be about to* or *just*: **Sie schreibt gerade einen Brief**, *She is about to write a letter.*

③ **den Tisch decken**, *to lay the table* (**decken**, *to cover*).

④ **legen**, *to lay, to put*. **Ich lege das Messer auf den Tisch**, *I put the knife on the table.*
The preposition **auf** is followed by the **accusative** because **legen** is a verb denoting a change in position. The corresponding question is: **Wohin legst du das Messer?**, *Where do you put the knife?* ▶

5 – In five minutes! I am about to lay the table.
6 – Where did you put the TV program *(n.)?*
7 – It is *(lies)* on the table *(m.)* next [to] the window *(m.)*. I will fetch it for you immediately.
8 Then, Mr. Kleinemann sat down in the armchair *(m.)* in front of the TV *(m.)*,
9 stretched out his legs *(of him)* and shouted: ???

10 – So, and what did Mr. Kleinemann shout?
11 If you don't have the right answer *(f.)* on the [tip of your] tongue,
12 turn your book *(n.)* upside down and you will find the solution *(f.)*:
13 – □ Where did you put my slippers?

▸ But: **liegen**, *to lie*, denotes no change in position therefore the respective preposition is followed by the dative and the question is: **Wo?**

⑤ **holen**, *to fetch, to get*. **Abholen**, *to go to get/fetch, to call for someone*. **Er holt die Kinder von der Schule ab**, *He goes to fetch the children from school*. **Er hat Paul abgeholt**, *He called for Paul*. **Er holt das Paket ab**, *He goes to get the parcel*.

⑥ **sich setzen**, *to sit down*, is also a verb denoting a change in position. Thus, the corresponding question is: **Wohin setzt er sich?**, *Where does he sit down?* The answer is: **In den** (acc.) **Sessel**, *In the armchair*.

⑦ **stellen**, *to put*, for something that "stands": **Ich stelle die Blumenvase auf den Tisch**, *I put the (flower) vase on the table*. But, **stehen**, *to stand*: **die Blumenvase steht auf dem Tisch**, *The vase stands/is on the table* (see lesson 26).

Übung 1 – Übersetzen Sie bitte

❶ Wann bist du nach Hause gekommen? – Gegen Mitternacht. ❷ Er hat eine Stunde auf seine Frau gewartet. ❸ Ich kann jetzt nicht kommen. Ich bin gerade beim Kochen. ❹ Falls Sie die richtige Antwort nicht finden, rufen Sie mich. ❺ Ich werde Ihnen helfen.

Übung 2 – Ergänzen Sie bitte mit den Verben: setzen, stellen, legen
Exercise 2 – Complete using the verbs: "to put, to sit"

❶ Where did Mr. Huber put his bicycle? – In the cellar.
Wohin . . . Herr Huber sein Fahrrad . . . . ?
– In . . . Keller.

❷ Where did you put the newspaper? – On the table.
Wohin . . . . . Sie die Zeitung . . . . . . ?
– Auf . . . Tisch.

Übung 3 – Ergänzen Sie bitte mit den Verben: sitzen, stehen, liegen
Exercise 3 – Complete using the verbs: "to sit, to stand, to lie"

❶ Where is *(stands)* your car? – In front of the garage.
Wo . . . . . dein Wagen? – Vor . . . Garage.

❷ Where are *(lie)* my letters? – On your desk.
Wo . . . . . . meine Briefe? – Auf . . . . . . Schreibtisch.

❸ Where are you sitting? – In the fifth row.
Wo . . . . . du? – In . . . fünften Reihe.

Answers to exercise 1

❶ When did you come home? – At around midnight. ❷ He has been waiting for his wife for an hour. ❸ I can't come now, I'm *(just)* cooking. ❹ Call me, if you don't find the right answer. ❺ I will help you.

❸ Where did you put the little cat? – In the basket.
Wohin .... du die kleine Katze .... ?
– In ..... Korb.

❹ Where shall I sit down? – On my right.
Wohin soll ich mich ...... ?
– Rechts neben ..... .

Answers to exercise 2

❶ – hat – gestellt – den – ❷ – haben – gelegt – den – ❸ – hast – gesetzt – ihren – ❹ – setzen – mich

Answers to exercise 3

❶ – steht – der – ❷ – liegen – deinem – ❸ – sitzt – der –

44 Vierundvierzigste Lektion

Lieber Christian!

1 Seit fast **ei**nem M**o**nat hast Du nichts mehr von mir geh**ö**rt. ①
2 Inzw**i**schen ist viel gesch**e**hen ②. Ich war sehr besch**ä**ftigt.
3 Vor ③ gut zwei W**o**chen h**a**be ich mich bei **ei**nem Z**i**rkus bew**o**rben ④.
4 Ich h**a**be die St**e**lle bek**o**mmen und sof**o**rt beg**o**nnen ⑤ zu **a**rbeiten.
5 Was war ich froh!
6 M**ei**ne beste N**u**mmer (du weißt schon: „der K**o**pfstand") hat den Z**u**schauern sehr gut gef**a**llen.
7 Sie h**a**ben viel gekl**a**tscht, und ich bin schnell ber**ü**hmt gew**o**rden.
8 Aber vor drei T**a**gen ist **e**twas Schr**e**ckliches pass**ie**rt.
9 Ich bin mit dem Kopf in **ei**nen r**o**stigen N**a**gel gef**a**llen ⑥,
10 und die W**u**nde hat sich so stark entz**ü**ndet,
11 daß ich m**i**ndestens **ei**ne W**o**che nicht **a**rbeiten kann.

Notes

① Try to remember the expression: **Hast du schon etwas von ihm gehört?**, *Have you heard (anything) from him?* **Ich habe noch nichts von ihm gehört**, *I haven't heard anything from him.*

② **geschehen**, **passieren**, *to happen*. **Was geschieht**, **passiert hier?**, *What is happening here?*
The past participle of **geschehen** = the infinitive. ▸

Dear Christian!

1 You haven't heard anything from me for about a month *(m.)*.
2 In the meantime many things have happened. I was very busy.
3 About a fortnight ago I applied for a job at a circus *(m.)*.
4 I got the job and started *(to)* work immediately.
5 I was very happy!
6 The audience liked my best number very much (you know what I mean: "the head-stand").
7 They applauded a lot, I became famous very quickly.
8 But three days ago something awful happened.
9 I fell on to a rusty nail *(m.)* with my head *(m.)*,
10 and the wound *(f.)* got so badly *(strong)* infected,
11 that I won't be able to work for at least one week *(f.)*.

Pronunciation Key
leeber kristyahn

③ **vor** (*time*), *ago*; **vor einem Jahr**, *one year ago (***vor** is followed by the dative); **vor zehn Minuten**, *ten minutes ago.*

④ **sich bewerben um**, *to apply for.* **Er bewirbt sich um diese Stelle**, *He applies for this job.* **Er hat sich um diese Stelle beworben**, *He applied for this job.*

⑤ **beginnen**, *to begin, to start* is followed by the infinitive with **zu**: **Es beginnt zu regnen**, *It begins to rain.* **Er hat vor drei Wochen begonnen Deutsch zu lernen**, *He started to learn German three weeks ago.*

⑥ **fallen**, *to fall* and **gefallen**, *to like, to be pleased*, have the same past participle: **das Kind ist ins Wasser gefallen**, *The child fell into the water*; **Der Film hat mir gut gefallen**, *I liked the film very much.*

44 **12** Man hat mich fristlos entlassen ⑦.
13 Kann ich ein Weilchen ⑧ zu Dir kommen?

Bis bald! Viele liebe Grüße

Dein Peter □

Notes

⑦ **entlassen**, *to fire, to dismiss*. The past participle is the same as the infinitive: **Der Direktor hat fünf Angestellte entlassen**, *The manager dismissed five employees.*

⑧ **eine Weile**, *a while*; **die Langeweile**, *boredom (long while).*

***

Übung 1 – Übersetzen Sie bitte

❶ Haben Sie schon etwas von Ihrem Mann gehört? ❷ Seit ein paar Wochen ist nichts Besonderes geschehen. ❸ Der Abend gestern hat allen sehr gut gefallen. ❹ Dieses Haus kostet mindestens dreihunderttausend Mark. ❺ Ich habe mich vor drei Wochen um diese Stelle beworben, und ich habe immer noch keine Antwort.

Übung 2 – Ergänzen Sie bitte

❶ I received your letter and answered [it] immediately.
Ich . . . . Ihren Brief gestern . . . . und . . . . sofort . . . .

❷ The audience liked the play very much. They applauded a lot *(for a long time).*
Das Theaterstück . . . den Zuschauern gut . . . . Sie . . . . . lange . . . .

❸ The company went bankrupt. All the employees were dismissed.
Die Firma . . . Bankrott . . . . Man . . . alle Angestellten . . . .

12 I was fired *(without notice)*.
13 May I come and stay with you for a little while? *(...I come to you...)*.

See you soon! (Many kind regards)
Love, Peter □

Answers to exercise 1

❶ Have you heard anything from your husband? ❷ Nothing special has been happening over the [last] few weeks. ❸ Everybody liked the party *(evening)* last night very much. ❹ This house costs at least three hundred thousand Marks. ❺ I applied for this job three weeks ago and I have not received an answer, yet.

❹ They have been living *(they live)* in Frankfurt for one year.
Sie wohnen . . . . in Frankfurt.

❺ He went *(drove)* to France two months ago.
Er . . . . nach Frankreich gefahren.

❻ Last week we were very busy.
Die letzte Woche waren wir sehr . . . .

Answers to exercise 2

❶ – habe – bekommen habe geantwortet ❷ – hat – gefallen – haben – geklatscht ❸ – hat – gemacht – hat – entlassen ❹ – seit einem Jahr – ❺ – ist vor zwei Monaten – ❻ – beschäftigt

45 Fünfundvierzigste Lektion

Neues Leben

(nach Kurt Tucholsky)

Berl**i**n, den 31. Dez**e**mber 1920
Berl**i**n, den 31. Dez**e**mber 1921
Berl**i**n, den 31. Dez**e**mber 1922
(**a**bends im Bett)

1 Von m**o**rgen ab fängt ① ein n**eu**es L**e**ben an ①.
2 G**e**stern h**a**be ich z**u**fällig D**o**ktor B**e**rgmann auf der Str**a**ße getr**o**ffen ②.
3 Er hat **ei**nen **o**rdentlichen Schreck bek**o**mmen und l**ei**se gefr**a**gt:
4 „Was m**a**chen Sie denn, l**ie**ber Freund? H**a**ben Sie **e**twas mit der L**e**ber?"
5 Ich soll ③ in den n**ä**chsten T**a**gen zu ihm k**o**mmen.
6 Nat**ü**rlich g**e**he ich hin.
7 Ich weiß schon, was er mir s**a**gen will, und er hat auch ganz recht.
8 So geht das nicht mehr w**ei**ter.

Pronunciation Key
*... koort toocH**o**lsky ... **i**ne-oont.dr**y**ssiçhstenn dets**e**mmber noyn-tsehn-h**oo**ndert-tsv**a**nntsiçh* **2** *... ts**oo**failliçh ...*

Notes

① **anfangen**, *to begin, to start*; past participle, **angefangen**. **Er hat um neun Uhr angefangen zu arbeiten**, *He began to work at* ▸

New Life *(m.)*

(adapted from Kurt Tucholsky)

Berlin, 31st December 1920
Berlin, 31st December 1921
Berlin, 31st December 1922
(in bed at night)

1 From tomorrow on a new life will begin.
2 Last night in the street I came across *(met accidentally)* Doctor Bergmann.
3 He was considerably frightened *(he got a considerable fright [m.])* and asked in a low voice *(quietly)*:
4 "But what is the matter with you *(do you do)* dear friend? Is something wrong with your liver *(f.)*?"
5 I have to see him within the next few days.
6 I will go there, of course.
7 I already know what he is going to tell me, and he is right after all.
8 It can't go on like this *(so)*.

9 o'clock. The infinitive following **anfangen** is preceded by **zu** *(= beginnen)*.

② **treffen – getroffen**, *to meet, met*. **Er trifft seine Freundin im Café**, *He meets his girlfriend in the cafe.*

③ **sollen**, *to have to*; an obligation imposed by a third person: **Der Doktor sagt, er soll weniger trinken und rauchen**, *The doctor says that he has to drink and smoke less.*

9 Also von morgen ab hört ④ mir das mit dem Bier bei Tisch auf ④.
10 Emmy darf ⑤ nicht mehr so fett kochen.
11 Ich stehe ⑥ früh um sechs auf ⑥ und fange wieder an, regelmäßig zu turnen.
12 („Wieder“ – denke ich deshalb, weil ich es mir schon so oft vorgenommen ⑦ habe.)
13 In drei Monaten bin ⑧ ich ein anderer Kerl ⑨. Schlank, elegant, gesund!

(Fortsetzung folgt) □

11 *... raygelmai'ssiçh ...*

Notes

④ **aufhören**, *to stop*; **es hat aufgehört zu regnen**, *It stopped raining.*

⑤ Remember that **dürfen** means to have the permission - *may*, **Er darf keinen Kaffee trinken**, *He mustn't drink coffee.* **Sie darf heute abend mit Freunden ausgehen**, *She may go out with friends tonight.*

***

Übung 1 – Übersetzen Sie bitte

❶ Wir haben gestern zufällig unseren Lehrer auf der Straße getroffen. ❷ Von morgen ab werde ich nicht mehr rauchen. ❸ Sie steht morgens um sieben Uhr auf und geht abends um elf Uhr ins Bett. ❹ Er hat sich vorgenommen, morgen früh aufzustehen. ❺ Hast du wieder angefangen, regelmäßig zu turnen?

9 Well, from tomorrow on, there will be no more beer at table.
10 Emmy mustn't cook such fatty food any more.
11 I will get up at six o'clock in the morning and start to exercise again.
12 (I think "again", because I have made up my mind to do it ever so often.)
13 In three months I will be another guy *(m.)*. Slim, elegant, in good health!

(To be continued) □

⑥ **aufstehen**, *to get up* and **aufwachen**, *to wake up*, form their perfect with **sein** because there is a change in position of state, **Ich bin um 6 Uhr aufgewacht, aber ich bin erst um 10 Uhr aufgestanden**, *I woke up at six o'clock, but I only got up at ten o'clock.*

⑦ **sich etwas vornehmen**, *to make up one's mind to do something*: **Ich nehme mir vor, ab morgen nicht mehr zu arbeiten**, *I have made up my mind to stop working from tomorrow onwards.*

⑧ In German you need not use the future tense if there is an adverb of time as: **morgen**, **übermorgen**, **nächste Woche**... E. g.: **Ich fliege übermorgen nach Paris**, *I will go (by plane) to Paris the day after tomorrow.*

⑨ **der Kerl**: **Er ist ein netter Kerl**, *He is a nice guy.*

***

Answers to exercise 1

❶ Yesterday we bumped into our teacher in the street *(we met accidentally)*. ❷ From tomorrow onwards I won't smoke any more. ❸ She gets up at seven o'clock in the morning and [she] goes to bed at eleven o'clock in the evening. ❹ He has made up his mind to get up early tomorrow. ❺ Did you start exercising regularly again?

46 Übung 2 – Ergänzen Sie bitte

❶ The film begins at eight o'clock and it ends at half past eleven.
Der Film . . . . . um acht Uhr . . und er . . . . um halb elf . . . .

❷ From tomorrow onwards I will get up earlier.
. . . morgen . . werde ich früher . . . .

❸ He asked in a low voice: "What is the matter with you?"
Er . . . leise . . . .: „Was . . . . ?"

❹ I already know what you want to tell me.
Ich . . . . schon, . . . Sie mir sagen . . . .

❺ We made up our minds not to smoke today.
Wir . . . . . uns . . . . heute nicht zu . . . .

❻ They mustn't go there.
Sie . . . . . . nicht dorthin gehen.

46 Sechsundvierzigste Lektion

Neues Leben (Fortsetzung)

1 Von **ü**bermorgen ab wird **a**lles ganz **a**nders ①.
2 **A**lso erst mal w**e**rde ich die Biblioth**e**k **au**fräumen.
3 Dann m**a**che ich nicht mehr **ü**berall d**ie**se kl**ei**nen Sch**u**lden ②,

Pronunciation Key
2 … owf'roymen

Answers to exercise 2

❶ – fängt – an – hört – auf ❷ Von – ab – aufstehen ❸ – hat – gefragt – machen Sie denn ❹ – weiß – was – wollen ❺ – haben – vorgenommen – rauchen ❻ – dürfen –

VON MORGEN AB WERDE ICH NICHT MEHR RAUCHEN

46th Lesson 46

New Life (continued)

1 From the day after tomorrow onwards everything will be completely different.
2 Well, firstly I will tidy up the bookshelves *(f.)*.
3 Then I won't continue to run up *(won't make any longer)* these small debts everywhere,

Notes

① **anders, verschieden**, *different*. **Der, die, das Andere** (m., f., n.).

② **die Schulden** (plur.), *debts*; **die Schuld,** *the guilt, fault.*

4 und die **a**lten bez**a**hle ich **a**lle ab.
5 Ich will w**ie**der jeden S**o**nntag ins Mus**e**um gehen,
6 das kann mir ja nichts sch**a**den.
7 **O**der l**ie**ber jeden ③ zw**ei**ten S**o**nntag – den **a**nderen S**o**nntag w**e**rden wir **Au**sflüge m**a**chen.
8 Man kennt ja sein **ei**genes Land nicht mehr.
9 Man kommt **e**ben zu nichts. Das hört jetzt auf.
10 Denn die H**au**ptsache ④ ist bei **a**lledem:
11 Man muß sich den Tag r**i**chtig **ei**nteilen.
12 Energ**ie**! H**o**pla! Das wird ein L**e**ben!
13 **A**nmerkung **ei**ner Fl**e**dermaus: „Wir w**e**rden ja s**e**hen! Ich werde n**ä**chstes Jahr w**ie**der vorb**ei**fliegen ⑤!“ □

*5 … mooz**ay**'oom … 7 … **ow**sflüge … 8 … **i**-genes … 10 … h**ow**pt'zacHe … 12 ennerg**ee**! … 13 forb**y**fleegen*

Notes

③ **Ich fahre jedes Wochenende auf das Land**, *Every weekend I go into the country.* **Sie besuchen jedes vierte Wochenende ihre Eltern**, *They go to see her parents every fourth weekend.* **Jeder zweite**, *every other*; **jeder dritte**, *one out of three, every third*. **Jedes zehnte Kind**, *one child out of ten*. ▸

***

Übung 1 – Übersetzen Sie bitte

❶ In einem Jahr wird alles ganz anders. ❷ Wir werden keine Schulden mehr haben und jeden Sonntag einen Ausflug machen. ❸ Die Hauptsache ist, daß wir gesund sind. ❹ Kommen Sie doch morgen nachmittag bei mir vorbei! ❺ Wir können ins Museum gehen oder einen Spaziergang machen. ❻ Habt ihr endlich euer Zimmer aufgeräumt? ❼ Ihr könnt ja eure eigenen Sachen nicht mehr finden!

4 and I will pay back all the old ones.
5 I want to go to the museum *(n.)* again every Sunday,
6 it can't do me any harm.
7 Or rather every other Sunday – *(every second Sunday)* – on the remaining *(other)* Sunday we will go on an excursion.
8 You don't even know your own country any more.
9 You don't have time to do anything. That will stop now.
10 For the main thing *(f.)* in all this is:
11 You have to organize *(divide)* your day correctly.
12 Energy! Whoops! That'll be a life!
13 Remark *(f.)* of a bat *(f.)*: "Wait and see! I'll fly past next year!" □

④ **das Haupt**, (fig.) *the head*. **Das Haupt dieser Bewegung ist Herr X**, *The head of this movement is Mr. X*. **Haupt** in a compound word means *principal, main, central*. **Der Hauptbahnhof**, *the main/central station*; **der Haupteingang**, *the main entrance*.

⑤ **vorbei** added to a verb as separable prefix means *past*. **Den ganzen Tag fahren Züge an meinem Fenster vorbei**, *All day long trains are coming past my window*. But: **Ich bin gestern bei dir vorbeigekommen**, *I dropped in on you yesterday*.

***

Answers to exercise 1

❶ Everything will be completely different in a year. ❷ We won't have any more debts and we will go on an excursion every Sunday. ❸ The most important *(main)* thing is that we are healthy. ❹ Come round to my house tomorrow afternoon! ❺ We can go to the museum or go for a walk. ❻ Have you tidied up your room after all? ❼ You can't find your own things any more!

46 Übung 2 – Ergänzen Sie bitte

❶ I will go to the swimming pool again every Monday.
Ich . . . . . wieder . . . . ins Schwimmbad gehen.

❷ This morning we went past your house but we didn't see you.
Wir . . . . heute morgen an Ihrem Haus . . . . aber wir . . . . . Sie nicht . . . .

❸ It can't do any harm!
Das kann nichts . . . . !

❹ He has to go to Kassel every other *(every second)* month.
Er muß . . . . nach Kassel fahren.

❺ Do you organize your day correctly?
. . . . . . Sie sich Ihren Tag richtig . . . ?

❻ Next month I will pay back all my small debts.
Nächsten Monat . . . . ich alle meine kleinen . . . .

Answers to exercise 2

❶ – werde – jeden Montag – ❷ – sind – vorbeigegangen – haben – gesehen ❸ – schaden ❹ – jeden zweiten Monat – ❺ Teilen – ein ❻ – bezahle – Schulden ab

47 Siebenundvierzigste Lektion

Drei Szenen einer Ehe ①

1 – Jetzt sind wir erst **ei**ne W**o**che verh**ei**ratet, und du kommst schon so spät nach H**au**se!
2 – Sei nicht b**ö**se ②! Ich h**a**be nur den L**eu**ten in der Kn**ei**pe erz**ä**hlt, wie gl**ü**cklich ich mit dir bin ③.

3 – Ich h**a**lte ④ das nicht mehr l**ä**nger aus ④! Ich g**e**he zu m**ei**ner M**u**tter zur**ü**ck!
4 – Zu spät! D**ei**ne M**u**tter hat **e**ben ⑤ **a**ngerufen. Sie hat sich mit d**ei**nem V**a**ter gez**a**nkt und ist zu d**ei**ner Großmutter zur**ü**ckgegangen.

Pronunciation Key
*... s'tsaynen ... **4** ... getsang'kt ...*

Notes

① **die Ehe**, *marriage*; **die Hochzeit**, *the wedding*. Some compound words: **das Ehepaar**, *the married couple*; **die Ehefrau**, *the spouse, the wife*; **der Ehemann**, *the spouse, the husband.*

② **böse**, *angry, cross*; *bad, naughty.* **Er ist sehr böse**, *He is very angry.* **Das ist ein böser Junge**, *He is a bad boy.* When the noun is qualified by an adjective we say **das ist/sind**, *he, she, it, is, they are*, e.g.: **Das ist eine schöne Frau**, *She is a beautiful woman.*

③ Pay attention to the place of the verb! It is at the end of the subordinate clause. ▶

Three Domestic Scenes

(scenes of a marriage [f.])

1 – Now we have only been married for one week and you already come home too late!

2 – Don't be angry! I just told the people in the pub how happy I am with you.

3 – I can't bear it any longer! I'll go back to my mother.

4 – Too late! Your mother has just phoned. She quarrelled with your father and returned to your grandmother.

HUNDE UND KATZEN ZANKEN SICH MIT VERGNÜGEN

④ **aushalten**, *to bear*, is an irregular verb. **Sie hält das nicht aus**, *She can't bear it*. **Sie hat ihn nicht mehr ausgehalten**, *She couldn't bear him any longer.*

⑤ **eben** = **gerade**, *just*.

47

5 – Warum erzählst du überall, daß du mich geheiratet ⑥ hast, weil ich so gut koche? Ich weiß doch nicht mal, wie man Spiegeleier brät ⑦!

6 – Weißt du 'was Besseres? Irgendeinen ⑧ Grund muß ich doch angeben! □

5 *... shpeegel'i-er brait* **6** *... irgennt-i-nen ...*

Notes

⑥ **heiraten**, *to marry*; **sich verheiraten**, *to get married*; **verheiratet sein**, *to be married*. **Sie haben sich vor zwei Wochen verheiratet**, *They got married two weeks ago*; or, **Sie haben vor zwei Wochen geheiratet**.

⑦ **braten**, *to roast*; *to fry*; *to grill*. **Der Braten**, *roast meat*; the past participle: **gebraten**. **Kochen**, *to cook*, *to boil*. **Das Wasser kocht**, *The water is boiling*. **Kochst du uns einen Kaffee?**, ▸

***

Übung 1 – Übersetzen Sie bitte

❶ Sie sind erst einen Tag hier und kennen schon fast die ganze Stadt. ❷ Warum kommst du immer so spät? ❸ Seien Sie bitte nicht böse, aber ich habe in der Kneipe erzählt, daß Sie viele Schulden haben. ❹ Hunde und Katzen zanken sich mit Vergnügen. ❺ Er ist seit zwanzig Jahren mit ihr verheiratet. ❻ Sie ist seit zwanzig Jahren mit ihm verheiratet.

5 – Why are you saying everywhere that you married me because I am a good cook *(I cook so well)*? I don't even know how to make fried eggs!

6 – Do you know a better reason *(anything better)*? I have to give [them] some reason *(m.)*! □

▸ *Will you make us a coffee?* Don't confuse **Kochen** with **der Kuchen**, *the cake*; **die Küche**, *the kitchen…* **die Kirche**, *the church.*

⑧ We already know **irgendwer/irgendwo/irgendwas**, *any-, some-one/any-, some-where/any-, something*. **Irgend** added to the indefinite article **ein** means *any.*

***

Answers to exercise 1

❶ They have only been here for one day and they almost know the whole town already. ❷ Why do you always come so late? ❸ Please don't be cross, but I said in the pub that you had a lot of debts. ❹ Cats and dogs quarrel happily *(with delight)*. ❺ He has been married to her for 20 years. ❻ She has been married to him for 20 years.

Übung 2 – Ergänzen Sie bitte

❶ How long have you been married? – Only *(for)* three months.
Wie lange sind Sie schon . . . . ? – . . . . drei Monate.

❷ Turn the radio down *(quieter)* please! I can't bear it any longer.
. . . . Sie bitte das Radio leiser! Ich . . . . es nicht mehr . . . .

❸ We have just eaten. You came too late.
Wir haben . . . . gegessen. Du kommst . . . .

❹ Why do you say everywhere that your wife is a good cook *(cooks well)*?
Warum . . . . Sie . . . . daß Ihre Frau gut . . . . . ?

---

48 Achtundvierzigste Lektion

Wer ist schuld daran? ①

1 **A**nne und Ralf über**le**gen ② **lan**ge, was sie **ih**rem **O**nkel **Ar**thur zum Ge**bur**tstag schen**ken kö**nnen.

2 Er lebt seit dem Tod s**ei**ner Frau all**ei**n und zur**ü**ckgezogen ③

Pronunciation Key
*... choult ... **1** ... geb**oo**rts'tak ... sheng'k*e̲*n ... **2** ... tsoor**ü**k'getsohg*e̲*n*

Notes

① **an etwas schuld sein**, *it's... fault*; *to be blamed for...* **Das ist meine Schuld, ich bin schuld daran**, *That's my fault.*

❺ Do you have any reason or are you always like that?
Haben Sie .... Grund oder sind Sie immer so?

❻ Your husband has just called and asked how to make fried eggs *(how you fry)*.
... Mann hat eben .... und .... man .... brät.

Answers to exercise 2

❶ – verheiratet – erst – ❷ Stellen – kann – aushalten ❸ – eben – zu spät ❹ – erzählen – überall – kocht ❺ – irgendeinen – ❻ Ihr – angerufen – gefragt – wie – Spiegeleier –

48th Lesson 48

Whose Fault is It?

1 Anne and Ralf have been wondering *(thinking)* for quite a while what they could give their uncle *(m.)* for his birthday *(m.)*.
2 Since the death *(m.)* of his wife he has been leading a lonely and retired life *(he lives)*

② **überlegen**, **nachdenken**, *to think about*. **Er hat lange über dieses Problem nachgedacht**, *He has been thinking about this problem for a long time*. **Überlegen** has a prefix which can't be separated from the verb, therefore the past participle is formed without **ge-**; but, **nachdenken** has a separable prefix. **Nachdenken** needs another preposition **über**: **Ich denke über etwas nach**, *I think about something*.

③ **zurückgezogen** is the past participle of **zurückziehen**, *to retire*; **ziehen** means *to pull*.

3 und sieht **kei**nen **Men**schen mehr.
4 **Schließ**lich **kau**fen sie ihm **ei**nen Pa**pa**gei und **las**sen ④ ihn an **sei**ne Ad**res**se **schi**cken.
5 Das **Wo**chenende da**rauf fah**ren sie zu Be**such** ⑤ zu ihm.
6 Der **Vo**gel ist **nir**gends ⑥ zu **se**hen.
7 Zu**erst wa**gen sie nicht zu **fra**gen; **a**ber nach **ei**niger Zeit **kön**nen sie **ih**re **Fra**ge nicht mehr zu**rück**halten ⑦:
8 – Wo ist der Pa**pa**gei, den ⑧ wir dir ge**schickt ha**ben?
9 – **Wel**cher ⑨ Pa**pa**gei? Ach, der **di**cke, **grü**ne **Vo**gel? Den **ha**be ich zum **Mit**tagessen ge**bra**ten.
10 – Ge**bra**ten? Bist du ver**rückt**? Das war ein **Vo**gel, der **spre**chen **konn**te!
11 – So? Wa**rum** hat er dann nichts ge**sagt**? ☐

***4** … shleessliçh … **6** … nirgents …*

Notes

④ **lassen** means *to let, to leave*, and *to have something done*: **Sie läßt sich ein Kleid machen**, *She has a dress made.* **Lassen Sie bitte die Türe offen!**, *Leave the door open, please!* **Lassen Sie mich Ihnen helfen**, *Let me help you.*

⑤ **der Besuch**, *the visit.*

⑥ **nirgends**, **nirgendwo**, *nowhere*; **anderswo**, *elsewhere.*

⑦ **zurückhalten**, *to keep/hold back*; **halten**, *to hold*; **gehalten**, *held.*

⑧ **den**, the relative pronoun refers to **Papagei**, a masculine noun; **die** is the feminine pronoun and **das** the neuter pronoun ▸

3 and he doesn't see anybody any more.
4 They finally buy a parrot *(m.)* and have it sent to his address.
5 The following weekend *(n.) (the weekend after)* they go to see him *(on visit (m.) to him)*.
6 The bird *(m.)* can't be seen anywhere *(is nowhere to see)*.
7 At first they daren't ask; but after some time they can't help asking *(keep back their question)*:
8 – Where is the parrot *(that)* we sent you?
9 – Which parrot? Ah, the fat, green bird? I roasted it for lunch.
10 – Roasted? Are you crazy? That was a bird which could speak!
11 – Was it *(so)*? Then, why didn't it say anything? □

▸ (= the article). **Wo ist die Katze, die ich dir geschenkt habe?**, *Where is the cat that I have sent you?* **Wo ist das Buch, das ich dir geliehen habe?**, *Where is the book that I lent you?*

⑨ **welcher, welche, welches**, *which.*

Übung 1 – Übersetzen Sie bitte

❶ Die Karte, die Sie uns geschickt haben, ist sehr schön. ❷ Wo ist das Bier, das ich mir gerade geholt habe? ❸ Der Brief, den ich heute bekommen habe, ist von meinem Vater. ❹ Warum überlegen Sie so lange? Das ist doch ganz einfach! ❺ Die Kinder sind nirgends zu sehen; und sie waren vor zwei Minuten noch im Garten. ❻ Welchen Vogel möchtest du? Den grünen oder den gelbblauen?

Übung 2 – Ergänzen Sie bitte

❶ First he sent her twenty roses and then he came personally *(himself)*.
...... hat er ihr zwanzig Rosen ....
und .... ist er ....

❷ Did you really think hard *(well)*?
..... Sie wirklich gut .... ?

❸ What will you give me for my birthday?
Was ..... du mir zum ....
.... ?

❹ He has been living abroad since the death of his parents.
Seit ... ... seiner Eltern .... er im Ausland.

Answers to exercise 1

❶ The card *(which)* you sent us is very nice. ❷ Where is the beer *(which)* I have just fetched *(me)*? ❸ The letter *(which)* I received today is from my father. ❹ Why are you thinking for such a long time? It's very easy! ❺ The children can't be seen anywhere *(are nowhere to see)*; and two minutes ago they were still in the garden. ❻ Which bird would you like? The green [one] or the yellow-blue [one]?

❺ Which coat is yours *(belongs to you)*? Have it brought!
. . . . Mantel gehört Ihnen? . . . . Sie ihn bringen!

❻ Why didn't you ask me ? – I didn't dare.
Warum haben Sie . . . . nicht . . . .?
– Ich . . . . es nicht . . . .

Answers to exercise 2

❶ Zuerst – geschickt – dann – selbst gekommen ❷ Haben – überlegt ❸ – wirst – Geburtstag schenken ❹ – dem Tod – lebt – ❺ Welcher – Lassen – ❻ – mich – gefragt – habe – gewagt

49 Neunundvierzigste Lektion

Wiederholung und Erklärungen

1 Conjugations and Verbs

Let's have a look at the verbs and their conjugations.

1.1 Verbs e→i and a→ä

Some verbs change the vowel of the stem in the second and third person of the singular:
Examples:
nehmen, *to take*: **ich nehme; du nimmst, er nimmt**...
geben, *to give*: **ich gebe, du gibst, er gibt**...
essen, *to eat*: **ich esse, du ißt, er ißt**...
e→i
sehen, *to see*: **ich sehe, du siehst, er sieht**...
lesen, *to read*: **ich lese, du liest, er liest**...
befehlen, *to order*: **ich befehle, du befiehlst, er befiehlt**...
e→ie
halten, *to hold*: **ich halte, du hältst, er hält**...
gefallen, *to like*: **ich gefalle, du gefällst, er gefällt**...
anfangen, *to begin*: **ich fange an, du fängst an, er fängt an**...
a→ä
laufen, *to run*: **ich laufe, du läufst, er läuft**...

All these verbs also have an irregular past participle: **genommen**, *taken*: **gegeben**, *given*; **befohlen**, *ordered*...
There are, however, verbs that have a regular present tense, but whose past participles are irregular: **denken**, *to think* → **gedacht**; **gehen**, *to go* → **gegangen**; **bringen**, *to bring* → **gebracht**; **bleiben**, *to stay* → **geblieben**...

Don't worry! Don't learn anything by heart! Only practice makes perfect!

1.2 Verbs with Prefixes

We have already seen several verbs with prefixes; do you know that a verb like **halten**, for example, can have a lot of different

prefixes which each time change the meaning of the word? Let's have a look at some of them:
halten, *to hold*:
anhalten, *to stop*; **zurückhalten**, *to hold back;* **aushalten**, *to bear*; **behalten**, *to keep*; **erhalten**, *to get...*
The past participle of **halten** is **gehalten**. What are the past participles of **anhalten**, **zurückhalten**...? You will find the answer at the end of the lesson. Don't forget that **an**, **zurück**, **aus** are separable prefixes, but that **be-** and **er-** are not!

2 Prepositions of Place

They either require the dative or the accusative.

2.1 Prepositions of Place Using Dative

The dative is used when the verb denotes a state of rest; the corresponding question is **wo**?
Die Wolke hängt über dem Haus, *The cloud is (hangs) above the house.*
Die Katze sitzt auf dem Dach, *The cat is sitting on the roof.*
Das Mädchen steht am (an dem) Fenster, *The girl stands at the window.*
Das Auto steht hinter dem Haus, *The car is (stands) behind the house.*

2.2 Prepositions of Place Using Accusative

The accusative is used when the verb denotes a change in position: the corresponding question is **wohin**?
Der Junge geht ins (in das) Bett, *The boy goes to bed.*
Die Maus läuft unter das Bett, *The mouse runs under the bed.*
Some other prepositions: **hinter**: *behind*; **vor**: *in front of*; **zwischen**: *between*; **neben**: *beside, next to...*

3 The Infinitive with *zu*

The infinitive, **zu** preceding the infinitive is translated by to:
Wir versuchen, pünktlich zu kommen, *We try to be on time.*

Er beginnt um acht Uhr zu arbeiten, *He starts to work at eight o'clock.*
Es scheint zu regnen, *It seems to be raining.*
Ich hoffe, dich bald wiederzusehen, *I hope to see you again soon.*
When the infinitive is preceded by a separable prefix, **zu** is put between the prefix and the stem: **wiederzusehen**.

4 Solution to paragraph 1.2

The five past participles are: **angehalten**, **zurückgehalten**, **ausgehalten**, **behalten**, **erhalten**.

50 Fünfzigste Lektion

Verkäufer ① sein ist nicht leicht

1 – Was w**ü**nschen Sie? Kann ich **I**hnen viell**ei**cht h**e**lfen?
2 – Ja, ich h**ä**tte gern ein T**a**schentuch.
3 – Ein **ei**nziges T**a**schentuch? Sie m**ei**nen ② wohl **ei**ne Gesch**e**nkpackung T**a**schent**ü**cher?
4 – Nein, nein, ich m**ö**chte ein sch**ö**nes, gr**o**ßes T**a**schentuch für m**ei**ne M**u**tter.

Pronunciation Key
... ferkoyfer ... ***2*** *... haitte ...* ***3*** *... ine-tsiges ... gesheng'kpakoong*

The Second Wave

Here we are at the end of the passive phase. Up to now, all we have asked you to do is to read and to understand the texts. Tomorrow the active phase starts, it will require about five or ten minutes more a day.
It's very simple. Finish Lesson 50 in the usual way, then go back to Lesson 1. From now on, each time you finish a new lesson, go back to the earlier one indicated in our Second Wave.
Listen to the Second Wave Lesson again, then read it aloud. Cover up the German text and translate back from the English. This is the best way to progress and revise at the same time.
You have now moved from the passive to the creative stage, and you will be speaking and thinking in German every day. You will be suprised how easy these first lessons seem!

50th Lesson 50

Being *(to be)* a Shop Assistant *(m.)* is not Easy

1 – What are you looking for *(would you like)?* May I possibly help you?
2 – Yes, I would like a handkerchief *(n.)*.
3 – Only one *(single)* handkerchief? You certainly mean a gift-box [of] handkerchiefs?
4 – No, no, I would like one beautiful [and] big handkerchief for my mother.

Notes

① **der Verkäufer**, *the shop assistant* (m.), **die Verkäuferin**, *the shop assistant* (f.), **verkaufen**, *to sell*, **der Käufer**, *the buyer*, **kaufen**, *to buy.*

② **meinen**, *to mean, to think, to believe*; **die Meinung**, *the opinion.*

5 – Na, gut, wenn Sie w**o**llen… An w**e**lche F**a**rbe h**a**ben Sie denn ged**a**cht ③?

6 – Mm, an nichts Best**i**mmtes. K**ö**nnen Sie mich nicht ber**a**ten ④?

7 – Sie ber**a**ten? Selbstverst**ä**ndlich! Hier h**a**be ich zum B**ei**spiel ein r**o**tes aus r**ei**ner ⑤ S**ei**de und hier…

8 – Rot? Ja rot, das ist hübsch. Rot steht ⑥ m**ei**ner M**u**tter sehr gut.

9 – Steht ihr gut? Na denn, um so b**e**sser! N**e**hmen Sie es?

10 – Ich d**e**nke ja. W**e**lches W**a**schmittel k**ö**nnen Sie mir daf**ü**r empf**e**hlen?

11 – Das W**a**schmittel ist eg**a**l ⑦; **a**ber Sie d**ü**rfen es nur in l**au**warmem ⑧ oder k**a**ltem ⑧ W**a**sser w**a**schen.

12 – Ach so! Man kann es nicht in der W**a**schmaschine w**a**schen? Das ist zu **u**npraktisch ⑨. V**ie**len Dank, **a**ber ich n**e**hme es doch nicht! Auf W**ie**dersehen!

13 So, **e**ndlich mal Deutsch gespr**o**chen, und ich h**a**be mich verst**ä**ndlich gem**a**cht! □

***6** … beshtimmtes … **7** … zelpstfershtaintliçh!*

Notes

③ **denken**, *to think*, is followed by the preposition **an** + accusative: **Ich denke nur an dich**, *I am only thinking of you.*

④ **raten** or **beraten**, *to recommend*; *to advise.* **Ich rate Ihnen, früh loszufahren**, *I advise you to leave early.* **Was suchen Sie? Kann ich Sie beraten?** *What are you looking for? May I recommend you [something]?* ▸

5 – So, well, as you like… which colour were you thinking of?

6 – Erm, nothing in particular. Can't you advise me?

7 – Advise you? Certainly! Here, for example, I have a red one made of pure silk, and here…

8 – Red? Yes, red, that is pretty. Red suits my mother very well.

9 – Does it suit her? Well, then all the better! Will you take it?

10 – I think so. Which detergent *(n.)* can you recommend me for it?

11 – The detergent does not matter; but you must only wash it in lukewarm or cold water.

12 – Oh, I see! You cannot wash it in the washing machine *(f.)*? That is not very practical. Thank you very much, but I won't take it after all. Goodbye!

13 So, I have finally spoken some German, and I have made myself understood! □

▸ ⑤ **aus** is followed by the dative; **die Seide**, *the silk*; the adjective **rein** ends in **-er** (dat. fem.) because there is no preceding article.

⑥ **stehen**, *to stand*; but, **Das Kleid steht Ihnen gut**, *The dress suits you well.*

⑦ **egal**, *equal*; **Das ist egal**, *That does not matter, that makes no difference*. **Das ist mir egal**, *It's all the same to me.*

⑧ **in** must be followed by the dative here; there is no article, so you have to decline the adjective. **Lauwarm**, *lukewarm*; **kalt**, *cold*; both end in **-em** (dative neuter).

⑨ **praktisch**, *practical*, **unpraktisch**, *unpractical*; **glücklich**, *happy*, **unglücklich**, *unhappy*. **Un-** is a negative prefix.

50 **Übung 1 – Übersetzen Sie bitte**

❶ Können Sie mir bitte helfen? – Selbstverständlich. ❷ Soll ich den blauen oder den roten Pullover nehmen? Was raten Sie mir? ❸ Das ist ganz egal. Beide sind sehr schön. ❹ Wer hat Ihnen diesen Arzt empfohlen? ❺ Haben Sie daran gedacht, die erste Lektion zu wiederholen? ❻ Ich hätte gern ein großes Stück Kuchen und eine Tasse Kaffee.

Übung 2 – Ergänzen Sie bitte

❶ Are you looking for anything special? May I help you?
Suchen Sie etwas . . . . ? Kann ich . . . . . helfen?

❷ Did you think of your tooth-brush?
Haben Sie . . . . Zahnbürste . . . . ?

❸ I really can recommend [you] this restaurant.
Ich kann . . . dieses Restaurant wirklich . . . .

❹ Green suits my brother. I prefer *(to wear)* blue.
Grün . . . . Bruder sehr gut. Ich trage . . . . . . blau.

❺ He would like a small white handkerchief.
Er möchte ein . . . . Taschentuch.

❻ You have spoken a lot of German and you have made yourself understood.
Sie . . . . . heute viel Deutsch . . . . und Sie haben sich gut . . . . gemacht.

Answers to exercise 1

❶ Can you help me please? – Certainly. ❷ Shall I take the blue or the red pullover? What do you recommend me? ❸ It does not matter. Both are very pretty. ❹ Who recommended you this doctor? ❺ Did you think of repeating your first lesson? ❻ I'd like a big piece of cake and a cup of coffee.

Answers to exercise 2

❶ – Bestimmtes – Ihnen – ❷ – an Ihre – gedacht ❸ – dir – empfehlen ❹ – steht meinem – lieber – ❺ – kleines weißes – ❻ – haben – gesprochen – verständlich –

Second Wave: First Lesson

51 Einundfünfzigste Lektion

Erinnern Sie sich auch daran?

1 – Erinnerst du dich an die Fußballweltmeisterschaft?
2 – Und ob ① ich mich daran erinnere!
3 – Algerien hat uns geschlagen ②, und ich hab' ③ 'nen Kasten Bier verloren.
4 – Mit wem ④ hast du denn gewettet?
5 – Mit **ei**nem Franzosen. Am **A**nfang war er ganz zufr**ie**den, und dann hat er sich f**ü**rchterlich ⑤ **ü**ber das Spiel Frankreich-BRD **au**fgeregt.
6 – Ich kann's verstehen. Ich habe mich auch darüber geärgert ⑥.
7 – Weißt du noch, wie sie mit dem Torwart geschimpft haben:
8 – „Sie sind kein ***Monsieur*** ⑦…". Das war trotz allem komisch!

Pronunciation Key
*er'innern … **1** … foossballveltmy-stershaft **3** algayri'enn …*

Notes

① Generally, the conjunction **ob** denotes doubt or an indirect question. It means *whether*. **Ich frage mich, ob er krank ist**, *I wonder whether he is ill*. **Wir wissen nicht, ob sie kommen**, *We don't know whether they are coming*. Subordinate clauses introduced by **ob** are separated from the main clause by a comma.

② **schlagen**, *to beat, to hit*; **verlieren**, *to lose*.

③ In spoken language we often leave out the **e** of **es**, the **ei** of the indefinite article or final **e** of the first person singular: **Ich** ▸

51st Lesson 51

Do you Remember It, Too?

1 – Do you remember the first world cup *(m.)* in football?
2 – Do I remember it? You bet!
3 – Algeria beat us and I lost a crate of beer.
4 – Who did you bet with?
5 – With a Frenchman. In the beginning he was rather satisfied, and then he got terribly excited about the match France-West Germany.
6 – I can understand it. I was annoyed about it too.
7 – Do you remember *(still know)* how they scolded the goalkeeper *(m.)*:
8 – "You are no ***Monsieur***...". That was funny nevertheless!

▸ **hab' 'nen Kasten Bier verloren**, *I lost a crate of beer.* (**Ich habe einen...).**

④ **mit**, *with*, is followed by the dative, so, after **mit** the interrogative pronoun **wer**, *who*, is **wem**, *who... with*, *with whom*. Ex.: **Mit wem spielt Peter?**, *Who is Peter playing with?*

⑤ **fürchterlich**, *terrible*, *awful*; **die Furcht**, *the fear*; the verb is **fürchten**, *to be afraid*. **Ich fürchte, wir verpassen den Zug**, *I am afraid we will miss the train.*

⑥ **sich aufregen** or **sich ärgern**, *to get excited about*; *to be annoyed about*, are followed by the preposition **über**. The part of the sentence introduced by the preposition can be replaced by **da** + preposition (or **dar-** when the preposition begins with a vowel); **Er erinnert sich an das Spiel**, *He remembers the match.* **Er erinnert sich daran**, *He remembers it.* **Sie sprechen über den Film**, *They are talking about the film.* **Sie sprechen davon**, *They are talking about it.*

⑦ ***Monsieur*** is French and means *Mister* or *Sir*. Here: *gentleman*.

51 **9** – Er hat sich offiziell entschuldigen müssen ⑧.

 10 – Was hat er eigentlich gemacht? Ich hab's vergessen.

 11 – Ich weiß es auch nicht mehr. Auf alle Fälle war's ein Skandal!

 12 Beim Endspiel war ich schon klüger. Ich habe um zwei Kästen Bier gewettet ⑨, daß wir verlieren;

 13 und so hab' ich dann hinterher wenigstens in Ruhe trinken können! □

Notes

⑧ Notice that: **müssen**, **sollen**, **dürfen**, **können** and **wollen** form their compound tenses with the infinitive instead of the past participle: **Wir haben arbeiten müssen**, *We had to work.* **Er hat kommen wollen, aber er hat nicht gekonnt**, *He wanted to come but he couldn't.* The **Perfekt** of the auxiliary verbs themselves is formed with the past participle: **gedurft**, **gesollt**, **gemußt**, **gekonnt**, **gewollt**.

⑨ **mit jemandem um etwas wetten**, *to bet someone something.* **Die Wette**, *the bet*; **der Wettbewerb**, *the competition.* Ex.: **Ich wette mit meinem Bruder um eine Flasche Champagner**.

<div align="center">***</div>

Übung 1 – Übersetzen Sie bitte

❶ Ich bin sicher, daß wir gewinnen werden. Wir können ja wetten. ❷ Ich habe gestern mein Portemonnaie verloren. ❸ Kannst du dich noch an die letzten Ausflüge im Schwarzwald erinnern? ❹ Die Leute haben sich alle fürchterlich aufgeregt. ❺ Am Anfang ist alles sehr gut gegangen, und wir waren ganz zufrieden, aber dann hatten wir kein Glück mehr.

9 – He had to apologize in public.
10 – What did he actually do? I have forgotten *(it)*.
11 – I don't remember [it] either. In any case, it was a scandal *(m.)*!
12 At the final I was even more cautious *(clever)*. I bet two crates of beer that we would lose;
13 and so, I was able to drink at my leisure *(quietly)* afterwards. □

DIE LEUTE HABEN SICH ALLE FÜRCHTERLICH AUFGEREGT

***

Answers to exercise 1

❶ I am sure that we will win. We can bet. ❷ I lost my purse yesterday. ❸ Do *(can)* you remember the last excursions to the Black Forest? ❹ People got very excited about it. ❺ In the beginning everything was *(went)* alright, and we were completely satisfied; but then we weren't lucky any more.

Übung 2 – Ergänzen Sie bitte

❶ At least he apologized.
Er hat sich ....

❷ We couldn't sleep quietly.
Wir haben nicht .. ..

❸ They bet a bottle of whisky.
Sie haben .. .. Whisky ....

❹ Were you annoyed about it, too?
Haben Sie sich auch .... ?

---

52 Zweiundfünfzigste Lektion

Das neue Rotkäppchen

1 **E**ines T**a**ges, als ① R**o**tkäppchen schon fast erw**a**chsen war, ist es w**ie**der **ei**nmal zu s**ei**ner Gr**o**ßmutter geg**a**ngen.
2 Unterw**e**gs hat es ein gr**o**ßes Stück S**a**hnetorte gek**au**ft,
3 denn es gab ② k**ei**nen Wald mehr, in dem man B**ee**ren s**a**mmeln k**o**nnte. ③

Pronunciation Key
... noye rotkaippçhen **1** *... ervaxen ...* **2** *oonterveks ...*
3 *... bayren ...*

Notes

① The conjunction **als**, *when*, is used when expressing a past action: **Als ich jung war, hatte ich Angst vor Hunden**, *When I was young, I was afraid of dogs*. Notice the inversion of subject and verb in the main clause. ▸

❺ Do you remember the second lesson?
. . . . Sie sich . . die zweite Lektion?

❻ Or have you already forgotten everything?
Oder haben Sie schon . . . . ?

Answers to exercise 2
❶ – wenigstens entschuldigt ❷ – in Ruhe schlafen können ❸ – um eine Flasche – gewettet ❹ – darüber geärgert ❺ Erinnern – an – ❻ – alles vergessen

Second Wave: Second Lesson

52nd Lesson 52

(The) New Little Red Riding Hood *(n.)*

1 One day when Little Red Riding Hood was nearly grown-up, she went to [see] her grandmother once again.
2 On the way, she bought a big piece *(n.)* of cream-tart *(f.)*,
3 because there was no more forest *(m.)* to pick berries in *(where you could pick berries)*.

② **es gab** is the simple past (**Imperfekt**) of *there is.*

③ **in** is followed by the dative here, because the corresponding question is: **Wo konnte man Beeren sammeln?**, *Where could you pick berries?* – **In dem Wald**, – *In the wood.* **Konnte** is the imperfect of **kann**: **Er konnte nicht kommen**, *He couldn't come.*

4 In der W**o**hnung der Gr**o**ßmutter war **a**lles in **U**nordnung.
5 Dem R**o**tkäppchen war **e**twas k**o**misch zum**u**te ④. **I**rgend **e**twas st**i**mmte nicht.
6 Die Gr**o**ßmutter war **i**mmer **ei**ne **o**rdentliche und s**au**bere Frau gew**e**sen.
7 H**o**ffentlich ⑤ ist ihr nichts pass**ie**rt, d**a**chte ⑥ R**o**tkäppchen und rief:
8 – Gr**o**ßmutter, wo bist du denn?
9 Aus dem Schl**a**fzimmer **a**ntwortete ⑦ **ei**ne t**ie**fe St**i**mme:
10 – Ich bin hier im Bett, R**o**tkäppchen. Schön, daß du gek**o**mmen bist!
11 Ich h**a**be schon so l**a**nge auf dich gew**a**rtet.

(F**o**rtsetzung folgt) □

Notes

④ **Es ist mir traurig zumute**, *I feel sad*. **Mir ist komisch zumute**, *I feel funny*. **Mein Bruder kennt viele komische Geschichten**, *My brother knows lots of funny stories*.

⑤ **hoffentlich** is the adverb of **hoffen**, *to hope*. You can say: **Hoffentlich kommt er pünktlich** or **Ich hoffe, daß er pünktlich kommt**, *I hope that he will be on time*. The first expression is smoother.

***

Übung 1 – Übersetzen Sie bitte

❶ Eines Tages ist er wieder einmal zu seinem Großvater gefahren. ❷ Ihm war komisch zumute, denn er konnte das Haus des Großvaters nicht mehr finden. ❸ Es gab viele neue Straßen. ❹ Als er jung war, war er ordentlich und sauber. ❺ Später hatte er keine Zeit mehr, und alles war in Unordnung. ❻ Dann hat er geheiratet.

4 In her grandmother's flat everything was in a mess *(disorder)*.
5 Little Red Riding Hood felt a bit funny. Something was wrong.
6 *(The)* grandmother had always been a clean and tidy woman.
7 I hope that nothing has happened to her, Little Red Riding Hood thought and shouted:
8 – Grandmother where are you?
9 A deep voice replied from the bedroom:
10 – I am *(here)* in bed Little Red Riding Hood. Nice of you to come *(that you have come)*.
11 I have been waiting for you [for] [a] long [time] *(already)*.

(To be continued) □

▸ ⑥ **denken**, *to think*, is an irregular verb. You already know the past participle: **gedacht**. Here is the third person singular of the simple past (**Imperfekt**): **dachte**. In German it is used in narratives or in the description of historical events. It is used less frequently in spoken language.

⑦ **antworten**, *to answer, to reply*. **Er antwortete**, *He replied*. We will look at the complete conjugation of the imperfect shortly.

***

Answers to exercise 1

❶ One day he once again went to [see] his grandfather. ❷ He felt funny because he could not find his *(the)* grandfather's house any more. ❸ There were a lot of new streets. ❹ When he was young, he was orderly and clean. ❺ Later he didn't have any time any more, and everything was in a mess. ❻ Then he got married.

52 Übung 2 – Ergänzen Sie bitte

❶ On the way, we met a lot of friends.
. . . . haben wir . . . . getroffen.

❷ Did you pick berries when you were young?
Haben Sie . . . . . . gesammelt, . . . Sie . . . . waren?

❸ Last night the moon was full *(full moon)*; he couldn't sleep.
Heute . . . . . war Vollmond; er . . . . . . nicht schlafen.

❹ How did you feel when you saw that?
. . . war Ihnen . . . . . . als Sie das . . . . ?

❺ A low voice answered and she thought: "There is something wrong!"
Eine . . . . . Stimme . . . . und sie . . . . . .: „Da . . . . . . etwas nicht!"

❻ Nice of you to come! I have been waiting for you for such a long time!
Schön, . . . Sie . . . .! Ich warte schon so lange . . . Sie!

Answers to exercise 2

❶ Unterwegs – viele Freunde – ❷ – Beeren – als – jung – ❸ – nacht – konnte – ❹ Wie – zumute – gesehen haben ❺ – tiefe – antwortete – dachte – stimmt – ❻ – daß – gekommen sind – auf –

Second Wave: Third Lesson

53 Dreiundfünfzigste Lektion

Das neue Rotkäppchen (Fortsetzung)

1 – Was ist los, Gr**o**ßmutter? War**u**m hast du so **ei**ne ti**e**fe St**i**mme?
2 – Ich h**a**be **ei**ne Gr**i**ppe und H**a**lsweh. Ich bin ein w**e**nig h**ei**ser. **A**ber komm ① doch her**ei**n ①!
3 R**o**tkäppchen ging ② in das d**u**nkle Schl**a**fzimmer. Die Gr**o**ßmutter sah ② ganz **a**nders aus als gew**ö**hnlich.
4 – Gr**o**ßmutter, war**u**m hast du so gr**o**ße **O**hren ③? fragte R**o**tkäppchen **ä**ngstlich.
5 – Dam**i**t ich dich b**e**sser h**ö**ren kann! ④
6 – Und Gr**o**ßmutter, war**u**m hast du so gr**o**ße **Au**gen?
7 – Dam**i**t ich dich b**e**sser s**e**hen kann!
8 – Ja, **a**ber Gr**o**ßmutter, war**u**m hast du **ei**nen so gr**o**ßen Mund?

Pronunciation Key

2 *… ha**ll**svay … h**i**-zer …* ***4*** *… **ai**ngstliçh*

Notes

① Do you remember the imperative form? **Hereinkommen**, *to come in*, *to enter*; **Komm herein!**, *Come in!* **Kommen Sie herein!**, *Come in!* **Kommt herein!** *Come in!*

② You already know that **gehen**, *to go*, and **sehen**, *to see*, are irregular verbs. The past participles are **gegangen**, **gesehen**. The third person singular of the **Imperfekt**, **er sah**, *he saw*; **er ging**, *he went*. ▶

Little Red Hiding Hood (cont.)

1 – What's the matter grandmother? Why do you have such a deep voice *(f.)*?
2 – I have got flu *(f.)* and a sore throat. I am a bit hoarse. But do come in!
3 Little Red Riding Hood went into the bedroom. Grandmother looked different than usual.
4 – Grandmother, why do you have such big ears? Little Red Riding Hood asked fearfully.
5 – So that I can hear you better!
6 – And grandmother, why do you have such big eyes?
7 – So that I can see you better!
8 – Yes, but grandmother, why do you have such a big mouth *(m.)*?

③ **das Ohr, die Ohren**, *the ear(s).*

④ **damit**, *so that, in order to*, is a conjunction introducing a subordinate clause. The word order is: **1**. conjunction, **2**. subject and the verb at the end: **damit ich... kann**.

53

9 – Damit ich dich besser küssen kann, sagte der Prinz lachend ⑤,
10 sprang ⑥ aus dem Bett und küßte Rotkäppchen.
11 Und wenn sie nicht gestorben ⑦ sind,
12 dann leben sie noch heute.

9 ... prinnts ... 10 shprang ...

Notes

⑤ **lachen**, *to laugh*; **lachend** is the present participle. It is formed by adding **-d** to the infinitive.

***

Übung 1 – Übersetzen Sie bitte

❶ Er sprang schreiend aus der Badewanne; das Wasser war zu heiß. ❷ Gib mir bitte meine Brille, damit ich dich besser sehe. ❸ Mein Großvater ist vor drei Jahren gestorben. ❹ Haben Sie heute mehr Arbeit als gewöhnlich? ❺ Sie ging in die Küche und sah nach dem Essen. ❻ Er fragte sie ängstlich: „Darf ich Sie küssen?“.

Übung 2 – Ergänzen Sie bitte

❶ She can hardly speak *(she nearly cannot speak)*; she is hoarse.
Sie . . . . fast nicht . . . .; sie ist . . . .

❷ She has nice big blue eyes.
Sie hat schöne . . . . . , ...

❸ I can't hear you *(understand)*. I have got ear-ache.
Ich . . . . dich nicht. Ich habe . . . .

❹ He sits down in the first row in order to see better.
Er setzt sich in die erste Reihe, ... besser sehen . . . . .

9 – So that I can kiss you better, the prince said laughing,
10 [he] jumped out of the bed and kissed Little Red Riding Hood.
11 And if they did not die,
12 then they still live today.

⑥ **springen**, *to jump*; past participle, **gesprungen.**

⑦ **gestorben** is the past participle of **sterben**, *to die*. In the present tense **e** → **i** in the second and third person singular: **du stirbst, er, sie, es stirbt. Und wenn sie nicht gestorben sind**... German fairy-tales frequently end with this sentence.

***

Answers to exercise 1

❶ He jumped out of the bathtub screaming: the water was too hot. ❷ Give me my glasses, please, so that I [can] see you better. ❸ My grandfather died three years ago. ❹ Do you have more work today than usual? ❺ She went into the kitchen to see to the meal *(and saw to)*. ❻ He nervously asked her: "May I kiss you?".

❺ When did Mozart die? Do you know [it]?
Wann ist Mozart . . . . ? . . . . Sie das?

❻ He has a ready tongue [He's not fallen on the mouth].
Er ist . . . . nicht auf . . . . gefallen!

Answers to exercise 2

❶ – kann – sprechen – heiser ❷ – große – blaue Augen ❸ – verstehe – Ohrenweh ❹ – damit er – kann ❺ – gestorben – Wissen – ❻ – wirklich – den Mund –

Second Wave: Fourth Lesson

54 Vierundfünfzigste Lektion

Ist Ihnen so was schon mal passiert?

1 – Worüber ① lachen Sie, bitte schön?
2 – Über Sie! – Über mich ②? – Ja, über wen denn sonst?
3 – Und warum, wenn ich fragen darf?
4 – Sie machen immer so ein langes Gesicht! – Ein langes Gesicht, ich?
5 – Ja, Sie sind immer schlechter Laune ③. Sie sind ein richtiger Miesepeter!
6 – Also das! Das hat mir noch niemand gesagt.
7 – Nein? Wirklich nicht? Na, dann wird's ja höchste ④ Zeit!
8 Lächeln Sie doch mal ein bißchen!… Ja, so! So ist es schon besser.
9 – Meinen Sie das ernst ⑤? Sie machen sich nicht über mich lustig ⑥?

Pronunciation Key
***4** … geziçht! **5** … lowne … meezepeter*

Notes

① The interrogative pronoun **wo** + preposition (**wor-** when the preposition begins with a vowel) refers to things: **Ich lache über den Film**, *I laugh at the film* → **Worüber lachst du?**, *What are you laughing at?* **Sie sprechen von ihrer Arbeit**, *They are talking about their work.* → **Wovon sprechen sie?**, *What are they talking about?*

② **über** is followed by the accusative when preceded by the verb **lachen**.

Has Anything like That Ever Happened to You?

1 – [Excuse me] What are you laughing at *(please)*?
2 – At you! – At me? – Yes, what did you think? *(At who else?)*
3 – And why, if I may ask?
4 – You always make such a long face *(n.)*! – A long face, me?
5 – Yes, you are always in a bad mood *(f.)*. You are a real crab!
6 – Is that so! Nobody has told me that before.
7 – No? Really *(not)*? Then it's high *(highest)* time somebody did *(does)*!
8 Come on, smile a little! Yes, like that! Like that, that's even *(already)* better.
9 – Are you serious *(do you mean that seriously)*? You are not making fun of me?

▸ ③ **Guter** or **schlechter Laune sein**, *to be in a good*, or *bad mood*. **Schlecht** and **gut** have the ending **-er**, because they are in the genitive form.

④ **Hoch**, *high*; its comparative form is irregular, **höher**, *higher*; **am höchsten**, *highest*. **Der Feldberg ist der höchste Berg vom Schwarzwald**, *The Feldberg is the highest mountain in the Black Forest.*

⑤ **ernst**, *serious*, *grave*, *severe*. **Ernst** is also a first name!

⑥ **sich über jemanden oder etwas lustig machen**, *to make fun of someone/something*. **Machen Sich sich nicht über meinen Akzent lustig**, *Don't make fun of my accent*. **Aber nein! Versuchen sie's noch mal!**, *Oh no! Try it again!*

10 – **A**ber nein, vers**u**chen Sie's n**o**chmal! S**e**hen Sie dort in den Sp**ie**gel!
11 – Ja, das ist ja w**i**rklich b**e**sser!
12 Auf der r**e**chten S**ei**te noch **e**twas mehr… ja, gut, und jetzt links…
13 – Halt! Ich kann nicht mehr **au**fhören… – Gut! Pr**i**ma! M**a**chen Sie w**ei**ter ⑦! Ha! Ha! Ha! Ha!

***10** … shpeeg<u>e</u>l*

Note

⑦ **weiter** (lit., "further") added to a verb means *to carry on*, *to continue*, **Sprechen Sie weiter**, *Carry on speaking.* **Mach weiter**, *Carry on.*

***

Übung 1 – Übersetzen Sie bitte

❶ Woran denken Sie? – An die Mittagspause. ❷ Er kann nicht mehr aufhören zu lachen. ❸ Warum kommen Sie so spät, wenn ich fragen darf? ❹ Auf der rechten Seite sehen Sie den Rhein und auf der linken das neue Industriegebiet. ❺ Meine Mutter ist eine phantastische Frau. Sie ist immer guter Laune!

10 – Certainly *(But)* not, try it again! Look in the mirror *(m.)* over there!
11 – Yes, that really is better!
12 Slightly more to your right *(side)*… yes, good, and now to your *(the)* left…
13 – Stop! I can't stop anymore…
– Fine! Super! Go on! Ha! Ha! Ha! Ha! □

***

Answers to exercise 1

❶ What are you thinking? – My *(the)* lunch-break. ❷ He can't stop laughing. ❸ Why do you come so late, if I may ask? ❹ On your right you can see the Rhine and on your left the new industrial area. ❺ My mother is a fantastic woman. She is always in a good mood!

Übung 2 – Ergänzen Sie bitte

1. He has lost his wallet. He is in a bad mood!
   Er . . . sein Portemonnaie . . . . Er ist . . . . Laune!

2. What did you laugh at, if we *(one)* may ask *(you)*?
   . . . . hast du gelacht, ... man fragen darf?

3. Smile a little please! You always look so serious *(make such a serious face)*.
   . . . . Sie bitte ein bißchen! Sie machen immer ein so ernstes . . . .

4. The train is leaving in two minutes.
   It is high *(highest)* time to get on board.
   Der Zug fährt . . . . Minuten.
   Es wird . . . . einzusteigen.

---

55 Fünfundfünfzigste Lektion

Der Engel mit Schuhen ①

1 Ein Pr**ie**ster beste**ll**te **ei**nmal bei **ei**nem bek**a**nnten M**a**ler ein gro**ß**es Bild für s**ei**ne K**i**rche ②.

2 Nach **ei**nigen W**o**chen war das Bild f**e**rtig. Es war ein M**ei**sterwerk ③.

Pronunciation Key
... engel ... shoohen ***1*** *... preester beshtellte ... kir'çhe*
2 *... mysterverk*

⑤ Who have you been talking to just now? You were so serious.
… … haben Sie gerade …………? Sie waren so …… .

⑥ Are you making fun of me or are you serious?
Machst du dich …. …. lustig oder …… du das ernst?

Answers to exercise 2

❶ – hat – verloren – schlechter – ❷ Worüber – wenn – ❸ Lächeln – Gesicht ❹ – in zwei – höchste Zeit – ❺ Mit wem – gesprochen – ernst ❻ – über mich – meinst –

Second Wave : Fifth Lesson

55th Lesson 55

The Angel *(m.)* with Shoes

1 Once, a priest *(m.)* ordered a big painting *(n.)* for his church from a famous painter *(m.)*.

2 Some weeks later the painting was finished. It was a masterpiece *(n.)*.

Notes

① **der Schuh**; **die Schuhe**, *the shoe(s)*.

② Beware of the pronounciation of the final consonant group. **Kirche** is pronounced *[çh]* and **Kirsche**, *cherry [sh]*.

③ **das Werk**, *the work (factory)*; achievement. **Das Kunstwerk**, *work of art*. **Der Meister**, *the master*.

55

3 Der Priester war begeistert und lobte den Maler in den Himmel. ④

4 Plötzlich stutzte er jedoch, trat ⑤ ungläubig näher ⑤ an das Bild heran und murmelte:

5 – Ich traue ⑥ meinen Augen nicht!

6 Das ist doch nicht möglich! Der Engel hat Schuhe!

7 – Aber ja, sagte der Maler. Warum denn nicht?

8 – Was haben Sie sich denn dabei gedacht?

9 Haben Sie jemals einen Engel mit Schuhen gesehen?

10 – Natürlich nicht! Und Sie, haben Sie schon mal ⑦ einen ohne Schuhe gesehen? □

***3** … beguy-stert … **4** … shtootste … oongloybiçh naiher … moormelte*

Notes

④ **der Himmel**, *the sky*. **Jemanden oder etwas in den Himmel heben oder loben**, *to praise someone/something to the skies*.

⑤ **nähertreten**, *to get closer*; or *to approach*, **näher herantreten**. ▶

***

Übung 1 – Übersetzen Sie bitte

❶ Sie bestellte eine Tasse heiße Schokolade und Schlagsahne. ❷ Er traut niemandem außer sich selbst. ❸ Warum hast du das gesagt? Was hast du dir dabei gedacht? ❹ Das Konzert war ausgezeichnet. Alle Leute waren begeistert. ❺ Nach einigen Monaten hatte der Maler das Bild fertig und der Priester lobte ihn.

3 The priest was enthusiastic and praised the painter to the skies.
4 Suddenly, however, he started, got closer to the painting incredulously and murmured:
5 – I can't *(don't)* believe my eyes!
6 That's impossible! The angel has got shoes on!
7 – Certainly! the painter said, Why not?
8 – What did you mean by that?
9 Have you ever seen an angel with shoes?
10 – Certainly not! And you, have you ever seen one without shoes? □

⑥ **vertrauen** or **trauen**, *to rely on*; *to trust* : **Ich vertraue dir**, *I rely on you*. **Das Vertrauen**, *confidence*.

⑦ **mal** is the abbreviation for **einmal**, *once*. **Kommen Sie mal**, *Come*. **Sag mal, was machst du da?**, *Say, what are you doing there?* But **einmal** also means *once* - referring to an event in the past, **Er war einmal mein Mann**, *He once was my husband*.

***

Answers to exercise 1

❶ She orders a cup of hot chocolate *(f.)* and whipped cream. ❷ He trusts nobody except himself. ❸ Why did you say that? What did you mean by it? ❹ The concert was excellent. Everybody *(all the people)* was enthusiastic. ❺ Several months later, the painter had finished the painting and the priest praised him.

Übung 2 – Ergänzen Sie bitte

1. Have you ever seen an angel?
   ..... Sie schon mal einen Engel ....?
2. What did you mean by that? That is impossible.
   Was ... er sich ....? Das ist ja ....
3. Where did you order the painting? – From a famous painter.
   Wo ..... Sie das Bild ....? – ....
4. Don't enter the mosque with shoes [on].
   Gehen Sie nicht ... . in diese Moschee.
5. This film is fantastic. It is a real masterpiece.
   Der Film ist .... Er ist ein richtiges ....
6. And you, have you ever met an angel without shoes?
   Und Sie, haben Sie jemals .... Schuhe getroffen?

56 Sechsundfünfzigste Lektion

Wiederholung und Erklärungen

1 *Das Imperfekt und das Perfekt*

Both **das Imperfekt** and **das Perfekt** express an event or an action in the past. The latter is more common in everyday language, but **das Imperfekt** is the tense used for narratives or historical events.
Here are the conjugations of a regular verb, **suchen**, and an irregular verb, **gehen**:

Answers to exercise 2

❶ Haben – gesehen ❷ – hat – dabei gedacht – unmöglich ❸ – haben – bestellt – bei einem bekannten Maler ❹ – mit Schuhen – ❺ – phantastisch – Meisterwerk ❻ – einen Engel ohne –

Second Wave: Sixth Lesson

56th Lesson 56

Imperfekt

ich suchte, *I looked for*	**ich ging**, *I went*
du suchtest	**du gingst**
er/sie/es suchte	**er/sie/es ging**
wir suchten	**wir gingen**
ihr suchtet	**ihr gingt**
sie suchten	**sie gingen**
Sie suchten (formal)	**Sie gingen** (formal)

Please note that the first and the third persons of the singular are the same and that the third person does not end in **-t**.
Irregular verbs often change the vowel of their stem in the **Imperfekt** and the past participle, but the vowel is not necessarily the same in both tenses: **sprechen** (*to speak*): **er sprach**: *he spoke*; **gesprochen**: *spoken*. At the end of the book you will find a list of irregular verbs.

2 Double Infinitive Construction

What does double infinitive mean?
In compound tenses **können**, **wollen**, **müssen**, **sollen**, **dürfen** and **lassen** are never found in the past participle. We have two infinitives:
Er hat schon gehen müssen, *He had to go already.*
Wir haben nicht kommen können, *We couldn't come.*
Sie haben mich rufen lassen, *You sent for me.*

3 Word Order in German

Let's look again at the word order in subordinate clauses introduced by a conjunction:
Ich hoffe, daß du morgen kommen wirst, *I hope that you will come tomorrow.* We have: **1**. conjunction, **2**. subject (you)… and

57 Siebenundfünfzigste Lektion

Wie der Vater, so die Söhne

1 Ein **a**lter, r**ei**cher G**ei**zhals ① h**a**tte in s**ei**nem Testam**e**nt beschl**o**ssen ②,
2 daß j**e**der s**ei**ner drei S**ö**hne t**au**send M**a**rk in sein Gr**a**b w**e**rfen s**o**llte,

Notes

① **der Geiz**, *miserliness, avarice*. The adjective is **geizig**, *miserly, stingy*.

the conjugated verb (**wirst**) at the end of the sentence.
The infinitive precedes the conjugated verb.

Try practising now with the following examples:

Ich bleibe im Bett, weil es draußen zu kalt ist, *I'm staying in bed because it is too cold outside.*
Kommen Sie etwas näher, damit ich Sie besser sehen kann, *Come nearer so that I can see you better.*
Sie wissen nicht, ob er kommt, *They don't know whether he is coming.*
Kannst du mich mitnehmen, wenn du morgen ins Büro fährst?, *Can you give me a lift when you go to the office tomorrow?*
Als er klein war, trug er keine Schuhe, *When he was young (little) he did not wear shoes.*

Hoffentlich denken Sie an die zweite Welle!, *Don't forget the second wave! You are already at the 7th lesson – It's easy,* **nicht wahr?**

57th Lesson 57

Like Father like Son *(sons)*

1 A rich old miser *(m.)* had decided in his will *(n.)*
2 that each of his three sons was to throw one thousand Marks into his grave *(n.)*

② **beschlossen** is the past participle of **beschließen**, *to decide*. Remember **schließen**, *to close*, and its past participle: **geschlossen**, *closed*.

3 um etwas zu ③ erben.
4 Am Tag der Beerdigung trat nun der Älteste als ④ erster an das Grab des Vaters
5 und ließ seufzend einen Tausendmarkschein hineinfallen.
6 Daraufhin kam der zweite
7 und warf langsam und widerwillig tausend Mark in Geldstücken hinein.
8 Sie klangen ⑤ auf dem Sarg wie Regen auf einem Blechdach.
9 Als letzter erschien ⑥ der Jüngste.
10 Ruhig näherte er sich dem Grab.
11 Dort angekommen schrieb er vor aller Augen einen Scheck über dreitausend Mark aus ⑦
12 und ließ ihn ruhig ins Grab flattern.
13 Dann stieg ⑧ er langsam in die Grube und sammelte die zweitausend Mark seiner Brüder ein…

Pronunciation Key
*4 … be'**ayr**digoong … 5 … **soy**ftsennt …*

Notes

③ **um… zu**, *in order to*; notice that **zu** is placed before the infinitive and that **um** introduces the subordinate clause: **Er arbeitet, um Geld zu verdienen**, *He works in order to earn money.*

④ **als**, *as*; **Sie arbeitet als Verkäuferin**, *She works as a shop-assistant.* **Martin ging als letzter nach Hause**, *Martin was the last to go home (went home as the last).*

3 in order to inherit something.
4 On the day of the funeral *(f.)* the eldest was the first to approach the grave of his father *(the eldest appeared as the first)*
5 and with a sigh, he dropped *(let fall)* a thousand Mark-note *(m.)* into it.
6 Then the second son followed *(came)*
7 and slowly and reluctantly he threw one thousand Marks worth of *(in)* coins into it.
8 They sounded on the coffin *(m.)* like rain *(m.)* on a tin roof *(n.)*.
9 The youngest [son] was the last to appear *(as the last the youngest)*
10 He approached the grave calmly.
11 [When he] arrived there he wrote out a check *(m.)* for three thousand Marks in front of everybody *(in front of the eyes of everybody)*
12 and let it flutter into the grave.
13 Then he slowly climbed down into the grave *(f.)* *(pit)* and collected the two thousand Marks of his brothers… □

⑤ **klangen** is the **Imperfekt** of **klingen**, *to sound*. Don't mix it up with **klingeln**, *to ring*. **Das Telefon klingelt**, *The phone is ringing*.

⑥ **erschien** → **Imperfekt** of **erscheinen**, *to appear*. But: **scheinen** (without the prefix), *to seem*; *to shine*.

⑦ **einen Scheck schreiben** or **ausschreiben**, *to write out a check*.

⑧ **stieg** → **Imperfekt** of **steigen**: *to climb* down or up according to the preposition: **Ich steige auf den Berg**, *I climb up the mountain*. **Sie steigen in die Höhle**, *They climb down into the cavern*.

Übung 1 – Übersetzen Sie bitte

❶ Sie haben gestern beschlossen, heute zu Hause zu bleiben. ❷ Eine alte, reiche Frau hat jedem ihrer Söhne eine Million Mark hinterlassen. ❸ Alle Leute waren schon in der Kirche. Als letzter erschien der Priester. ❹ Der Polizist näherte sich ruhig dem Auto. Dort angekommen schrieb er vor aller Augen einen Strafzettel aus. ❺ Seufzend und widerwillig bezahlte der Autofahrer zwanzig Mark.

Übung 2 – Ergänzen Sie bitte

❶ He is very kind to this old woman in order to inherit something one day.
Er ist sehr . . . . zu der . . . . Frau, . . eines Tages etwas . . erben.

❷ The eldest was the first to arrive *(came as the first)*, and the youngest, as usual the last.
Der . . . . kam . . . erster, und der . . . . wie immer . . . letzter.

❸ Write me out a check for thousand Marks, please!
. . . . Sie mir bitte einen Scheck . . . . tausend Mark . . . !

❹ The day of his exam, he had a terrible *(strong)* stomach-ache.
. . . . . seiner Prüfung hatte er starke . . . .

❺ Each of my brothers has a big car, and each of my sisters has a bicycle *(n.)*.
. . . . . meiner Brüder hat ein . . . . . . Auto, und . . . . meiner Schwestern hat ein Fahrrad.

Answers to exercise 1

❶ Yesterday they decided to stay at home. ❷ A rich old woman left *(behind)* one million Marks to each of her sons. ❸ Everybody was already in the church. The priest was the last to appear. ❹ The policeman approached the car calmly. [When he] arrived [there] he wrote out a parking ticket in front of everybody. ❺ With a sigh, the conductor reluctantly paid the twenty Marks.

❻ She decided to stop smoking *(not to smoke any more).*
Sie . . . . , nicht mehr . . . .

Answers to exercise 2

❶ – nett – alten reichen – um – zu – ❷ – Älteste – als – Jüngste – als – ❸ Schreiben – über – aus ❹ Am Tag – Magenschmerzen ❺ Jeder – großes – jede – ❻ – hat beschlossen – zu rauchen

WIE DER VATER, SO DIE SÖHNE

Second Wave: Eighth Lesson

58 Achtundfünfzigste Lektion

Gemüse auf einem Spaziergang

(**Heu**te d**ü**rfen Sie st**o**ttern; und Sie m**ü**ssen sog**ar** st**o**ttern, wenn Sie l**a**chen w**o**llen!)

1 – Kennt ihr schon die W**i**tze von den **E**rbsen, M**ö**hren und Tom**a**ten? ①
2 – Nein! Die hast du uns noch nicht erz**ä**hlt. Los! Erz**ä**hl doch mal!
3 – **A**lso: Zwei **E**rbsen g**e**hen spaz**ie**ren ②.
4 Da sagt pl**ö**tzlich die **ei**ne zur ③ **a**nderen:
5 V**o**rsicht, da ist **ei**ne Tr**e**ppe, -pe, -pe, -pe, -pe…
6 – Ha, ha, ist das k**o**misch! Wo hast du den denn her ④?
7 – W**a**rtet 'mal! Der mit den M**ö**hren ist noch besser:
8 Zwei M**ö**hren fl**ie**gen zum Mond.
9 Da sagt pl**ö**tzlich die **ei**ne der b**ei**den ⑤:

Pronunciation Key
1 *vitse … erpsen, merenn … tomatenn* ***4*** *plertsslịch*

Notes

① **die Erbse**; **die Möhre**; **die Tomate**. But: **der Witz**, *the joke* or *wit*.

② **spazierengehen** is the infinitive. **Spazieren** is used as a separable prefix. The past participle is **spazierengegangen**. ▸

Vegetables out for a Walk *(m.)*

(Today you may stutter; in fact, you have to stutter if you want to laugh!)

1 – Do you already know the jokes about the peas, the carrots and the tomatoes?
2 – No, you haven't told them to us yet. Go ahead! Tell us!
3 – Well: two peas go for a walk.
4 Suddenly one of them says to the other:
5 Be careful there is a step *(f.)*, -p, -p, -p *(steps)*…
6 – Ha, ha, that's funny! Where did you pick that one up?
7 – Wait! The one with the carrots is even better:
8 Two carrots are flying to the moon *(m.)*.
9 Suddenly one of them says:

③ **zur** is the contraction of **zu der**; **zu** is always followed by the dative → **der** is the dative of the feminine article **die**.

④ Remember that **woher** can be separated in spoken language: **Wo kommst du her?**, *Where do you come from?*

⑤ **die beiden**, *both*; **der beiden** is the genitive plural.

10 – V**o**rsicht, da kommt ein H**u**bschrapp ⑥, -schrapp, -schrapp, -schrapp…

11 – Ha, ha, ha, ha… Gut, daß ich k**ei**ne M**ö**hre bin! Und wie ist der mit den Tom**a**ten?

12 – Den erz**ä**hle ich euch ein **a**nderes Mal, wenn ihr euch ⑦ **e**twas erh**o**lt habt.

13 Ihr lacht euch sonst ja tot. □

Notes

⑥ **der Hubschrauber**, *the helicopter.*

⑦ Notice that the informal form of address is used here: **euch** is the dative and accusative of the personal pronoun **ihr**.

***

Übung 1 – Übersetzen Sie bitte

❶ Es gibt Menschen, die viel Witz haben und andere, die keinen haben. ❷ Können Sie gut Witze erzählen? ❸ Habt ihr euch in den Ferien gut erholt? ❹ Eßt nicht soviel vor dem Essen, ihr habt sonst keinen Hunger mehr. ❺ Haben Sie das Ende verstanden? ❻ Plötzlich haben die beiden Frauen laut gelacht und gerufen: „Vorsicht, hinter Ihnen steht ein dicker Stier!“

10 – Be careful, there comes a helicop,-op,-op,-op… **58**
11 – Ha, ha, ha, ha,… Luckily *(good)* I am not a carrot *(f.)*. And how about the one with the tomatoes?
12 – I will tell it another time when you will have recovered a little.
13 Otherwise you will die of laughter. □

***

Answers to exercise 1

❶ There are people who have a lot of ready wit and others who haven't any. ❷ Do you know how to tell jokes *(Can you tell jokes well)*? ❸ Did you recover *(well)* during your *(the)* holidays? ❹ Don't eat so much before the meal otherwise you won't be hungry any more *(you won't have any hunger…)*. ❺ Did you understand the end? ❻ Suddenly the two women burst out laughing *(laughed loudly)*: "Be careful, there is a big bull standing behind you *(behind you stands a big bull)*!"

Übung 2 – Ergänzen Sie bitte

❶ I prefer to come another time when you have more time.
Ich komme lieber . . . . wenn ihr mehr . . . . habt!

❷ They haven't told us yet what happened to you yesterday.
Sie haben . . . noch nicht erzählt, . . . Ihnen . . . . passiert ist.

❸ It is pouring. I'm glad that I'm home now.
Es . . . . . . in Strömen. . . . , . . . ich schon zu Hause bin.

❹ Suddenly one of them says to the other: "You really are very pretty!"
. . . . sagt die eine . . . anderen: „Sie sind . . . . !"

59 Neunundfünfzigste Lektion

Was halten Sie davon?

1 – Schl**a**fen Sie gern ① l**a**nge? K**ö**nnen Sie **o**hne **A**rbeit l**e**ben?
2 – R**u**hen Sie sich gern aus und sind Sie ganz zufr**ie**den, wenn ② Sie nichts tun?

Pronunciation Key
2 … tsoofreeden …

Notes

① Do you remember: **Ich schlafe gern**, *I like to sleep (sleeping)*. **Ich schlafe lieber**, *I prefer to sleep (I'd rather sleep)*? ▸

❺ We have to hurry up, otherwise the shops will be closed *(close)*.
Wir müssen uns beeilen .... die Geschäfte.

❻ Did you go for a walk on Sunday?
Sind Sie .. .. ?

Answers to exercise 2
❶ – ein anderes Mal – Zeit – ❷ – uns – was – gestern – ❸ – regnet – Gut – daß – ❹ Plötzlich – zur – wirklich sehr schön ❺ – sonst schließen – ❻ – am Sonntag spazierengegangen

Second Wave: Ninth Lesson

59th Lesson 59

What Do you Think of That?

1 – Do you like to sleep in *(long)*? Can you live without work?
2 – Do you like to rest and are you completely satisfied when you have nothing to do *(when you do nothing)*?

② *when* is translated by **wenn**, if it does not refer to a unique action in the past : **Wenn er kommt, essen wir**, *When he comes [will be here] we will eat.*

3 – Dann denken Sie vielleicht, Sie sind ein neuer Menschenschlag und die folgenden ③ Sprichwörter sind nicht von Ihnen erfunden, nicht wahr?
4 – Aber täuschen Sie sich nicht, es gab auch schon früher Leute wie Sie,
5 und die haben die traditionellen Sprichwörter ganz einfach zu ihren Gunsten verändert ④.
6 – Zum Beispiel sagten sie nicht: Arbeit hält gesund, sondern ⑤:
7 – Arbeit macht krank und legten sich dann auf die faule Haut. ⑥
8 – Und sie sagten nicht: Was du heute kannst besorgen, das verschiebe nicht auf morgen, ⑦
9 – sondern: Morgen ist auch ein Tag, und gingen ins Kino oder ganz einfach ins Bett.
10 – Also dann: Bis morgen ⑧! □

***3** … menshenshlak … shpriçhverter … **4** … toy'shen … **5** … feraindert*

Notes

③ **folgend** is the present participle of **folgen**, *to follow*. When it precedes a noun it functions as an adjective and must be declined. **Das folgende Kapitel**, *the following chapter*.

④ **verändern**, *to change*. **Mein Freund hat sich in den letzten Jahren sehr verändert**, *My friend has changed a lot in the last few years*. **Ändern** (without prefix), *to change*. E.g.: **Er hat seine Meinung geändert**, *He has changed his mind*. *To change* is translated by **wechseln**: **Ich habe Geld gewechselt**, *I changed some money* (you change something in return for something else). ▶

3 – Then maybe you think you are a new sort of man *(m.)* and the following sayings were not your invention *(are not invented by you)*, don't you?
4 – But don't be mistaken; there were already people like you before,
5 and they simply changed the traditional sayings to their advantage.
6 – They didn't say for example *(n.)*: Work keeps healthy, but:
7 – Work makes you ill, and they didn't do anything any more.
8 – And they didn't say: Don't put off until tomorrow what you can do today,
9 – but: Tomorrow is another day, and they simply went to the cinema or to bed.
10 – Well, then: See you tomorrow *(until…)*! □

▸ ⑤ **sondern**, *but*, after negative sentences. **Ich heiße nicht Martin, sondern Horst**, *My name is not Martin but Horst.*

⑥ **sich auf die faule Haut legen** is an expression that means *to do nothing*. Word for word: "to lay down on the lazy skin".

⑦ **verschieben**, *to put off, to postpone*; *to remove*. **Ich muß leider unsere Verabredung verschieben**, *Unfortunately I have to postpone our appointment*. **Besorgen**, *to see to, to do.*

⑧ **der Morgen**, *the morning*. But, **morgen**, *tomorrow*; **morgen früh**, *tomorrow morning*. **Morgen abend**, *tomorrow evening.*

59 **Übung 1 – Übersetzen Sie bitte**

❶ Gehen Sie gern ins Kino oder sehen Sie lieber zu Hause fern? ❷ Wissen Sie, wer die pasteurisierte Milch erfunden hat? ❸ Mein Großvater ist ganz zufrieden, wenn er mit einer Zigarre auf der Gartenbank sitzt. ❹ Heute nachmittag werde ich mich ausruhen. ❺ Haben Sie schon die Karten für das Theater besorgt?

Übung 2 – Ergänzen Sie bitte

❶ Don't be mistaken! That's more difficult than you think.
. . . . Sie . . . . nicht! Das ist . . . . als Sie . . . .

❷ I will be happy *(glad)* when I am at home again.
Ich bin . . . . , ... ich wieder . . . . bin.

❸ Can you change *(me)* Euros into Dollars?
Können Sie mir Euro in Dollar . . . . ?

❹ He often changes his mind.
Er . . . . . . oft seine Meinung.

❺ Tomorrow morning I will buy new wallpaper and [I will] completely change my bedroom.
. . . . werde ich mir eine neue Tapete besorgen und mein Schlafzimmer ganz . . . .

❻ No, we don't live in *(the)* Adelbert Street any longer, but in *(the)* Freiligrath Street.
Nein, wir wohnen . . . . in der Adeibertstraße, ... in der Freiligrathstraße.

Answers to exercise 1

❶ Do you like going to the cinema or do you prefer to watch the TV at home? ❷ Do you know who invented pasteurized milk? ❸ My grandfather is fully content when he sits on the garden bench [smoking] a cigar. ❹ This afternoon I will rest. ❺ Have you already bought the theatre tickets?

Answers to exercise 2

❶ Täuschen – sich – schwerer – denken ❷ – zufrieden – wenn – zu Hause – ❸ – wechseln ❹ – ändert – ❺ Morgen früh – verändern ❻ – nicht mehr – sondern –

60 Sechzigste Lektion

Der kleine Blonde ① und sein roter Koffer

1 – Erinnerst du dich noch an den kl**ei**nen Bl**o**nden mit dem r**o**ten K**o**ffer, d**a**mals in **A**msterdam?

2 – Ja, er ist uns überallh**i**n gef**o**lgt. ②

3 – Als ③ wir in St**u**ttgart in den Zug **ei**nstiegen, saß er in **u**nserem Abt**ei**l.

4 – Ja, und er h**a**tte s**ei**nen gr**o**ßen, r**o**ten K**o**ffer auf dem Schoß und ließ ihn nicht **ei**ne Sek**u**nde los ④.

5 – Und als wir in Fr**a**nkfurt **u**msteigen m**u**ßten, stieg er auch um.

6 – Und er saß w**ie**der im s**e**lben ⑤ Abt**ei**l wie wir und s**a**gte kein Wort.

7 – Ja, und ich fr**a**gte ihn **ei**nmal, ob er ein Keks m**ö**chte, **a**ber er sch**ü**ttelte nur den Kopf.

Pronunciation Key
2 *... überall'h**i**nn ...* ***3*** *... Appt**i**le* ***4*** *... Zek**oo**nnde ...* ***5*** *... **oo**mmshty'gen ...* ***7*** *... sh**ü**ttelte ...*

Notes

① Adjectives used as nouns are nevertheless declined like an adjective: **der Blonde**, *the fair-haired (guy)*; **ein Blonder**, *a fair-haired...*

② Notice that the **Perfekt** of **folgen** is formed with **sein** because it is a verb denoting movement. That is why we must add **hin** to **überall**, *everywhere*.

The Little Fair-Haired [Man] and his Red Suitcase

1 – Do you still remember the little fair-haired [man] with the red suitcase *(m.)* back in those days in Amsterdam?
2 – Yes, he followed us everywhere.
3 – When we got on the train at *(in)* Stuttgart he was sitting in our compartment *(n.)*.
4 – Yes, and he had a big red suitcase on his knees *(lap)* and he didn't leave it for a second.
5 – And when we had to change at *(in)* Frankfurt he changed, too.
6 – And again he sat in the same compartment as we [did] and didn't say a word.
7 – Yes, and I asked him once whether he wanted a biscuit *(n.)* but he just shook his head.

▸ ③ *when* is translated by **als** because it refers to an action in the past (see lesson 63, paragraph 1).

④ You already know **los**, meaning: *to leave*. **Wir fahren in einer Stunde los**, *We'll leave in an hour*. Here it means *to untie*, *to let loose go*. **Der Hund ist los**, *The dog is loose*. **Los** (adjective) is the opposite of **fest**, *firm*.

⑤ **derselbe**, **dieselbe**, **dasselbe**, *the same* (m., f., n.). The definite article + **selb** + the ending of an adjective: **Ich saß heute auf demselben Platz wie gestern**, *Today I have been sitting on the same seat as [I did] yesterday*. **Wir wohnen im selben (= in demselben) Haus**, *We live in the same house*.

8 – Und dann sind wir in Amsterdam **au**sgestiegen, und er ging w**ie**der h**i**nter uns her... bis zum **Au**sgang ⑥.

9 – Und dort n**a**hmen wir ein T**a**xi.

10 – Er **a**ber blieb am **Au**sgang st**e**hen, halb verd**e**ckt von s**ei**nem gr**o**ßen, r**o**ten K**o**ffer und w**i**nkte ⑦.

11 – Ja, so war's! Und seit J**a**hren fr**a**ge ich mich, was er wohl in s**ei**nem r**o**ten K**o**ffer h**a**tte... □

Notes

⑥ **der Ausgang**, *the exit*; **der Eingang**, *the entrance.*

⑦ **winken**, *to wave, to make a sign.*

***

Übung 1 – Übersetzen Sie bitte

❶ Als ich sie fragte, ob sie etwas essen möchte, schüttelte sie nur den Kopf. ❷ Sie sind in Frankfurt eingestiegen und in Hamburg ausgestiegen. Sie mußten nicht umsteigen. ❸ Der Mann von Frau Meier trägt immer denselben Hut. ❹ Wir wohnen seit zehn Jahren in derselben Wohnung. ❺ Sie blieben stehen, um einem Taxi zu winken. ❻ Das Kind hat plötzlich die Hand seiner Mutter losgelassen und gesagt: „Ich kann allein laufen".

8 – And then we got off at *(in)* Amsterdam and again he followed us to the exit *(m.)*.
9 – And there we took a taxi *(n.)*.
10 – But he stayed at the exit partly hidden *(half covered)* by his big red suitcase and was waving.
11 – Yes, that was it. And I have been wondering for years what might have been in his red suitcase… *(What he had…)*. □

SIE BLIEBEN STEHEN, UM EINEM TAXI ZU WINKEN
TAXI
H.CA.311

***

Answers to exercise 1

❶ When I asked her whether she wanted something to eat, she just shook her head. ❷ They got on at Frankfurt and they got off at Hamburg. They didn't have to change. ❸ Mrs. Meier's husband always wears the same hat. ❹ We have been living in the same flat for 10 years. ❺ They stopped in order to make a sign to the taxi [driver]. ❻ Suddenly the child let go of her mother's hand and said: "I can walk by myself".

Übung 2 – Ergänzen Sie bitte

❶ Is there a seat left *(free)* in this compartment, please?
Ist in diesem . . . . . . noch . . . . frei, bitte?

❷ There is no through train *(direct communication)*. You have to change at Bonn.
. . . . keine direkte Verbindung. Sie müssen in Bonn . . . .

❸ Get on, please! The train is leaving immediately.
. . . . Sie bitte . . . ! Der Zug . . . . . gleich . . . .

❹ I wonder what the man over there is doing.
. . . ., . . . der Mann dort macht.

61 Einundsechzigste Lektion

Kein Wunder!

1 – Guten Morgen! Was ist denn mit dir los? Hast du schlecht geschlafen?
2 – Ja, das kann man wohl sagen! Ich fühle mich hundselend ①.
3 – Du hast wohl 'nen Kater ②, was? Was hast du denn gestern abend gemacht? Gesteh'!
4 – Ich war auf einer Party bei Freunden. Wir haben das Semesterende gefeiert.

Pronunciation Key
... voonder ***2*** *... hoonntselennt*

❺ She always travels with her small black suitcase.
Sie verreist immer mit ihrem . . . . ,
. . . . Koffer.

❻ Everybody got off because the bus broke down.
Alle . . . . weil der Bus . . . .
. . . . . hatte.

Answers to exercise 2

❶ – Abteil – ein Platz – ❷ Es gibt – umsteigen ❸ Steigen – ein – fährt – los ❹ Ich frage mich – was – ❺ – kleinen – schwarzen – ❻ – sind ausgestiegen – eine Panne –

Second Wave: Eleventh Lesson

61st Lesson 61

No Wonder *(n.)*!

1 – Good morning! What's the matter with you? Did you sleep badly?

2 – You can say that again! I really feel miserable *(like a dog)*.

3 – No doubt you have a hangover *(m.)*, haven't you? What did you do last night? Confess!

4 – I went *(was)* to a party *(f.)* with friends. We celebrated the end of the term.

Notes

① **das Elend**, *the misery*; **elend**, *miserable*.

② **einen Kater haben**, lit. "to have a cat", *to have a hangover*.

5 Gestern früh hatten wir die letzte Prüfung.
6 – Was für eine Prüfung war das denn?
7 – Deutsche Wirtschaft. Wir mußten einen Bericht über die Arbeitslosigkeit ③ schreiben und Lösungen finden…
8 – Um Gotteswillen! Hast du da was schreiben können?
9 – Ehrlich ④ gesagt, nicht sehr viel.
10 – Kein Wunder! Die Regierung weiß ja auch nicht, was sie tun soll. ⑤
11 – Ja, deshalb ⑥ haben wir gestern abend auch einen Brief an den Wirtschaftsminister geschrieben, in dem ⑦ wir ihm unsere Dienste anbieten. □

7 … virtshaft …

Notes

③ **die Arbeitslosigkeit**, *the unemployment*; **arbeitslos**, *unemployed*. When you add **-los** to a noun it becomes an **adjective** and means, *without*... or... *less*, **heimatlos**, *homeless*; **kinderlos**, *childless*; **mittellos**, *without means*. ▸

***

Übung 1 – Übersetzen Sie bitte

❶ Was ist denn mit Ihnen los? Sind Sie krank? ❷ Können Sie uns helfen? Wir wissen nicht, was wir machen sollen. ❸ Meinem Mann geht es nicht gut. Ich glaube, er hat einen Kater. ❹ Gestern früh habe ich einen Wirtschaftsbericht geschrieben. ❺ Die Regierung findet keine Lösung für das Problem der Arbeitslosigkeit.

5 Yesterday morning we took *(had)* the last exam *(f.)*. **61**
6 – What kind of exam was it?
7 – German economy *(f.)*. We had to write a report *(m.)* on unemployment *(f.)* and to find solutions.
8 – For God's sake! Where you able to write anything?
9 – Honestly speaking, not a lot.
10 – No wonder! The government doesn't know what to do either.
11 – Yes, that is why we wrote a letter *(m.)* to the Minister *(m.)* of the Economy offering our services *(in which we offer...)*. □

④ **ehrlich**, *honest*; **die Ehre**, *the honour*; **ehren**, *to honour*. Do you remember, **sehr geehrte Herren**, **sehr geehrte Damen** (lesson 29).

⑤ Notice the expression: **Ich weiß nicht, was ich tun soll**, *I don't know what to do*. In German we must introduce a subordinate, **was ich tun soll**, *what I am to do*. **Er weiß nicht, was er antworten soll**, *He doesn't know what to answer*.

⑥ **deshalb**, *therefore, that is why*. Pay attention to the inversion of subject and verb.

⑦ **der Brief**, *the letter*, a masculine noun, therefore we must say: **der Brief, in dem...**, *the letter...*

***

Answers to exercise 1

❶ What is the matter with you? Are you ill? ❷ Can you help us? We don't know what to do. ❸ My husband doesn't feel good. I think *(believe)* he has a hangover. ❹ Yesterday morning I wrote a report on economy *(an economic report)*. ❺ The government doesn't find a solution to the problem of unemployment.

Übung 2 – Ergänzen Sie bitte

❶ What's the matter with you? Aren't you coming to Fritz's party?
Was ist . . . . ? . . . . du nicht . . . die Party von Fritz?

❷ Honestly speaking, I don't like going *(there)*.
. . . ., ich habe keine Lust, dorthin . . . .

❸ Can you swim?
. . . . . . Sie schwimmen?

❹ He has been unemployed for a year *(he is unemployed...)*.
Er ist . . . . einem Jahr . . . .

❺ I can only speak English. That is why I prefer to stay in England during the holidays.
Ich . . . . nur English . . . . bleibe ich in den Ferien . . . . . . in England.

❻ I have eaten too much. I feel very miserable *(like a dog)*.
Ich habe . . . . Ich fühle mich . . . .

62 Zweiundsechzigste Lektion

Ein glücklicher Zufall

1 – Entschuldigen Sie! Was trinken Sie da? Ein Alsterwasser ①? Was ist denn das?
2 – Das ist Bier gemischt mit Limonade: halb Bier, halb Zitronenlimonade.

Note

① Names of drinks or specialities may vary from one region to another. In Berlin, beer mixed with lemonade is sometimes ▸

Answers to exercise 2

❶ – mit dir los – Kommst – auf – ❷ Ehrlich gesagt – zu gehen ❸ Können – ❹ – seit – arbeitslos ❺ – kann – sprechen – Deshalb – lieber ❻ – zuviel gegessen – hundselend

Second Wave: Twelfth Lesson

62nd Lesson 62

Lucky Chance *(m.)*

1 – Excuse me! What are you drinking there? An Alsterwasser *(shandy)*? What is that?
2 – *(That is)* beer mixed with lemonade. [One] half [of it is] beer, [the other] half [is] lemonade.

▸ called **Havelwasser** (the Havel is the river which flows through Berlin).

3 – Ach so! Bei uns in M**ü**nchen heißt das „R**a**dler".
4 – Ah**a**, Sie sind also M**ü**nchner? Wohl ② zum **e**rsten Mal in H**a**mburg, was?
5 – Ja, so ist es, obw**o**hl ③ m**ei**ne M**u**tter H**a**mburgerin ist.
6 **A**ber mein V**a**ter ist ein **e**chter ④ B**a**yer und haßt **a**lles, was n**ö**rdlich von B**a**yern liegt… Und Sie? Sind Sie von hier?
7 – Ja, ich bin w**a**schechter ④ H**a**mburger und k**e**nne die Stadt wie m**ei**ne W**e**stentasche.
8 – Na, dann k**ö**nnen Sie mir best**i**mmt s**a**gen, was man an **ei**nem tr**au**rigen Sonntagm**o**rgen hier m**a**chen kann?
9 – Klar! Schon mal was geh**ö**rt von Sankt P**au**li, dem **a**lten H**a**fenviertel? ⑤
10 – Ja, **a**ber das ist doch das Vergn**ü**gungsviertel ⑥, wo nur nachts was los ⑦ ist, **o**der nicht?

Pronunciation Key
9 *… zang'kt* ***pow****li …* ***10*** *… fergn****ü****goongsfeertel …*

Notes

② **wohl** is one of the little words which often are not or cannot be translated. Here, one of its uses: **wohl** in a question (direct or indirect) shows that the person who is asking thinks he knows the answer, but wants to be sure: **Morgen hast du wohl keine Zeit?**, *No doubt you are not free tomorrow, am I right?* **Das ist wohl das Autos deines Vaters?**, *That's your father's car, isn't it?* Two possible translations are, the question tag, or, No doubt...

③ **obwohl**, *although*, introduces a subordinate clause → the verb is placed at the end of the sentence, and when you start your sentence with the subordinate clause, subject and verb ▸

3 – I see! In Munich we call it "Radier".
4 – Oh, you are from Munich? No doubt the first time you are in Hamburg, *(am I right?)*.
5 – Yes, that's right, although my mother is from Hamburg.
6 But my father is a real Bavarian and hates everything north of Bavaria. And what about you *(and you)*? Are you from here?
7 – Yes, I am a real Hamburger and know the town like my pocket *(of my waistcoat)*.
8 – Well, so you surely can tell me what to do here on a sad Sunday morning.
9 – Certainly! Have you ever heard of St. Pauli, the old harbour *(m.)* district *(n.)*?
10 – Yes, but that's the entertainment *(n.)* district, where there is only something happening at night, isn't it?

▸ are inverted in the main clause: **Obwohl es regnet, gehe ich spazieren**, *Although it is raining I am going for a walk.*

④ **echt**, *real*, *true*; the opposite is **unecht**, **künstlich**, *false*, *artificial*. **Waschecht** means that washing does not deteriorate the colour of the clothes. **Waschecht** used to qualify a person is a colloquial expression meaning *typical*.

⑤ **der Hafen**, *the harbour*; **das Viertel**, *the district*, *the quarter*, *area*. **Das Hafenviertel** in this sentence depends on the preposition **von** which requires the dative: **Ich habe von St. Pauli, (von) dem alten Hafenviertel gehört**, *I have heard of St. Pauli, the old harbour district.*

⑥ **das Vergnügen**, *the pleasure*, *entertainment*. **Mit Vergnügen**, *with pleasure*. **Die Vergnügung(en)**, *The amusement(s)*, *entertainment*.

⑦ You already know the expression **Was ist los?**, *What is the matter?* – **Dort ist etwas los** means *there is something happening*.

11 – Nee ⑧, nee, s**o**nntag m**o**rgens ist da F**i**schmarkt; das m**ü**ssen Sie ges**e**hen h**a**ben.
12 K**o**mmen Sie, ich begl**ei**te Sie, ich h**a**be auch ger**a**de nichts zu tun, und **au**ßerdem kann ich dort gleich Fisch für h**eu**te **a**bend **ei**nkaufen… □

Note

⑧ **nee** is equivalent to *nope* – an informal way of saying no. The pronounciation is *[nay]*.

***

Übung 1 – Übersetzen Sie bitte

❶ Er hat sich ein neues Auto gekauft, obwohl er kein Geld hatte. ❷ Haben Sie schon mal etwas von dieser Person gehört? ❸ Ich bin letztes Jahr zum ersten Mal nach Berlin gefahren. ❹ Sonntag morgens sind normalerweise alle Geschäfte geschlossen. ❺ Sie kommen wohl aus der Schweiz? ❻ Dann können Sie mir bestimmt zeigen, wie man Müsli macht? – Klar, mit Vergnügen!

11 – No, no, on Sunday mornings there is the fish-market *(m.)*; you must see it *(have seen it)*.
12 Come on, I will come with you *(accompany)*. I don't have anything to do and what's more I can buy fish *(m.)* for tonight there. □

***

Answers to exercise 1

❶ He bought a new car although he didn't have any money. ❷ Have you ever heard of this person? ❸ Last year I went to Berlin for the first time. ❹ On Sunday mornings the shops are generally closed. ❺ You come from Switzerland, don't you? ❻ Then you can certainly show me how to make muesli – Certainly, with pleasure!

Übung 2 – Ergänzen Sie bitte

1. His mother was from Hamburg *(was a Hamburger)* and his father from Munich.
   Seine Mutter war . . . . und sein Vater . . . .
2. He is a real Bavarian and he knows Bavaria like his pocket.
   Er ist ein . . . . und kennt . . . . . . wie seine . . . .
3. Is the fish-market open on Sunday mornings?
   Ist der Fischmarkt . . . . geöffnet?
4. She won't come with him although she hasn't got anything to do.
   Sie . . . . ihn nicht . . . . . . sie nichts zu . . . hat.

63 Dreiundsechzigste Lektion

Wiederholung und Erklärungen

1 The Translation of "When"

There are three ways of translating when: **als**, **wenn** and **wann**. To be on the safe side, try to remember the following explanations. In German we make certain distinctions.

1.1 *Als*

Als is used for something that only happened once in the past.

Als ich gestern nach Hause gekommen bin, war ich sehr müde, *When I came home yesterday I was very tired.* **Als er vier Jahre alt war, hatte er die Masern**, *When he was four years old he had the measles.*

❺ Come on, let's go to the harbour district. There are always a lot of things happening.
Komm, wir gehen ... . Dort ist ..... viel .... .

❻ Freiburg is situated north of Basel *(... lies north...).*
Freiburg .... von Basel.

Answers to exercise 2

❶ – Hamburgerin – Münchner ❷ – echter Bayer – Bayern – Westentasche ❸ – sonntags morgens – ❹ – begleitet – obwohl – tun – ❺ – ins Hafenviertel – immer – los ❻ – liegt nördlich –

Second Wave: Thirteenth Lesson

63rd Lesson 63

1.2 *Wenn*

Wenn is used to refer to a present or future event, or to an event which was repeated once or more.

Wenn ich am Abend nach Hause komme, bin ich immer sehr müde, *When I come home in the evening I am always very tired.*
Wenn wir in Frankfurt ankommen, müssen wir unsere Freunde anrufen, *When we arrive in Frankfurt we must phone our friends.*

1.3 *Wann*

Wann: *when?* is only used in questions (direct or indirect):

63 **Wann kommen Sie in Frankfurt an?**, *When do you arrive in Frankfurt?*
Können Sie mir sagen, wann der Zug nach Heidelberg abfährt?, *Can you tell me when the train for Heidelberg is leaving?*

1.4 Translation

That's not too difficult, is it?
Try and translate the following sentences to make use of your newly acquired knowledge:

When Hans was ten years old his grandfather gave him his first watch. When Hans looks at this watch nowadays he thinks of his grandfather; and he wonders when he will give him a new one after all.
(Solution at the end of the lesson).

2 Infinitive with *um… zu* or *damit*

2.1 *Um… zu*

When there is the same subject in both main and subordinate clauses.
Ich arbeite, um Geld zu verdienen, *I work in order to earn money.*
Er kommt, um mit uns zu sprechen, *He comes in order to speak with us.*

2.2 *Damit*

When there are two different subjects:
Komm näher, damit ich dich besser verstehe, *Come closer so that I understand you better.*
Die Kinder spielen draußen, damit die Mutter in Ruhe schlafen kann, *The children are playing outside so that the mothe can sleep in peace.*

3 Adverbs of Time

- **Damals, früher, vor kurzem, gerade** locate an event in the past:

Damals, als wir in Frankfurt wohnten, gab es keine U-bahn, *In those days when we lived in Frankfurt there was no Underground.*

Früher war alles ganz anders, *In former times everything was totally different.*
Ich habe ihn vor kurzem gesehen, *I have seen him recently.*
Ich habe ihn gerade gesehen, *I have just seen him.*

• **Gleich/sofort**, **bald**, **später** locate a future event.

Ich komme gleich, *I will come immediately.*
Er wird bald kommen, *He will come soon.*
Später wirst du dich darüber freuen, *You will be happy about it later.*

Don't learn anything by heart! We will see everything again in more detail. We only want to draw your attention to certain details.

The adverbs of time **danach**, **vorher**, **hinterher** link two situations:

Ich mache zuerst meine Übungen, danach werde ich Fußball spielen, *First I will do my exercises, afterwards I will play football.*
Ich werde Ihnen das Geld geben, aber vorher muß ich mit Ihrem Vater sprechen, *I will give you the money but I have to talk to your father beforehand.*
Kommen Sie bitte hinterher zu mir!, *Come and see me afterwards, please!*

4 Solution to Paragraph 1.4

Als Hans zehn Jahre alt war, hat ihm sein Großvater seine erste Uhr geschenkt. Wenn Hans heute diese Uhr ansieht, denkt er an seinen Großvater; und er fragt sich, wann er ihm endlich eine neue schenken wird.

64 Vierundsechzigste Lektion

Der Auserwählte ①

1 – Na, wie war denn gestern **a**bend der Empf**a**ng ② beim Gener**a**ldirektor?
2 – Och, **a**nfangs ③ ganz **a**ngenehm. Es gab Champ**a**gner und **ei**ne M**e**nge L**eu**te.
3 – Ja ja, es h**a**ben nicht **a**lle ④ das Glück, s**o**lche ⑤ **Ei**nladungen zu bek**o**mmen!
4 – Glück? Was heißt hier Glück? W**a**rte, wie's w**ei**tergeht.
5 Sp**ä**ter beim **E**ssen h**a**tte ich als T**i**schpartnerin ⑥ die Schw**e**ster des Gener**a**ldirektors.
6 Man hat mich ansch**ei**nend für sie **ei**ngeladen.
7 – Siehst du! Ich w**u**ßte ja gleich, du bist ein **Au**serwählter!
8 – Mach' dich r**u**hig **ü**ber mich l**u**stig! Du hast sie nicht ges**e**hen und nicht geh**ö**rt…

Pronunciation Key
*…**ow**sservaihlt**e** **1** …emm'pf**a**ng …gener**a**l …**2** shammp**a**nyer…*

Notes

① **wählen**, *to choose, to vote*; **auswählen**, *to choose, to select*, contains the idea of elite. E.g.: **ein auserwähltes Volk**, *a chosen people*. **Eine auserwählte Speise**, *an exquisite dish*. **Man hat uns auserwählt**, *We were chosen*. Don't mix it up with **auswählen = wählen, Welchen Pullover hat du ausgewählt?** *Which pullover did you choose?* ▸

The Chosen *(m.)*

1 – So, what was the reception *(m.)* at the general manager's like last night?
2 – Oh, in the beginning it was quite pleasant. We had *(there was)* champagne and there were a lot of people.
3 – Yes, not everyone is lucky enough to get such invitations!
4 – Luck? What do you mean by luck *(what does luck mean here)*? Wait [for] what comes next *(how it goes on)*.
5 Later, during the meal, the manager's sister was my neighbour at table *(I had the... as neighbour)*.
6 I was apparently invited for her.
7 – You see! I immediately knew you are a lucky man.
8 – [I don't mind if you] make fun of me *(quietly)*! You neither saw nor heard her…

▸ ② **der Empfang**, *the reception; receipt.* **Empfangen**, *to receive, to welcome.* **Er hat mich freundlich empfangen**, *He gave me a friendly reception [he kindly received me].* **Ich habe deinen Brief gestern empfangen**, *I received your letter yesterday.* **Der Empfänger**, *the addressee*; **der Absender**, *the sender.*

③ **anfangs** or **am Anfang**, *in the beginning.* **Ganz** preceding an adjective means *completely* or *quite.*

④ The subject of this sentence is **alle**, not **es**. That is why the verb is in the third person plural (see lesson 70, paragraph 3).

⑤ **ein solcher**, **eine solche**, **ein solches**, *such a* (m./f./n.).

⑥ **der Partner**, **die Partnerin**, *the partner.* **Der Tischpartner**, *the neighbour at table.*

64 9 Während des ⑦ ganzen Essens ⑦ hat sie sich beklagt:
10 wie allein sie ist, wie gemein ⑧ die Leute sind, und wie traurig das Leben ist.
11 – Na und was hast du ihr empfohlen ⑨?
12 – Nichts. Ich habe mich so schnell wie möglich auf französisch empfohlen. □

Notes

⑦ **während** is followed by the genitive.

⑧ **gemein**, *common, nasty*, **Du bist gemein**, *You are nasty.* **Wir haben nichts mit ihnen gemein**, *We have nothing in common with them.* **Die Gemeinschaft**, *the community.*

⑨ **empfehlen**, *to recommend*, but **sich empfehlen**, *to take one's leave.*

***

Übung 1 – Übersetzen Sie bitte

❶ Anfangs war das Wetter sehr schön, aber dann begann es zu regnen. ❷ Es haben nicht viele Leute das Glück, eine solche Reise machen zu können. ❸ Dieser Mann ist anscheinend sehr reich. ❹ Während der ganzen Reise habe ich an dich gedacht. ❺ Warum hast du keinen Absender auf deinen Brief geschrieben? ❻ Als Tischpartner hatte ich gestern abend den Bruder meines Chefs.

9 She was complaining during the whole meal:
10 how lonely she is, how mean people are and how sad life is.
11 – So, and what did you recommend *(her)*?
12 – Nothing. I took French leave *(I recommended myself in French)*.

***

Answers to exercise 1

❶ In the beginning the weather was very nice, but then it started raining. ❷ There are not many who [few people] are lucky enough to make such a journey. ❸ Apparently this man is very rich. ❹ I thought of you during the whole journey. ❺ Why didn't you write the name of the sender on your letter? ❻ Yesterday my boss' brother was my neighbour at table.

Übung 2 – Ergänzen Sie bitte

❶ What was the film like *(which)* you saw yesterday?
... ... denn ... ., ... Sie gestern gesehen haben?

❷ Oh, quite good in the beginning but the end was very sad.
Och .... ganz gut. aber das Ende ....

❸ Don't complain all the time *(always)*! You should [had better] go to the cinema more often.
.... Sie sich nicht immer! .... öfters ins Kino!

❹ What do you want to eat? Have you already chosen something?
... .? .... schon etwas ....?

65 Fünfundsechzigste Lektion

Und Sie, sind Sie schon einmal einem Nationalisten begegnet ①?

1 Man sagt, daß **Lie**be und **Haß na**he beiein**an**der st**e**hen.
2 Gilt ② das auch für V**a**terlandsliebe und V**a**terlandshaß?

Pronunciation Key
*... natsyonalisten ... **1** ... by'i-nannder ...*

Notes

① **begegnen,** *to come across* + dat. in German. **Ich bin meinem Freund begegnet,** *I came across my friend.* Its past participle

⑤ On Sunday there will be a reception at the Krämers. Are you invited too?

Am . . . . ist ein . . . . bei Krämers. . . . .
. . . auch . . . . ?

⑥ They all made fun of me.

. . . . alle . . . . lustig . . . .

Answers to exercise 2

❶ Wie war – der Film – den – ❷ – anfangs – war sehr traurig ❸ Beklagen – Gehen Sie lieber – ❹ Was wollen Sie essen – Haben Sie – ausgewählt ❺ – Sonntag – Empfang – Sind Sie – eingeladen ❻ Sie haben sich – über mich – gemacht

Second Wave: Fifteenth Lesson

65th Lesson 65

And You, Have You ever Met a Nationalist?

1 It is said that love *(f.)* and hate *(m.)* are very close to one another.
2 Is this also true for [the] love and [the] hatred of *(one's)* native land *(n.)*?

is formed with **sein**. **Treffen**, *to meet* + acc.: **Ich habe meinen Freund getroffen**, *I met my friend.*

② **gelten**, *to be valid, to be effective*; **Dieser alte Zehnmarkschein gilt nicht mehr**, *This old ten-Mark-note is no longer valid.* **Gelten für**, *to be true for, to apply to*: **Diese Bestimmung gilt nur für Ausländer**, *This law only applies to foreigners.*

3 Vielleicht kennen Sie die folgende Geschichte schon oder vielleicht kennen Sie sogar Herrn K.?

4 Herr K. hielt es nicht für nötig ③, in einem bestimmten Land zu leben.

5 Er sagte: „Ich kann überall hungern".

6 Eines Tages aber ging er durch eine Stadt ④, die vom Feind des Landes besetzt war, in dem er lebte.

7 Da kam ⑤ ihm ein feindlicher Offizier entgegen ⑤ und zwang ⑥ ihn, vom Bürgersteig hinunterzugehen.

8 Herr K. machte Platz, und in demselben Augenblick bemerkte er,

9 daß er diesen Mann haßte und nicht nur diesen Mann,

10 sondern das ganze Land, zu dem der Offizier gehörte ⑦.

Notes

③ **es für nötig halten**, *to consider it necessary.* **Ich halte es nicht für nötig ihn einzuladen**, *I don't consider it necessary to invite him.*

④ **Ich gehe durch die Stadt/den Garten** either means *to go through* or *to walk in the town/garden. To cross the street* is translated by **über die Straße gehen**.

⑤ **entgegenkommen** or **entgegengehen**, *to go/come to meet somebody* or *to come/walk up to somebody.* **Das Kind läuft seiner Mutter entgegen**, *The child runs up to his mother.*

⑥ **zwingen**, *to force, to compel*; (*to oblige* + **zu** + infinitive): **Ich bin leider gezwungen, dieses Haus zu verlassen**, ▸

3 Maybe you already know the following story or maybe you even know Mr K. **65**

4 Mr K. didn't consider it necessary to live in a particular country.

5 He said: "I can be hungry everywhere."

6 But one day he was walking in a town which was occupied by the enemy *(m.)* of the country he lived in.

7 There a hostile officier *(m.)* came up to him and forced him to get off the pavement *(m.)*.

8 Mr. K. made way for him and at the same instant *(m.)* he noticed

9 that he hated this man and not only this man,

10 but the whole country the officier was part of.

WIR SIND AUF DER STRAßE UNSERM NACHBARN BEGEGNET

▸ *Unfortunately I am compelled to leave this house*. **Zu** is placed between the separable prefix and the infinitive.

(7) **gehören**, *to belong to*. **Das Buch gehört meiner Freundin**, *This book belongs to my friend*. **Gehören zu**, *to be part of/member of*. **Er gehört zu dieser Gruppe**, *He is member of this group*.

65 11 „Wodurch bin ich in diesem Augenblick Nationalist geworden?“ fragte er sich.

12 „Weil ich einem Nationalisten begegnet bin“, war die einzige Antwort,

13 die er finden konnte.

(Nach B. Brecht) □

***

Übung 1 – Übersetzen Sie bitte

❶ Wir sind auf der Straße unserm Nachbarn begegnet. ❷ Diese Bestimmung gilt für Franzosen aber nicht für Deutsche. ❸ Sie hielten es nicht für nötig, ihren Wagen abzuschließen. Aber als sie zurückkamen, war ihr Wagen nicht mehr da. ❹ Er wollte seine Frau pünktlich vom Zug abholen, aber als er am Bahnhof ankam, kam sie ihm schon entgegen.

Übung 2 – Ergänzen Sie bitte

❶ Do you really consider it necessary to do that?
. . . . wirklich . . . . das zu tun?

❷ The bad economic situation forces people to live more modestly.
Die schlechte Wirtschaftslage . . . . bescheidener . . . .

❸ Are you member of a political party?
. . . . einer politischen Partei?

❹ We prefer walking home across the forest rather than the town *(the forest than)*.
Wir . . . . . lieber . . . . . den Wald als . . . . . die Stadt . . . .

11 “Why *(by what)* did I turn nationalist at this moment?” he wondered.
12 “Because I came across a nationalist”, was the only reply
13 *(which)* he could think of *(find)*.
(According to B. Brecht) □

***

Answers to exercise 1

❶ We met our neighbour in the street. ❷ This law applies to Frenchmen but not to Germans. ❸ They didn’t consider it necessary to lock their car. But when they came back, their car wasn’t there any more. ❹ He wanted to go to meet his wife at [the arrival of] the train, but when he arrived at the station she was already coming towards him.

❺ All his life he hated dogs and cats, whereas he liked horses very [much].
Er . . . . . sein ganzes Leben Hunde und Katzen. Pferde dagegen . . . . sehr.

❻ When he was sixty years old he became general director.
. . . . . sechzig . . . . , . . . er Generaldirektor . . . .

Answers to exercise 2

❶ Halten Sie es – für nötig – ❷ – zwingt die Leute – zu leben ❸ Gehören Sie zu – ❹ – gehen – durch – durch – nach Hause ❺ – haßte – liebte er – ❻ Als er – Jahre alt war – ist – geworden

Second Wave: Sixteenth Lesson

66 Sechsundsechzigste Lektion

Nehmen Sie nicht alles wörtlich ①!

1 Wenn **I**hnen zum B**ei**spiel ein Bek**a**nnter ② sagt:
2 „Jetzt sind Sie **a**ber ins F**e**ttnäpfchen getr**e**ten ③",
3 s**e**hen Sie nicht kr**i**tisch ④ **I**hre Sch**u**he an,
4 s**o**ndern überl**e**gen Sie l**ie**ber, was Sie ger**a**de ges**a**gt h**a**ben.
5 **O**der wenn ein Freund beim M**i**ttagessen sagt:
6 „Das ist **a**lles für die Katz'", ⑤
7 **e**ssen Sie r**u**hig w**ei**ter,
8 g**e**ben ihm **a**ber vielleicht **ei**nen g**u**ten Rat **o**der ein Ber**u**higungsmittel.

Pronunciation Key
2 *… fettnaipfçhenn …* ***8*** *… ber**oo**higoongs …*

Notes

① **wörtlich**, *literally*; when you add **-lich** to certain nouns they become adjectives (if necessary you add the **Umlaut** too): **Wort** → **wörtlich**; **der Sinn**, *sense* → **sinnlich**, *sensual*, *sensuous*; **der Mensch** → **menschlich**, *human*; **der Tag** → **täglich**, *daily*.

② **ein Bekannter**: a "weak" noun has to be declined like an adjective: **ein Bekannter** but **der Bekannte**. A woman: **die Bekannte** or **eine Bekannte** and the plural is **die Bekannten**. ▸

Don't Take Everything Literally!

1 If someone *(an acquaintance [m.])* tells you, for example:
2 "Now, you've put your foot in it *(you walked into the little grease bowl)*",
3 don't look suspiciously at your shoes,
4 but you'd better think about what you have just said.
5 Or if a friend tells you during lunch [when you are having lunch]:
6 "That's all of no use", *(that's all for the cats)*,
7 go on eating quietly,
8 but perhaps you will give him some good advice *(m.)* or a sedative *(n.)*.

③ **in** or **auf etwas treten**, *to step/walk into* or *on something.*

④ **die Kritik**, *criticism*; **der Kritiker**, *the critic*; **kritisch**, *critical.* **Das ist eine kritische Situation**, *This is a critical situation*; **Das ist ein kritischer Mensch**, *He is a critical person.*

⑤ This expression goes back to a fable in the 15th century. Every time the smith was not paid by his customer, he would say this would be for the cat, so the poor cat was soon starved to death.

9 Und falls ⑥ **ei**nmal ein **Au**tofahrer, den Sie ger**a**de rechts überh**o**lt ⑦ h**a**ben, bei der n**ä**chsten r**o**ten **A**mpel ⑦ **au**ssteigt
10 und Sie fragt, ob Sie **ei**nen V**o**gel h**a**ben,
11 denken Sie nicht l**a**nge nach,
12 s**o**ndern fr**a**gen Sie ihn l**ie**ber,
13 ob er nicht aus **ei**ner M**ü**cke **ei**nen Elef**a**nten macht!

(F**o**rtsetzung folgt) □

Notes

⑥ *if* in a conditional clause is translated by **wenn** or **falls**.

⑦ **überholen**, *to pass*, *to overtake*. The stress is on the **o** of **holen**, as the prefix **über** cannot be separated. You certainly remember that only separable prefixes are stressed. **Die Ampel**, *the traffic light*.

***

Übung 1 – Übersetzen Sie bitte

❶ Wenn Sie mir noch einmal sagen, daß ich einen Vogel habe, werde ich niemals mehr mit Ihnen sprechen. ❷ Sehen Sie mich nicht so kritisch an! Ich habe Ihnen die Wahrheit gesagt. ❸ Ich habe gestern einen Bekannten getroffen, den ich seit zehn Jahren nicht mehr gesehen hatte. ❹ Du kannst den Lastwagen jetzt nicht überholen. Es kommen zu viele Autos entgegen. ❺ Frage ihn doch, ob er nicht noch einmal darüber nachdenken will.

9 And if one day *(once)* a driver *(m.)* you just passed on the right gets out of his car at the next red light *(f.)* **66**

10 and asks you whether you have a bee *(a bird [m.])* [in your bonnet],

11 don't think about it too long,

12 *(but)* you'd better ask him

13 whether he isn't making a mountain *(a gnat [f.])* out of a molehill *(an elephant [m.])*!

(To be continued) □

FRAGE IHN DOCH, OB ER NICHT NOCH EINMAL DARÜBER NACHDENKEN WILL

***

Answers to exercise 1

❶ If you say again that I have a bee in my bonnet I will never speak to you again. ❷ Don't look at me in such a critical [way]! I have told you the truth. ❸ Yesterday I met a friend [of mine] I had not seen for ten years. ❹ You cannot overtake the lorry now. There are too many cars *(coming up)* on the opposite side of the road. ❺ Ask him whether he doesn't want to think about it again *(once)*.

Übung 2 – Ergänzen Sie bitte

❶ Why are you looking at me in such a critical way? Don't you like my dress?
. . . . . siehst du mich so . . . . an? . . . . dir mein Kleid nicht?

❷ Turn *(drive)* right at the next light please.
Fahren Sie bitte an der nächsten . . . .

❸ It was all useless because I fell ill.
. . . . denn ich bin krank geworden.

❹ Don't you know whether my husband is still at the office?
. . . . , . . mein Mann noch im Büro ist?

67 Siebenundsechzigste Lektion

Nehmen Sie aber bitte auch ab und zu etwas wörtlich!

1 – „Du hast doch nicht die Spaghettisoße mit dem Hackfleisch,
2 das ganz hinten ① im untersten Fach im Kühlschrank war, gemacht?
3 Das war für die Katze!"

Note

① **hinten**, *behind*; *at the back*, is an adverb. The preposition is **hinter**. **Dort hinten ist die Post**, *The post-office is at the back*. ▸

⑤ If you see him, please tell him to call me *(that he shall call me).*

. . . . , sagen Sie ihm bitte, daß er . . . . soll.

⑥ Did you really think about it?

Haben Sie . . . . nachgedacht?

Answers to exercise 2

❶ Warum – kritisch – Gefällt – ❷ – Ampel links ❸ Das war alles für die Katz' – ❹ Wissen Sie – ob – ❺ Wenn Sie ihn sehen – mich anrufen – ❻ – wirklich darüber –

Second Wave: Seventeenth Lesson

67th Lesson 67

Nevertheless, Take Things Literally from Time to Time Please!

1 – "You didn't make the spaghetti sauce *(f.)* with the minced meat *(n.)*
2 which was at the back of the bottom compartment *(n.)* of the refrigerator *(m.)*, [did you]?
3 It was for the cat!"

Die Post ist hinter dem Bahnhof, *The post-office is behind the station* (See lesson 70, paragraph 4).

67

4 Also in diesem Fall gießen ② Sie die Soße am besten ③ sofort weg ②, falls Sie sie noch nicht gegessen haben, oder geben Sie sie der Katze!

5 Sie sind überarbeitet. Ihr Kanarienvogel ist weggeflogen, und Ihre Kinder weinen jämmerlich.

6 Es klingelt an der Tür. Es ist die Frau von gegenüber.

7 – Sie fragt: „Hatten Sie nicht einen kleinen, gelben Vogel?"

8 Dieses Mal haben Sie keinen Grund böse zu werden ④.

9 – Antworten Sie lieber mit einem freundlichen Lächeln: „Doch!"

10 Und Ihre Nachbarin wird Sie bitten, zu ihr zu kommen,

11 um den Vogel, der verschreckt auf einer Vorhangstange im Wohnzimmer sitzt, einzufangen ⑤.

12 Genug der guten Ratschläge ⑥!

13 Ab jetzt verlassen ⑦ wir uns auf Ihren gesunden Menschenverstand ⑧. □

Notes

② **gießen**, *to pour*; the separable prefix **weg-** means *away*. **Ich gieße den Wein weg**, *I pour the wine away*. **Er wirft seine Schuhe weg, sie sind zu alt**, *He is throwing his shoes away; they are too old*.

③ Remember the following expression: **Am besten gehen wir sofort**, *It's best to leave immediately*. **Am besten schläfst du** ▸

4 Well, in this case if you haven't already eaten it, pour it away immediately or give it to the cat!
5 You are overworked. Your canary has flown away, and your children are crying piteously.
6 The door bell is ringing *(it rings at the door)*. It is the woman across the road.
7 – She asks: "Didn't you have a little yellow bird?"
8 This time you have no reason *(m.)* to get angry.
9 – Rather *(you)* answer kindly, smiling *(with a kind smile)*: "Yes, I did!"
10 And your neighbour will ask you inside
11 in order to catch the bird which is sitting frightened on the curtain rod *(f.)* in the living room.

12 No more advice *(enough of the good advice)*!
13 From now on we rely on your common sense *(m.) (on your healthy human intelligence)*. □

▸ **erst einmal ein wenig**, *The best thing for you would be to sleep a little bit first.*

④ **böse sein**, *to be angry*: **Sei nicht böse**, *Don't be angry.* **Böse werden**, *to get angry.*

⑤ **fangen**, *to catch*; **einfangen** is used when you really get hold of the animal or person. **Sie brauchen viel Zeit um den kleinen Vogel einzufangen**, *It took them a long time to catch get hold of the little bird.*

⑥ **der Rat**, *piece of advice*; pl.: **die Ratschläge**.

⑦ **sich verlassen auf**, *to rely on*. This verb is reflexive in German: **Ich verlasse mich auf dich**, *I rely on you.* But **Ich verlasse dich**, *I leave you.*

⑧ **der Verstand**; **die Vernunft**, *reason, common sense.*

67 **Übung 1 – Übersetzen Sie bitte**

❶ Meine Nachbarn sind gestern weggefahren und haben mir ihren Kanarienvogel gegeben. ❷ Kannst du mir bitte beim Tischdecken helfen? Du findest die Teller ganz oben im Schrank. ❸ Seine Kinder haben jämmerlich geweint, als er das Haus verlassen hat. ❹ Sie haben keinen Grund sich aufzuregen. Das ist alles nur halb so schlimm! ❺ Meine Freundin hat mich gebeten, mit ihr ins Kaufhaus zu kommen, um ein Kleid für sie auszuwählen.

Übung 2 – Antworten Sie bitte *(Please answer)*

❶ Wo war das Hackfleisch für die Katze?

. . . .

❷ Was mache ich mit der Soße, die nicht mehr gut ist?

. . . . (. . . . . .) . . . . !

❸ Warum weinen die Kinder jämmerlich?

. . . .

❹ Wer klingelt an der Tür?

. . . .

❺ Wo sitzt der kleine, gelbe Vogel?

. . . .

❻ Worauf verlassen wir uns ab jetzt?

. . . . !

Answers to exercise 1

❶ My neighbours left yesterday and gave me their canary. ❷ Can you help me to lay the table please? You'll find the plates at the top of the cupboard. ❸ His children were crying piteously when he left the house. ❹ You have no reason to get excited. It's not as bad as that *(it's half as bad)*. ❺ My friend asked me to come to a department store with her to choose a dress for her.

Answers to exercise 2

❶ Ganz hinten im untersten Fach im Kühlschrank. ❷ Sie werfen (gießen) sie am besten weg! ❸ Weil der Kanarienvogel weggeflogen ist. ❹ Die Nachbarin klingelt an der Tür. ❺ Er sitzt auf der Vorhangstange im Wohnzimmer. ❻ Auf Ihren gesunden Menschenverstand!

Second Wave: Eighteenth Lesson

68 Achtundsechzigste Lektion

Der öffentliche Fernsprecher ① (I)

1 – Oh, Mist ②! Ich **h**abe verg**e**ssen, **O**nkel Kurt **a**nzurufen.
2 Halt 'mal b**i**tte an! Dort dr**ü**ben ③ ist **e**ine Telef**o**nzelle.
3 – Muß das sein? Wir sind schon so spät dran ④…
4 und **au**sgerechnet **O**nkel Kurt! Der r**e**det ⑤ **i**mmer st**u**ndenlang am Telef**o**n.
5 – Ich weiß ja, **a**ber's muß sein! Ich hab's ihm verspr**o**chen, und
6 wer weiß, wie l**a**nge er noch lebt…
7 – **A**lso gut! **A**ber mach es b**i**tte so kurz wie ⑥ m**ö**glich!
8 – Das verst**e**he ich nicht! Ich kr**ie**ge ⑦ k**ei**ne Verb**i**ndung.
9 Da kommt **i**mmer: „Kein **A**nschluß **u**nter d**ie**ser N**u**mmer…" Da wird doch ⑧ nichts pass**ie**rt sein?

Notes

① See lesson 70 paragraph 5.

② **Mist**, literally "dung", but in spoken language you find it in expressions like **Mach keinen Mist!**, *Don't do anything silly!* **Dein Zimmer ist ein reiner Misthaufen**, *Your room is a real jumble.*

③ **drüben**, *over there.*

④ **spät dran sein** is a familiar expression for **zu spät kommen** or **Verspätung haben**, *to be late.* ▸

The Public Telephone *(m.)* (Part One)

1 – Oh, dash it! I have forgotten to phone Uncle Kurt.
2 Stop for a moment please! There is a telephone box *(f.)* over there.
3 – Is that really necessary *(must that be)*? We are already so late…
4 and especially Uncle Kurt! He always talks for hours on the phone *(n.)*.
5 – Yes, I know, but it really is necessary! I promised him and
6 who knows how long he is going to live…?
7 – Well, okay! But make it as brief as possible.
8 – I don't understand that! I can't get through *(I don't get the connection [f.])*.
9 I can only hear *(there always comes)*: "Your call cannot be connected *(no connection (m.) under this number [f.])...*" I hope nothing happened.

⑤ **reden** or **sprechen**, *to speak*, **reden** often means *to chat*. But **die Rede**, *the speech*.

⑥ **so... wie**: **Er kommt so schnell wie möglich**, *He comes as quickly as possible.*

⑦ **kriegen** is used in spoken language for **bekommen**, **erhalten**, *to get, obtain*. **Er kriegt kein Geschenk**, *He doesn't get any present.*

⑧ **doch** is often introduced when we hope something will not happen: **Es wird doch morgen nicht regnen!**, *I hope it is not going to rain tomorrow!* **Er wird doch nicht kommen**, *I hope he will not come!*

68 **10** – Nein, natürlich nicht! Du mußt nur 089 vorwählen ⑨. Wir sind hier schon außerhalb ⑩ von München.
11 – Ach ja! Hallo Onkel Kurt? Ja, ich bin's. Ich wollte nur schnell…
12 – Ach Kindchen, das ist ja schön, daß du anrufst. Heute morgen bin ich mit dem Hund spazierengegangen, weißt du, es ging mir etwas besser als gewöhnlich, und da habe ich Frau Becker, die Frau, die dir immer die Pfefferminzbonbons geschenkt hat, wenn du in den Ferien hier warst, auf der Straße getroffen und… (N.1)
13 – Onkel Kurt, ich wollte nur…
(Fortsetzung folgt) □

Notes

⑨ **eine Telefonnummer wählen**, *to dial a telephone number*, **eine Nummer vorwählen**, *to dial the code*. **Vorwahlnummer**, *the dialling code*.

⑩ **außerhalb** (+ genitive), *outside, out of*. **Innerhalb**, *inside*.

***

Übung 1 – Übersetzen Sie bitte

❶ Wenn Sie von außerhalb telefonieren, müssen Sie vorwählen. ❷ Er ist mit seinem Hund spazierengegangen und hat auf der Straße seine Nachbarin getroffen. ❸ Ich habe heute morgen einen Brief von meiner Bank gekriegt, in dem sie mir schreiben, daß ich kein Geld mehr auf meinem Konto habe. ❹ Machen Sie bitte so schnell wie möglich! Ich bin sehr spät dran. ❺ Hinter uns fährt die Polizei. Die werden uns doch nicht anhalten wollen?

10 – No, certainly not! You just have to dial the code 089. We are already outside Munich here.
11 – Ah, yes! Hallo Uncle Kurt? Yes, it's me. I just wanted…
12 – Ah, my child, how nice of you to call me. This morning I went for a walk with the dog, you know, I felt a little bit better than usual and there I met Mrs. Becker in the street. [You know], the woman who used to give you peppermint drops when you were here on holiday…
13 – Uncle Kurt, I only wanted…

(To be continued) □

***

Answers to exercise 1

❶ If you phone from outside you have to dial the code. ❷ He went for a walk with his dog and met his neighbour in the street. ❸ This morning I got a letter from my bank [saying] that I haven't got any money in my bank account. ❹ Be as fast as possible please! I am very late. ❺ The police are *(driving)* behind us. I hope they are not going to stop us *(they don't want to...)*.

69 Übung 2 – Ergänzen Sie bitte

❶ I forgot to buy sugar and salt.
. . .   . , Zucker und Salz . . . .

❷ I know that you don't like doing that. But it is necessary.
. . . . , daß du das nicht gern machst. Aber . . . .

❸ He wants to phone his uncle but he can't get through.
. . . . . . seinen Onkel . . . . , aber . . . . keine Verbindung.

❹ Yesterday he felt a little better than usual.
Gestern . . . .   etwas   . . . .

69 Neunundsechzigste Lektion

Der öffentliche Fernsprecher (II)

1 – Hallo! Sie da drinnen! Beeilen Sie sich ① mal ein bißchen! Das ist eine öffentliche Telefonzelle!
2 – Du, Onkel Kurt, es tut mir leid, aber ich muß jetzt auflegen ②. Da draußen warten Leute…

Notes

① **sich beeilen**, *to hurry up*. **In Eile sein** or **es eilig haben**, *to be in a hurry*, **Ich habe es eilig/ich bin in Eile**, *I am in a hurry*. ▸

❺ Do you remember the man who gave you the bicycle?
Erinnerst du dich an den Mann, … … das Fahrrad … … … … ?

❻ Who is speaking? – It's me, Anne.
… … … ? – … … … Anne.

❼ We don't know how long we will be able to stay.
… … … … … , … … … wir bleiben können.

Answers to exercise 2
❶ Ich habe vergessen – zu kaufen ❷ Ich weiß – es muß sein ❸ Er will – anrufen – er kriegt – ❹ – ging es ihm – besser als gewöhnlich ❺ – der dir – geschenkt hat ❻ Wer ist da – Ich bin's – ❼ Wir wissen nicht – wie lange –

Second Wave: Nineteenth Lesson

69th Lesson 69

The Public Telephone (Part Two)

1 – Hey! You there! Hurry up a bit! This is a public telephone!
2 – *(You)* Uncle Kurt, I am sorry but I have to hang up now. There are people waiting outside…

② **auflegen**, *to hang up* (the telephone); **abnehmen/abheben**, *to pick up the receiver* or *to answer the telephone.*

3 – Die k**ö**nnen w**a**rten! Ich h**a**be in m**ei**nem Leben auch oft w**a**rten m**ü**ssen.
4 **Ei**nmal stand ③ ich bei 15 Grad K**ä**lte **ei**ne St**u**nde vor **ei**ner Telef**o**nzelle.
5 Das war d**a**mals, als sich noch nicht **a**lle ein Telef**o**n l**ei**sten ④ k**o**nnten und…
6 – H**a**llo! Sie da! Jetzt reicht's ⑤ **a**ber! Sie sind nicht all**ei**n auf der Welt.
7 Es gibt noch **a**ndere L**eu**te, die telefon**ie**ren w**o**llen.
8 – Hörst du, **O**nkel Kurt? Die L**eu**te dr**au**ßen r**e**gen sich **i**mmer mehr auf.
9 Ich muß jetzt w**i**rklich Schluß m**a**chen ⑥. **A**lso dann tschüs! Ich r**u**fe dich w**ie**der an.
10 Uff! Das war nicht **ei**nfach.
11 **A**ber glaubst du, es war w**i**rklich n**ö**tig, die Telef**o**nzelle halb **ei**nzureißen? □

Notes

③ The vowel of the following verbs changes in the **Imperfekt**: **stehen - ich stehe →ich stand**; **sitzen - ich sitze →ich saß**; **legen - ich liege →ich lag**.

④ **sich etwas leisten**, *to afford something*. But **leisten** (without the reflexive pronoun), *to perform*, *to accomplish*, *to achieve*. **Die Leistung**, *the performance*, *achievement*.

⑤ **es reicht**, *that is enough*; **reichen**, *to suffice*, or *to present*, *to offer*, *to pass*, **Reich mir bitte den Zucker**, *Pass me the sugar please*.

⑥ **der Schluß**, *the end*; **Schluß machen**, *to end*, *to come to an end* (**aufhören**).

3 – They can wait! I often had to waft in life too.
4 Once I spent one hour waiting *(I stood)* in front of a telephone box in a – 15 °C cold *(coldness)*.
5 That was back in the days when not everybody could afford to be on the telephone and…
6 – Hey! You there! That's enough! You are not alone in the world *(f.)*.
7 There are other people who want to telephone.
8 – Do you hear [that] Uncle Kurt? The people [waiting] outside are getting more and more angry.
9 I really have to come to an end now. Well, bye-bye then! I will call again.
10 Phew! That wasn't easy.
11 But *(do you think it)* was it really necessary to nearly pull the phone box down? □

69 **Übung 1 – Übersetzen Sie bitte**

❶ Wir essen lieber drinnen, draußen im Garten ist es zu kalt. ❷ Wir haben uns sehr beeilt, um nicht zu spät zu kommen. ❸ Er hat einmal eine halbe Stunde vor einer Telefonzelle gewartet, und als sie endlich frei war, hat er bemerkt, daß er kein Geld hatte. ❹ Er kann sich kein Auto leisten. Das Benzin ist zu teuer. ❺ Glauben Sie, Sie sind allein auf der Welt?

Übung 2 – Ergänzen Sie bitte

❶ We are very late. We have to hurry up.
Wir sind .... Wir müssen ... .

❷ Inside it is very hot, but outside it is icy cold.
.... ist es sehr warm, aber .... ist es eiskalt.

❸ Do you want another beer? – No, thanks! I have already had three; that is enough!
...... Sie .... ? – Nein danke! ... . schon drei ....; das ...... !

❹ I don't have enough money. I can't afford that.
... ... Ich kann mir das nicht ....

Answers to exercise 1

❶ We prefer to eat inside; outside in the garden it is too cold. ❷ We hurried in order to arrive on time *(in order not to come late)*. ❸ He had been waiting half an hour in front of a telephone box; when it was free at last he noticed that he hadn't got any money. ❹ He can't afford a car. *(The)* petrol is too expensive. ❺ Do you think you are alone in the world?

❺ He spent one hour standing in front other door. Then he went away.
Er . . . . . eine Stunde . . . ihrer Tür. Dann . . . . er . . . . .

❻ Don't get excited please! I will finish immediately.
. . . . bitte nicht . . . ! Ich . . . . . sofort . . . .

Answers to exercise 2

❶ – sehr spät dran – uns beeilen ❷ Drinnen – draußen – ❸ Wollen – noch ein Bier – Ich habe – getrunken – reicht ❹ Ich habe nicht genug Geld – leisten ❺ – stand – vor – ging – weg ❻ Regen Sie sich – auf – mache – Schluß

Second Wave: Twentieth Lesson

70 Siebzigste Lektion

Wiederholung und Erklärungen

1 Constructing German Sentences

We want to give you some more details about the construction of German sentences:
Als er sah, daß es nichts mehr zu sehen gab, nahm er sein Fahrrad, das er auf dem Trottoir gelassen hatte, und fuhr nach Hause.
When he saw that there was nothing more to see he took his bicycle, which he had left on the pavement, and rode home.
Please note the following points in this sentence.

1.1 The Verb of a Subordinate Clause

The conjugated verb is placed at the end of the subordinate clause, and subject and verb are inverted when the main clause follows the subordinate clause: **Als er das sah**, **nahm er sein Fahrrad**, *When he saw this he took his bicycle.*

1.2 The Rule of the Comma

Main clause and subordinate clause are always separated by a comma, and when there are several subordinate clauses there is a comma after each: **Er nahm sein Fahrrad, das er auf dem Trottoir gelassen hatte, und fuhr nach Hause**: *He took his bicycle, which he had left on the pavement, and rode home.*

One of the difficulties for learners of German is the position of the past participle or the infinitive.
You have to wait until the end of the sentence to discover its exact meaning since the verb is not mentioned until then:
Ich bin mit meiner Freundin, die ich seit zehn Jahren kenne, dieses Jahr zum ersten Mal... everything is still possible!... **in Ferien gefahren**.
In English we get this information at the beginning:
This year I went on holiday for the first time with my girlfriend, whom I have known for ten years.

2 The Infinitive with *zu*

You have to pay attention to the prefix when the infinitive is preceded by **zu**: when the prefix is separable, **zu** is placed between the prefix and the infinitive; if not, **zu** precedes verb + prefix:
Ich habe vergessen, das Radio auszumachen, *I forgot to switch off the radio.*
Er versucht, sein altes Auto zu verkaufen, *He is trying to sell his old car.*
Sie hat Angst, ihn wiederzusehen, *She is afraid of seeing him again.*
Er hat mir versprochen, seine Schulden zu bezahlen, *He promised me to pay his debts.*
After **wollen**, **können**, **sollen**, **dürfen**, **müssen**, there is always an infinitive without **zu** :
Ich muß gehen, *I must go.*
Er kann nicht kommen, *He cannot come.*

3 *Es* at the Beginning of a Sentence

Es is often placed at the beginning of a sentence when the verb is in the third person singular or plural and when there is another "real" subject in the sentence:
Es gehen jetzt alle = Alle gehen jetzt, *Everybody is leaving now.*
Es wird der Tag kommen, wo sie darüber nur noch lachen können, *The day will come when you will only (be able to) laugh about it.*

4 Adverbs and Prepositions of Place

Adverbs and prepositions of place are often similar but never identical:
Mein Hausbesitzer wohnt in der Wohnung unter mir, *My landlord lives in the flat below mine (me).*
Er wohnt unten und ich wohne oben, *He lives downstairs and I live upstairs.*
Er steht vor der Tür, *He is standing in front of the door.*
Er steht davor, *He is standing in front of it (the door).*

71 When an adverb of location is used with a verb denoting a change in position, a preposition must precede the adverb, or **hin** must be added to the adverb:
Die Post ist dort drüben, *The post-office is over there.*
Gehen wir hinüber, *Let's go over there, on the other side.*
Wir essen draußen, *We eat outside.*
Wir gehen nach draußen (or: **hinaus**), *We go outside.*
Drinnen ist es warm, *Inside it is warm.*
Ich gehe hinein, *I go inside.*
Mein Wagen steht dort, *My car is standing there.*
Ich stelle meinen Wagen dorthin, *I put my car there.*
Mein Vater ist oben, *My father is upstairs.*
Gehen Sie nach oben (or: **hinauf**), *Go upstairs!*

71 Einundsiebzigste Lektion

Klein-Fritzchen

1 Wir wollen Ihnen heute eine deutsche Persönlichkeit vorstellen, deren ① Name sowohl den Jungen als auch ② den Alten geläufig ist.
2 Warten Sie! Sie werden gleich selbst ③ sehen, wer das ist.
3 Na, wo ist er denn gerade? Ach ja, natürlich, in der Schule…

Pronunciation Key
kline-fritss'çhen **1** … *perzernlichkite* …

Notes

① The relative pronoun *whose* is translated by **dessen** (m./n.) and **deren** (f. and plural): **Der Mann, dessen Frau gestern** ▸

5 Some information about telecommunications

Ein Fernsprecher ist ein Telefon. Es gibt Ferngespräche, *long-distance calls*, **Auslandsgespräche**, *international calls*, **und Ortsgespräche**, *local calls.* **Wenn Sie mit einer Person in einer anderen Stadt sprechen wollen, müssen Sie die Vorwahlnummer**, *dialling code*, **dieser Stadt kennen.**
Das Handy, *the cell phone*; **das Internet**, *the Internet*; **jemandem (dat.) eine Mail schicken,** *to send an e-mail to someone.*

71st Lesson 71

Little Fritz

1 Today we want to introduce you to a German personality *(f.)* whose name is familiar to the young as well as to the old.
2 Wait! You'll see [by] yourself immediately who it is.
3 Well, where is he just now? Oh yes, at school, of course...

weggelaufen ist, findet seine Pantoffeln nicht, *The man whose wife went away yesterday can't find his slippers.* **Die Personen, deren Namen mit K beginnen, kommen bitte an den Schalter 6**, *The persons whose names begin with K come to counter [number] 6 please.* (See lesson 77, paragraph 4).

② **sowohl... als auch**, *as well... as*; *both... and.* **Er ist sowohl größer als auch dicker als ich**, *He is both taller and fatter than I am.*

③ **selbst** or **selber** (spoken language), *self (-ves),* **selbst** can be separated from the personal pronoun, **Ich mache das selbst = ich selbst mache das,** *I do it [by] myself.*

71 **4** Der Lehrer fragt die Kinder in der Deutschstunde:
5 – Na, Kinder, welche deutschen Vornamen kennt ihr denn so?
6 – „Hannes“, sagt sofort die kleine Erika, die immer die Schnellste ist.
7 – „Sehr gut“, lobt sie der Lehrer, „aber der richtige ④ Name ist Johannes“.
8 – „Achim“, ruft dann ein anderer Schüler.
9 – „Ja, aber das heißt Joachim“, verbessert ihn der Lehrer.
10 Daraufhin meldet sich ⑤ stürmisch ⑥ Klein-Fritzchen.
11 Der Lehrer ruft ihn auf und fragt ihn lächelnd ⑦:
12 – „Na, welchen Vornamen kennst du denn, mein Junge?“
13 – „ ⑧ Jokurt“, antwortet Fritzchen strahlend.* □

* **Falls Sie nicht verstanden haben, lesen Sie schnell den Anfang der nächsten Lektion.** *If you haven't understood, read the beginning of the next lesson!*

7 *... yohannes* ***9*** *... yo'açhimm ...* ***10*** *... shtürmish ...* ***13*** *... yokoort ... shtrahlennt*

Do you remember the first name Kurt? (See lesson 68). Notice that yoghourt is not written with **k** but with **gh** in German: **Joghurt!**

Notes

④ **richtig**, *proper, exact, right.* **Das ist nicht der richtige Weg**, *This is not the right way.* ▸

4 The teacher asks the children during the German lesson:
5 – Well, children, which German first names do you know?
6 – Little Erika, who is always the quickest, immediately says "Hannes".
7 – "Very good", the teacher praises her, "but the proper name is Johannes".
8 – "Achim", another pupil shouts.
9 – "Yes, but we say *(that means)* Joachim", the teacher corrects him.
10 Thereupon little Fritz eagerly puts his hand up.
11 The teacher calls him, and asks him, smiling:
12 – Well, which first name do you know, my boy?
13 – "Jokurt" [yoghourt], little Fritz answers beamingly. □

▸ ⑤ **sich melden**, *to present oneself, to put up one's hand.* But on the phone, **Es meldet sich niemand**, *Nobody answers.*

⑥ **stürmisch**, *impetuous, eager.*

⑦ The present participle has to be declined when it precedes the noun, **das lächelnde Kind**, *the smiling child*, **ein lächelndes Kind**, *a smiling child.*

⑧ In German, direct speech is introduced by quotation marks at the bottom of the line.

71 **Übung 1 – Übersetzen Sie bitte**

❶ Können Sie mir bitte Ihren Freund vorstellen? ❷ Die Mütter, deren Kinder drei Jahre alt sind, melden sich bei Frau Braun. ❸ Der alte Mann, dessen Haus vorgestern abgebrannt ist, sitzt jetzt auf der Straße. ❹ Ich habe heute alles gewußt, was mich der Lehrer gefragt hat. Er hat mich gelobt. ❺ Ist Ihnen dieser Ausdruck nicht geläufig? ❻ Nicht so stürmisch, Kinder, ich bin nicht mehr die Jüngste!

Übung 2 – Ergänzen Sie bitte

❶ Which famous German personality do you know?
.... kennen Sie?

❷ She has both French and German nationalities.
Sie hat ...... die französische ... . die deutsche Staatsbürgerschaft.

❸ Call in [by] yourself! Your husband can't do it for you.
Kommen Sie doch bitte ...... vorbei! ... .

❹ Aunt Erika, have you got any chocolate? – You mean: Have you got any chocolate please?
Tante Erika, ... Schokolade? – ... .: .... bitte Schokolade?

Answers to exercise 1

❶ Can you please introduce your friend to me? ❷ The mothers whose children are three years old present themselves at Mrs. Brown's. ❸ The old man whose house burnt down the day before yesterday is in the streets now. ❹ Today I knew everything the teacher asked me. He praised me. ❺ Aren't you familiar with this expression? ❻ Gently, gently children *(not so quickly)*, I am no longer as young as I used to be.

❺ I waited for an hour at the bank. My number was the last to be called.

. . . . eine Stunde auf der Bank . . . .
. . . . . . meine Nummer als letzte . . . .

❻ She says, beaming: I love both of you!

. . . . sagt sie: . . . . euch alle beide!

Answers to exercise 2

❶ Welche deutsche Persönlichkeit – ❷ – sowohl – als auch – ❸ – selbst – Ihr Mann kann das nicht für Sie machen ❹ – hast du – Das heißt – Hast du – ❺ Ich habe – gewartet – Man hat – aufgerufen ❻ Strahlend – Ich liebe –

Second Wave: 22nd Lesson

72 Zweiundsiebzigste Lektion

Quark und Schwarzbrot

1 – Übrigens, da wir gerade von ① Joghurt sprechen, muß ich an „Quark“ denken. Weißt du, was „Quark“ ist?
2 – Selbstverständlich weiß ich, was „Quark“ ist.
3 Wer kennt nicht weißen Käse und Käsekuchen mit oder ohne Rosinen!
4 – Um so besser! Ich wußte nicht, daß das so bekannt ist.
5 – Na, hör mal! Quark gehört genau so wie Schwarzbrot und Gemüsesäfte zum Thema: „Gesünder essen – länger leben“ oder so ähnlich ②,
6 und du mußt wirklich taub und blind sein, wenn du in Deutschland daran vorbeigehen ③ kannst...
7 Die Bio-Läden ④ schießen ja bei euch wie Pilze ⑤ aus der Erde.

Pronunciation Key
kvark ... shvartsbrot ***1*** *... yoghourt ...* ***3*** *... kaize ... rozeenenn*
5 *... gemüzezaifte ...* ***7*** *... bi'o-laiden sheessen ... piltse ...*

Notes

① A lot of verbs are followed by prepositions: **sprechen**, *to speak*, can be followed by **von** + dat. or by **über** + acc.: **Ich spreche von meiner Mutter**, *I am speaking about my mother.* **Er spricht über seine Arbeit**, *He is speaking of his work.* ▸

Soft White Cheese and Brown Bread

1 – By the way, we are speaking about yoghourt *(m.)*, I *(have to)* think of "Quark" *(m.)*. Do you know what "Quark" is?
2 – Of course I know what "Quark" is.
3 Who doesn't know soft white cheese and cheese *(m.)* cake with or without raisins!
4 – All the better! I didn't know that it was so well-known.
5 – But, listen! Soft white cheese is, like brown bread *(n.)* and vegetable juices, part of the topic *(n.)*: "Eat healthier – live longer" or something like that,
6 and you must really be dumb and blind if *(when you manage)* you fail to see them in Germany.
7 The organic shops are springing up *(out of the earth)* like mushrooms in your country.

▸ During the second wave you will see that you are already familiar with quite a number of verbs plus their corresponding prepositions.

② **ähnlich**, *similar.* **Ihre Schwester sieht Ihnen sehr ähnlich**, *Your sister looks very much like you.* **Das sieht dir ähnlich**, *That's you.* But the expression **oder so ähnlich** means *something like that.*

③ **vorbeigehen**, *to fail to see, to go past.*

④ **der Laden**, *the shop.* Organic shops sell natural products, fruit and vegetables without chemicals (**naturrein**).

⑤ **der Pilz**, **die Pilze**, *the mushroom/s.*

8 – Ja, das ist, Gott sei Dank, wahr! Und ich bin sehr froh dar**ü**ber ⑥!

9 **A**ber **ei**gentlich d**a**chte ich an **e**twas ganz **a**nderes.

10 – Oh, entsch**u**ldige! Wor**a**n ⑦ denn?

11 – Ich d**a**chte an den Frosch, der in ein M**i**lchgeschäft kommt,

12 und die Verk**äu**ferin fragt ihn: „Was darf' s sein?" ⑧

13 „Quak", sagt der Frosch. □

Notes

⑥ **froh sein über**, *to be glad about*... **Ich bin froh über das, was du mir gesagt hast**, *I am glad about what you told me.*

⑦ **Woran denken Sie**? *What are you thinking of?* But, **An wen denken Sie?** *Who are you thinking of?* (See lesson 54, note 1).

⑧ **Was darf's sein?** is an expression meaning **was wollen Sie?** or **was wünschen Sie?**, *What would you like?*

***

Übung 1 – Übersetzen Sie bitte

❶ Wir haben gestern viel von Ihnen und Ihrer Frau gesprochen. ❷ Ich mußte die ganze Zeit an den Film von gestern abend denken. ❸ Selbstverständlich können Sie bei mir vorbeikommen. Ich werde ab zehn Uhr in meinem Büro sein. ❹ Er sah so arm und traurig aus. Ich konnte nicht an ihm vorbeigehen. Ich habe ihm fünf Mark gegeben. ❺ Der Arzt hat mir „Benozidim" oder so etwas ähnliches gegeben. ❻ Die Video-Läden schießen wie Pilze aus der Erde.

8 – Yes, thank God, this is true! And I am very glad [about it]!
9 But actually I was thinking about something completely different.
10 – Oh, excuse me! What about?
11 – I was thinking about the frog who enters a dairy shop,
12 and the sales-girl asks him: "What would you like?"
13 "Quak" the frog says. □

***

Answers to exercise 1

❶ Yesterday we talked a lot about you and your wife. ❷ I had to think about last night's film all the time. ❸ Of course you can call on me. I'll be at my office from 10 o'clock onwards. ❹ He looked so poor and sad. I couldn't go past him. I gave him 5 marks. ❺ The doctor gave me "Benozidim" or something like that. ❻ Video shops are springing up like mushrooms.

Übung 2 – Ergänzen Sie bitte

❶ Today there is much talk about chemicals in food.
... . heute .... „Chemie in Lebensmitteln".

❷ I don't know what "Quark" is.
... ..., ... „Quark" .... .

❸ She was thinking all the time of the cake [which was] in the oven.
Sie mußte die ganze Zeit .. .. im Ofen ....

❹ The street is called "Kreuzhirdiweg" or something like that.
... . „Kreuzhirdiweg" ....

73 Dreiundsiebzigste Lektion

Bitte anschnallen ①!

1 – Wir b**i**tten ② Sie, sich w**ie**der **a**nzuschnallen!
2 Es h**a**ndelt sich nur um ③ **ei**ne S**i**cherheitsm**a**ßnahme,

Pronunciation Key
2 ... *ziçherhites-massnahme*

Notes

① We simply say **anschnallen** for *fasten your seatbelt*. You can also say **die Sicherheitsgurte anlegen**. **Der Sicherheitsgurt**, *the safety belt*, **der Gürtel**, *the belt*. The infinitive is often ▸

❺ When the frog came in, the sales-girl asked him: What would you like?
Als ... . eintrat, fragte ... die Verkäuferin: ... .?

❻ If you want to live healthily you must eat soft white cheese and brown bread.
Wenn Sie .... wollen, müssen Sie ..... und .... essen.

Answers to exercise 2

❶ Man spricht – viel von – ❷ Ich weiß nicht – was – ist ❸ – an den Kuchen – denken ❹ Die Straße heißt – oder so ähnlich ❺ – der Frosch – ihn – Was darf's sein ❻ – gesund leben – Quark – Schwarzbrot –

Second Wave: 23rd Lesson

73rd Lesson 73

Fasten Your Seatbelts Please!

1 – We ask you to fasten your seatbelt again!
2 This is only a safety measure *(f.)*,

used as imperative: **Ziehen!**, *Pull!* - **Drücken!**, *Press!* - **Nicht hinauslehnen!**, *Do not lean out of...!*

② **bitten**, *to ask*, can be followed by **zu** + infinitive – **Ich bitte Sie, mich zu entschuldigen**, *Please excuse me* – or by the preposition **um** + acc., when you ask for something: **Ich bitte Sie um Geduld**, *Please be patient.* (I ask you to excuse me;... for patience).

③ **sich handeln um**, *to be concerned.* **Es handelt sich um meine Mutter**, *My mother is concerned.* (See lesson 77, paragraph 3).

73

3 es besteht keinerlei Grund ④ zur Beunruhigung.

4 – „Jetzt ist es also passiert“, dachte er sofort.

5 Normalerweise hatte er keine Angst vorm ⑤ Fliegen.

6 Aber heute morgen hatte er ein komisches Gefühl gehabt, als er das Haus verließ.

7 Und noch bevor ⑥ er beim Flughafen ankam, hatte er mehrmals gezögert umzukehren.

8 Auch nachdem ⑦ er ins Flugzeug eingestiegen war, verließ ihn dieses Gefühl nicht.

9 Im Gegenteil, es wurde immer stärker. Etwas lag in der Luft! Etwas stimmte nicht!

10 Dabei hatte er allen Grund ruhig und glücklich zu sein:

11 Drei Wochen Urlaub in Aussicht, fern von allen Verpflichtungen, sich um nichts und niemanden kümmern ⑧ müssen…

12 Himmel! Emmanuela! Daher kam also sein komisches Gefühl!

13 Er hatte die Katze in den Keller gesperrt, weil sie ihn beim Kofferpacken ⑨ gestört hatte…

***3** … be'**oo**nrooigoong **7** … gets**er**gert …*

Notes

④ **der Grund**, *the reason for something.* **Es besteht kein Grund zu**, *There is no reason to.* **Es besteht kein Grund zum Schreien** (n.), *there is no reason to cry.* Verbs used as nouns are always neuter.

3 there is no reason *(m.)* to worry.
4 – "Now it has happened", he immediately thought.
5 Normally he didn't fear flying.
6 But this morning he had a strange feeling *(n.)* when he left the house.
7 And even before he arrived at the airport he had almost returned several times.
8 Even when he had got on the plane *(n.)* this feeling didn't leave him.
9 On the contrary, it became stronger and stronger. Something was in the air *(f.)*! Something was wrong!
10 Yet, he had every reason to be calm and happy:
11 Three weeks holiday in view, far from every obligation, to worry about nothing and nobody…
12 Heavens! Emmanuela! So that was why he had this strange feeling!
13 He had locked the cat in the cellar *(m.)* because it had bothered him when he packed his suitcase… □

▸ ⑤ **Angst haben vor** (+ dat.), *to be afraid of, to fear.* **Ich habe Angst vor dem Hund**, *I am afraid of the dog.* **Vorm** is the contraction of **vor + dem**, it is only used in spoken language.

⑥ **bevor** (conj.), *before.*

⑦ **nachdem** (conj.): *after, when.* **Nachdem er gegessen hatte, ging er ins Bett**, *When he had eaten he went to bed.*

⑧ **sich kümmern um**, *to take care of, to look after, to see to*: **Wer kümmert sich heute um die Kinder?**, *Who will look after the children today?*

⑨ **den Koffer** (m.) **packen**, *to pack one's things, to prepare one's suitcase.* **Beim (dei dem) Kofferpacken**, *While you prepare your suitcase.*

73 **Übung 1 – Übersetzen Sie bitte**

❶ Warum haben Sie sich nicht angeschnallt? Es ist Pflicht, sich anzuschnallen. ❷ Nachdem Herr und Frau Meier im Hotel angekommen waren, packten sie sofort ihre Koffer aus. ❸ Bevor ich endlich nach Hause gehen konnte, hatte ich noch zwei Briefe schreiben müssen. ❹ Herr Helm geht niemals ins Restaurant. Dabei hat er soviel Geld! ❺ Es bestand kein Grund plötzlich aufzustehen und zu gehen. Warum haben Sie das gemacht?

Übung 2 – Ergänzen Sie bitte

❶ Please fasten your seatbelt in my car.
... ., ... in meinem Wagen ....

❷ It is about your cat.
. . . . Ihre Katze.

❸ Normally he wasn't afraid of dogs.
. . . . hatte er .... Hunden.

❹ After having put the potatoes on the stove Mrs. Meier looked after the baby.
. . . . Frau Meier . . . . aufgesetzt hatte, ... das Baby.

❺ Before going home Mr. Meier quickly drank *(had drunk)* a schnaps.
. . . . . Herr Meier . . . . , ... er schnell noch . . . . getrunken.

Answers to exercise 1

❶ Why didn't you fasten your seatbelt? It is compulsory to fasten your seatbelt. ❷ When Mr and Mrs Meier [had] arrived at the hotel they immediately unpacked their suitcases. ❸ Before I could finally go home I had to write another two letters. ❹ Mr. Helm never goes to restaurants, yet he has got so much money! ❺ There was no reason to get up suddendly and leave. Why did you do that?

❻ He always makes such a long face. Yet he has every reason to be happy.

. . . . immer ein so langes . . . .
hat er allen . . . . . glücklich . . . .

Answers to exercise 2

❶ Ich bitte Sie – sich – anzuschnallen ❷ Es handelt sich um – ❸ Normalerweise – keine Angst vor – ❹ Nachdem – die Kartoffeln – kümmerte sie sich um – ❺ Bevor – nach Hause ging – hatte – einen Schnaps – ❻ Er macht – Gesicht – Dabei – Grund – zu sein

Second Wave: 24th Lesson

74 Vierundsiebzigste Lektion

Vater und Sohn

1 – **Pau**lchen, war**u**m hast du dir **au**sgerechnet d**ei**nen **ä**ltesten Pull**o**ver mit den L**ö**chern **a**ngezogen ①, um in den Zoo zu g**e**hen?
2 – D**a**rum ②!
3 – Hör mal! Sei nicht so frech! „D**a**rum" ist k**ei**ne **A**ntwort.
4 Geh dich schnell **u**mziehen ③, sonst n**e**hme ich dich nicht mit.
(Sp**ä**ter im Zoo)
5 – V**a**ti, war**u**m st**e**hen die L**ö**wen nicht auf?
6 – Weil sie m**ü**de sind, n**e**hme ich an.
7 – V**a**ti, woz**u** ④ h**a**ben die Eleph**a**nten **ei**ne so l**a**nge N**a**se?
8 – Zum F**u**ttersuchen. **Ü**brigens sagt man nicht „N**a**se" s**o**ndern „R**ü**ssel" bei **ei**nem Eleph**a**nten.
9 – V**a**ti, war**u**m darf ich die T**ie**re nicht f**ü**ttern?

Notes

① **sich anziehen**, *to dress*, **sich ausziehen**, *to undress*. The reflexive pronoun is in the accusative when there is no other direct object: **Ich ziehe mich an**, *I dress,* but it is in the dative when there is another direct object: **Ich ziehe mir den Pullover an**, *I put (me) my pullover on* (see lesson 77 paragraph 2).

② **Warum?** → **Darum**. **Weshalb?** → **Deshalb**. **Wozu?** → **Dazu**. These three pairs are more or less interchangeable. **Warum/weshalb/wozu lernen Sie Deutsch?**, *Why are you* ▸

Father and Son

1 – *(Little)* Paul, why exactly did you put on your oldest pullover with the holes in to go to the zoo *(m.)*?
2 – Because! *(For that)*
3 – Listen! Don't be so naughty! "Because" is no answer.
4 Go and change quickly, otherwise I won't take you with me.
(Later on at the zoo)
5 – Daddy, why don't the lions get up?
6 – Because they are tired I suppose.
7 – Daddy, why do the elephants have such long noses?
8 – To look for food. By the way, you don't say "nose" *(f.)* but "trunk" *(m.)* for an elephant.
9 – Daddy, why mustn't I feed the animals?

▸ *learning German?* – **Ich soll in Deutschland arbeiten, darum/deshalb/dazu brauche ich Deutsch**, – *I have to work in Germany; that's why I need German.*

③ **sich umziehen**, *to change*; but, **umziehen**, *to move.*

④ We use **wozu** when the answer is going to be introduced by **zum**: **Wozu nimmst du dieses Medikament?** – **Zum Schlafen**, *What do you take this medicine for? – In order to sleep.*

10 – Weil es verb**o**ten ist. Hör jetzt **e**ndlich auf mit d**ei**ner d**u**mmen Frager**ei**!
(Nach l**ä**ngerem Schw**ei**gen ⑤)

11 – V**a**ti, war**u**m bist du h**eu**te so schl**e**chter L**au**ne?

12 – D**a**rum!

13 – V**a**ti, du hast mir v**o**rhin ⑥ ges**a**gt, daß… □

Notes

⑤ **schweigen**, *to be silent*; **das Schweigen**, *the silence.*

⑥ **vorhin**, *a little while ago*; **später** or **nachher**, *later* ; **Hermann ist vorhin vorbeigekommen**. **Er wird später wiederkommen**, *Hermann dropped in a little while ago. He will come back later.*

***

Übung 1 – Übersetzen Sie bitte

❶ Sie hat sich ihr schönstes Kleid angezogen, um ins Theater zu gehen. ❷ Ich habe vorhin versucht, meinen Vater anzurufen, aber es hat sich niemand gemeldet. ❸ Ich werde es später nochmal versuchen. ❹ Ich bin heute erst um elf Uhr aufgestanden. ❺ Reden ist Silber*, Schweigen ist Gold. ❻ Wozu brauchen Sie denn so viele Zehn-Pfenning-Stücke? – Zum Telefonieren.

* **das Silber**, *silver.*

10 – Because it is forbidden. Do stop [asking] stupid questions [after all]! **74**
(After a while of silence *(a longer silence)*)
11 – Daddy, why are you in such a bad mood today?
12 – Because!
13 – Daddy, you have just told me that *(you told me a little while ago)*… □

***

Answers to exercise 1

❶ She put on her most beautiful dress to go to the theatre. ❷ I tried to phone my father just a little while ago but nobody answered. ❸ I will try again later. ❹ Today I only got up at eleven o'clock. ❺ Speech is silver* but silence is golden *(gold)*. ❻ Why do you need so many 10-pfennig coins? – To telephone.

74 Übung 2 – Ergänzen Sie bitte

❶ Did you hear the thunderstorm last night? – Yes, that's why I got up at two o'clock.
. . . . . Sie heute nacht das Gewitter . . . . . . ? – Ja, ... um zwei Uhr früh . . . .

❷ Put your coat on. It is cold outside.
. . . . deinen Mantel . . . .

❸ Yesterday he was in a bad mood all day long.
Er war gestern den ganzen Tag . . . .

❹ Do you also feed the birds in winter?
. . . . im Winter auch . . . . ?

⑤ Why don't you cross the street [when the lights are] red? – Because it is forbidden.

. . . . bei Rot über die Straße?
– . . . .

⑥ Excuse me for a moment please! I have to change.

. . . . bitte einen Augenblick. Ich muß . . . .

Answers to exercise 2

❶ Haben – gehört – deshalb bin ich – aufgestanden ❷ Zieh dir – an – Es ist kalt draußen ❸ – schlechter Laune ❹ Füttern Sie – die Vögel ❺ Warum gehen Sie nicht – Weil es verboten ist ❻ Entschuldigen Sie mich – mich umziehen

Second Wave: 25th Lesson

75 Fünfundsiebzigste Lektion

Die Rückkehr

1 – Verzeihung! Kommen Sie aus diesem Haus? – Ja.
2 – Wohnen Sie dort? – Ja.
3 – Liegt auf der Treppe ein dicker, roter Teppich und hängt im Treppenhaus ein Gemälde von Caspar David Friedrich? – Ja, so ist es.
4 – Und steht hinter dem Haus ein alter Nußbaum? – Ja, der steht dort.
5 – Und wenn ① man im Herbst auf der Terrasse sitzt, muß man vorsichtig sein, weil die Nüsse runterfallen ②? – Ja, das ist wahr.
6 – Und die Gartentür läßt sich nur öffnen, indem ① man sie gleichzeitig etwas anhebt? – Ja, auch das ist richtig.
7 – Ja, das war schwierig für ein Kind; ich erinnere mich gut daran.
8 Es ist unglaublich! Fast nichts hat sich verändert, seitdem ③ ich mit meinen Eltern vor gut dreißig Jahren dieses Haus verlassen habe.

Notes

① In German, present participles are often translated by subordinate clauses introduced by **wenn**, **als**, *when*; **während**/**indem**, *while*, or **indem**, indicating the way in which something is done: **Er ging schnell die Treppe hinauf, indem er** ▸

The Return *(f.)*

1 – Excuse me! Have you just left this house? – Yes.
2 – Do you live there? – Yes.
3 – Is there a thick red carpet *(m.)* lying on the stairs *(n.)*, and is there a painting *(n.)* by Caspar David Friedrich hanging on the staircase? – Yes, that's right.
4 – And is there an old nut-tree *(m.)* standing behind the house? – Yes, there is one standing there.
5 – And when you sit on the terrace in autumn you have to be careful, because the nuts fall down. – Yes, that is true.
6 – And the garden door can only be opened by lifting it a little bit at the same time? – Yes, that is right, too.
7 – Yes, that was difficult for a child; I remember that well.
8 It is incredible! Nearly nothing has changed since I left this house with my parents some 30 years ago.

▸ **zwei Stufen auf einmal nahm**, *He quickly went up the steps taking two steps at a time.* You'll find other examples in the following lessons.

② **hinauf** or **herauf** is reduced to **rauf** in spoken language. **Hinaus** and **heraus** to **raus**; **hinunter** or **herunter** to **runter**, **herein to rein...**

③ **seit** (+ dat.), *since, for.* **Seit einer Woche**, *for a week*; **seitdem**, **seit**, *since*, **Sie haben sich sehr verändert, seitdem (seit) ich Sie gesehen habe**, *You have changed a lot since I [last] saw you.*

9 Ich h**a**be mir oft v**o**rgestellt ④, **ei**nes T**a**ges zur**ü**ckzukommen.

10 – **A**ber ich b**i**tte Sie, k**o**mmen Sie doch rein ② und s**e**hen Sie sich **a**lles an!

11 – Oh, nein d**a**nke! Das ist sehr fr**eu**ndlich von **I**hnen, **a**ber ich muß w**ei**ter ⑤.

12 Ich w**o**hne nicht sehr weit entf**e**rnt ⑥ von hier. Ich k**o**mme ein **a**nderes Mal wieder. Auf W**ie**dersehen! □

Notes

④ **sich vorstellen**, *to imagine; to introduce oneself.* The reflexive pronoun is in the dative when there is a direct object. **Ich stelle mir ein Haus vor, in dem ich glücklich sein werde**, *I imagine a house where I will be happy (in which I will be...)*. **Ich habe mich bei meinem neuen Chef vorgestellt**, *I introduced myself to my new boss.*

⑤ **Ich muß weiter** = **ich muß weitergehen**, *I have to go on* (see lesson 54, note 7).

⑥ **entfernt sein**, *to be... from; far away.* **Berlin ist von Hannover circa 300 km entfernt**, *Berlin is about 300km from Hannover.* **Ist das weit entfernt?**, *Is that far away?*

***

Übung 1 – Übersetzen Sie bitte

❶ Seitdem wir uns gesehen haben, ist viel passiert. ❷ Er hat sich oft vorgestellt, ein kleines Haus mit Garten zu haben. ❸ Die Katze ist auf den Nußbaum geklettert und kann nicht mehr runter. ❹ Die Post ist nicht weit entfernt von hier. ❺ Wenn er ißt, kann er nicht singen. ❻ Mein Vater und mein Bruder waschen das Geschirr ab, indem sie es in die Badewanne stellen und das Wasser laufen lassen!

9 I often imagined coming back one day…
10 – But do come in please and have a look at everything!
11 – Oh, no thank you! That is very kind of you, but I have to go on.
12 I don't live very far away from here. I will come back another time. Goodbye! □

DIE KATZE IST AUF DEN NUßBAUM GEKLETTERT
UND KANN NICHT MEHR RUNTER

***

Answers to exercise 1

❶ Since we last met *(saw)* a lot has happened. ❷ He often imagined having a little house with a garden. ❸ The cat has climbed the nut tree and cannot get down any more. ❹ The post-office is not far from here. ❺ He cannot sing while he is eating. ❻ My father and my brother do the dishes by putting them into the bath-tub and letting the water run!

Übung 2 – Ergänzen Sie bitte

❶ Since you have been here I [feel] am better.
. . . . hier . . . ., ... es mir . . . .

❷ For ten years nothing has changed.
. . . . zehn Jahren . . . . nichts . . . .

❸ Can you imagine being rich one day?
Können Sie . . . ., eines Tages
. . . .

❹ When he is back he will buy the red carpet.
Wenn . . . . wird er . . . .
. . . . kaufen.

76 Sechsundsiebzigste Lektion

„Onkel" Christoph

1 – War**u**m sitzt du denn da so tr**au**rig und all**ei**n?
2 – Ich bin nicht tr**au**rig. Ich d**e**nke nach ①!
3 – Wor**ü**ber ① denkst du denn nach?
4 – Ich möchte so gern r**ü**ber ②, auf die **a**ndere **S**eite!

Pronunciation Key
*ong'kel … **1** … trowrich … **4** … zi-te*

Notes

① **nachdenken**, *to think*, is followed by the preposition **über** (+ acc.), the question *what about?* is translated by **worüber?** ▸

⑤ Frankfurt is not far from Mainz.
Frankfurt . . . nicht . . . . von Mainz . . . .

⑥ He opened the door by lifting it.
Er . . . . . . die Tür, ... er sie . . . .

Answers to exercise 2
❶ Seitdem du – bist – geht besser ❷ Seit – hat sich – verändert ❸ – sich vorstellen – reich zu sein ❹ – er zurückkommt – den roten Teppich – ❺ – ist – weit – entfernt ❻ – öffnet – indem – anhebt

Second Wave: 26th Lesson

76th Lesson 76

"Uncle" Christopher

1 – Why are you sitting here so sad and lonely?
2 – I am not sad. I am thinking.
3 – What are you thinking about?
4 – I would so much like to go over there to the other side!

② It is not necessary to add a verb of movement to an adverb which denotes a movement or a change in position: **Ich will hinüber (rüber)**, *I want [to go] on the other side.*

5 – Wenn du nach dr**ü**ben willst, mußt du **ei**nen Übergang ③ s**u**chen.

6 – Es gibt k**ei**nen. Ich h**a**be schon **ü**berall ges**u**cht!

7 – Dann mußt du **e**ntweder r**ü**berspringen **o**der d**u**rchwaten.

8 – Hin**ü**berspringen? Das sch**a**ffe ④ ich n**ie**mals! M**ei**ne B**ei**ne sind viel zu kurz.

9 Und d**u**rchwaten kann ⑤ ich nicht, weil ich m**ei**ne H**o**se nicht n**a**ßmachen darf ⑤. Das sieht mein V**a**ter nicht gern.

10 – Ah**a**, ich gl**au**be, ich verst**e**he. Du meinst, ich soll dich hin**ü**bertragen?

11 – Oh, w**ü**rden ⑥ Sie das w**i**rklich m**a**chen? Das w**ä**re aber nett von **I**hnen!

12 – Na, dann komm schnell! Setz dich auf m**ei**ne Sch**u**lter und h**a**lte ⑦ dich gut fest ⑦.

13 – W**a**rten Sie! Meine Kamer**a**den sind auch da!… Kommt schnell! Er trägt uns!

14 – Du kl**ei**ner Schl**au**meier ⑧! **Ei**gentlich h**a**tte ich h**eu**te n**a**chmittag **e**twas **a**nderes vor…

15 Na ja, wenn schon! Dann stellt euch mal **o**rdentlich in 'ne Schl**a**nge ⑨ und nennt mich **ei**nfach „**O**nkel Chr**i**stoph"! □

Notes

③ We say **Übergang** when you take a passage which is for example across a river… and we say **Durchgang** for a passage through or under…: **Ich gehe durch diesen kleinen Garten**, *I go through this little garden*. A notice forbidding passage would read **Durchgang verboten.**

④ **etwas schaffen** (fam.), *to manage*, *to make*… Otherwise **schaffen** means *to produce*, *to create* and (fam.), *to work*. ▸

5 – If you want to go to the other side you have to look for a crossing *(m.)*.
6 – There is none. I have already looked everywhere!
7 – Then you either have to jump over or wade through.
8 – Jump over? I'll never make it! My legs are much too short.
9 And I can't wade through because I mustn't get my trousers *(f.)* wet. My father doesn't like *(to see)* that.
10 – Oh, I think I understand. You mean you want me to carry you across?
11 – Oh, would you really do that? That would be nice of you!
12 – So, come on quickly! Sit down on my shoulders and hold tight.
13 – Wait! My friends are there too!… Come on quickly! He'll carry us!
14 – You are a bright one! Actually I had planned something else for this afternoon…
15 Well, yes after all! So, queue up properly and simply call me "Uncle Christopher"! □

⑤ Did you notice that all the auxiliary verbs are present in this lesson? Have a look at lesson 21, paragraph 2.

⑥ **würden** is the form of the **Konjunktiv II** of **werden** and, followed by the infinitive, it expresses the conditional: **Ich würde sagen**, *I would say...* that we'll talk about it later.

⑦ **sich festhalten**, *to hold tight.*

⑧ **der Schlaumeier** is the name for someone who is smart or bright. **Meier** is a very familiar name in Germany and **schlau** means *clever*, *smart*, a little like the English expression "a clever Dick".

⑨ **Schlange stehen**, *to queue up* (**die Schlange**, *the snake*); **sich in eine Schlange stellen**, *to join the queue.*

76

Übung 1 – Übersetzen Sie bitte

❶ Wenn Sie über die Straße gehen wollen, müssen Sie warten bis es grün ist. ❷ Er hat lange über dieses Problem nachgedacht. ❸ Ich hatte eigentlich vor, heute abend ins Kino zu gehen. ❹ Aber jetzt muß ich zu Hause bleiben, weil mein Cousin zu Besuch kommt. ❺ Stellen Sie sich bitte in die Schlange und warten Sie wie die anderen! ❻ Die Prüfung war zu schwierig. Ich habe sie nicht geschafft.

Übung 2 – Ergänzen Sie bitte

❶ You do not want to get your feet wet? Well, I will carry you across.

Du . . . . . . deine Füße nicht . . . . ? Gut, ich . . . . . dich . . . .

❷ Do you see the chapel over there on the mountain? I would so much like [to go] up there.

. . . . die Kapelle dort oben . . . dem Berg? Ich . . . . dort hinauf.

❸ We either have to queue up or come back tomorrow.

Wir müssen . . . . Schlange . . . . . . oder morgen . . . .

❹ He is not able *(does not manage)* to jump over. His legs are too short.

. . . . es nicht hinüberzuspringen. . . . . sind . . kurz.

❺ Will you come to the cinema with [me]? Or have you already planned something else?

. . . . mit ins Kino? Oder . . . . schon etwas vor?

Answers to exercise 1

❶ When you want to cross the street you have to wait until the lights are green. ❷ He has been thinking about this problem a long time. ❸ Actually I had planned to go to the cinema tonight. ❹ But now I have to stay at home because my cousin is coming to see us. ❺ Join the queue please and wait like everybody else *(the others)*! ❻ The exam was too difficult. I didn't manage it.

❻ What have you been thinking about for such a long time? – About life!

.... haben Sie so lange ....?
– .... Leben!

Answers to exercise 2

❶ – willst – naßmachen – trage – hinüber ❷ Sehen Sie – auf – möchte so gern – ❸ – entweder – stehen – wiederkommen ❹ Er schafft – Seine Beine – zu – ❺ Kommen Sie – haben Sie – ❻ Worüber – nachgedacht – Über das –

WENN SIE ÜBER DIE STRAßE GEHEN WOLLEN, MÜSSEN SIE WARTEN BIS ES GRÜN IST

Second Wave: 27th Lesson

77 Siebenundsiebzigste Lektion

Wiederholung und Erklärungen

1 The Pluperfect

The *pluperfect*, **Plusquamperfekt**, is generally used when one action or fact precedes another action/fact in the past:

Weil er den Bus verpaßt hatte, nahm er ein Taxi, *Because he had missed the bus he took a taxi.*

The pluperfect is formed with the **Imperfekt** of **haben** or **sein** + the past participle. (See lesson 42, paragraph 1 for the usage of **haben** and **sein**).

Sie war nach Hause gegangen, *She had gone home.*
Er hatte gearbeitet, *He had worked.*

The past perfect is used for an action which precedes another action in the past:

Wir hatten schon zwei Stunden gewartet, als das Schiff endlich kam, *We had been waiting for two hours when the boat came at last.*
Nachdem er seine Arbeit beendet hatte, ging er ins Kino, *After having finished his work he went to the cinema.*

Notice that you have to make a subordinate clause introduced by **nachdem** or **bevor**, and that the conjugated verb is placed at the end of the sentence.

Sicher! Nachdem wir so oft darüber gesprochen hatten, konnten Sie das nicht vergessen! *Of course! After having talked about it so many times you could not forget it!*

2 Reflexive Pronouns

With some reflexive verbs the reflexive pronoun may be in the accusative or in the dative; the dative is used when there already is a direct object:

Ich wasche mich, *I wash.* But,
Ich wasche mir die Hände, *I wash my hands* (lit. "I wash myself the hands").
Du siehst dich an, *You look at yourself.* But,
Du siehst dir einen Film an, *You watch a film.*

For the other pronouns (**er, sie, wir...**) there is no difference between the forms of the dative and the accusative:

Er stellt sich vor, *He introduces himself.* But,
Er stellt sich ein Land vor, wo..., *He imagines a country where...*
Wir waschen uns, *We wash.* But,
Wir waschen uns die Füße, *We wash our feet* (lit. "we wash ourselves the feet").

3 The Meaning of *handeln*

Es handelt sich hier um das Verb handeln.
A brief word about the verb **handeln** which has several meanings:
– *to act, to bargain* or (reflexive):
– **sich handeln um**, *to be a question* or *matter of;*
Meine Frau handelt immer unüberlegt, wenn sie handelt, *My wife always acts in a thoughtless way when she is bargaining.*

– **Der Handel**, *the trade, the business*; **verhandeln**, *to negotiate*; **die Verhandlung**, *the negotiation.*
Dieser Paragraph handelte von dem Verb handeln. *This paragraph was about the verb* **handeln.**

4 Relative Pronouns

Below we give you the relative pronoun in the four cases (the genitive is the only one we have not seen up to now):

77

	masculine	feminine	neuter	plural
Nom.:	**der**	**die**	**das**	**das**
Acc.:	**den**	**die**	**das**	**die**
Dat.:	**dem**	**der**	**dem**	**denen**
Gen.:	**dessen**	**deren**	**dessen**	**deren**

As you see with the exception of the genitive and the dative plural the forms are identical with those of the definite article:

Der Junge, dessen Mutter einen Bonbonladen hat, hat es gut, *The boy whose mother has a candy shop is lucky.*
Die Mutter, deren Junge viele Bonbons ißt, ist die Freundin des Zahnarztes, *The mother whose boy [son] eats a lot of candies is the girlfriend of the dentist.*

Welcher/welche/welches can also be used as a relative pronoun, but it is rarely used in spoken language:
Der Man, welchen (den) sie heiraten würde, ist noch nicht geboren, *The man (whom) she would marry has not been born yet.*

Eine kleine Übung! Ergänzen Sie bitte die Relativpronomen:

Der Zug, . . . ich nehmen wollte, ist schon weg. Der Freund, mit . . . ich in Ferien fahren wollte, sitzt in dem Zug. Meine Koffer, . . . ich meinem Freund gegeben habe, sind auch in dem Zug, und ich habe nicht die Adresse der Leute, bei . . . . . wir übernachten sollten.
The train which I wanted to take has already left. The friend with whom I wanted to go on holiday is (sits) in this train. My suitcases which I gave to my friend are also in the train and I don't have the address of the people (with whom) we were to spend the night with.
(Solution at the end of the lesson).

5 Coordinating Conjunctions

Do you remember the coordinating conjunctions?
sowohl ... als auch, *as well... as*; *both... and*;
weder... noch, *neither... nor*; **entweder... oder**, *either... or.*

Check your knowledge with the following text:

Die Tante fragt Klein-Fritzchen, nachdem er den ganzen Geburtstagskuchen allein gegessen hat, Fritzchen, bist du auch wirklich satt?* Worauf Fritzchen antwortet, Satt kenne ich nicht. Entweder habe ich Hunger oder mir ist schlecht.
* *satisfied* (not to be hungry any more).

6 Answer Key

Solution to paragraph 4: – **den** – **dem** – **die** – **denen** –

78 Achtundsiebzigste Lektion

Wußten Sie schon...

1 – daß die **Bu**ndesrepublik **De**utschland ein **Bu**ndesstaat ① ist, der aus sechzehn **Lä**ndern best**e**ht,
2 – daß die **Bu**ndesrepublik und die **De**utsche Demokr**a**tische Republ**i**k mehr als v**i**erzig J**a**hre nebeneinander ② exist**ie**rten,
3 – daß eine Mauer die b**ei**den d**eu**tschen St**aa**ten und Berlin **a**chtundzwanzig **Jah**re **tei**lte,
4 – daß sie fast so lang h**ie**lt wie der dr**ei**ßigjährige Krieg und d**o**ppelt so lang wie ③ die W**ei**marer Republ**i**k (1919-1933),
5 – daß B**o**nn w**äh**rend d**ie**ser Zeit die H**au**ptstadt der B**u**ndesrepublik war und nicht Berl**i**n,
6 – daß man Fr**a**nkfurt die H**au**ptstadt des G**e**ldes nennt, weil es über die meisten Bür**o**hochhäuser verf**ü**gt ④, und weil dort die w**i**chtigste europ**ä**ische B**ö**rse ihren Sitz hat,

Pronunciation Key
1 ... boondes'shtaat ... 2... neben'yne'annder ...
4...drysich'yairige...6...büroh'hocH'hoyzer...oyropai'ishe...

Notes

① **der Staat**, *the nation*, but **die Stadt**, *the town*. The **aa** of **Staat** is long.

Did You Know *(already)*...

1 – that the Federal Republic of Germany is a federal system *(m.) (state)* which is composed of 16 Länder *(Federal States)*,
2 – that the Federal Republic of Germany and the Democratic Republic of Germany [had] co-existed *(existed side by side)* for more than 40 years,
3 – that a wall *(f.)* separated the two German states and Berlin for 28 years,
4 – that it endured for almost as long as the Thirty Year's War *(m.)*, and twice as long as the Republic of Weimar (1919-1933)?
5 – that Bonn was the capital of the Federal Republic of Germany during that period, and not Berlin,
6 – that Frankfurt is called "the money capital" *(capital of the money)* because it contains the greatest number of corporate skyscrapers and because it's the seat *(m.)* of the most important European stock exchange *(f.)*,

② **nebeneinander**, *side by side*; **miteinander**, *with each other, together*; **hintereinander**, *one behind the other*, etc.

③ **doppelt so lang wie**, *twice as long as*, **dreimal so groß wie**, *three times as big as...* or: **halb so groß wie**, *half as big as*; but, **mehr als**, *more than*; **größer als**, *bigger than* (see lesson 35, paragraph 2).

④ **verfügen über** + acc., *to dispose of, to have*, **die Verfügung**, *the disposal, the disposition*. **Ich stehe zu Ihrer Verfügung**, *I'm at your disposal*. **Ich verfüge über 2.000 Euro pro Monat**, *I have 2,000 euros a month*.

78 **7** – daß in M**ü**nchen beim Okt**o**berfest, das **u**ngefähr zwei W**o**chen dauert, rund ⑤ 4 Milli**o**nen L**i**ter Bier getr**u**nken werden ⑥,
8 – und daß z**ah**lreiche Tour**i**sten aus aller Welt nach M**ü**nchen kommen ⑦, um die D**eu**tschen bei diesem Unterf**a**ngen zu unterst**ü**tzen? □

*8 … tsa**h**l'ry'che' … oontershtü**tz**en*

Notes

⑤ **rund**, *round* – **der Ball ist rund**, *the ball is round*. As an adverb, **rund** means *about* – **Rund 4.000 Leute**, *about 4,000 people*.

⑥ Notice that Germans say **getrunken werden** and not **getrunken sind** (*are drunk*, as we would say in English). We will explain this later.

⑦ You probably noticed that in each of these sentences the verb is placed at the end because they are all introduced by **daß**.

***

Übung 1 – Übersetzen Sie bitte

❶ Wußtest du schon, daß es mehr als 40 Jahre zwei deutsche Staaten gab? ❷ Die Bundesrepublik ist ein Bundesstaat, der aus sechzehn Bundesländern besteht. ❸ Wissen Sie, wie lange der dreißigjährige Krieg dauerte? ❹ Bayern ist doppelt so groß wie Nordrhein-Westfalen, aber Nordrhein-Westfalen hat die meisten Einwohner. ❺ In China leben rund fünfzehnmal soviel Menschen wie in der Bundesrepublik.

7 – that about four million litres of beer are drunk at the Oktoberfest in Munich which lasts for about two weeks, **78**

8 – and that many *(numerous)* tourists from all over the world come to Munich to assist the Germans in this venture? □

DIE KNEIPEN UND GASTSTÄTTEN SIND IN BERLIN LÄNGER GEÖFFNET ALS ANDERSWO

***

Answers to exercise 1

❶ Did you *(already)* know that there had been *(were)* two German nations for more than 40 years? ❷ The Federal Republic of Germany is a federal system which is composed of 16 states. ❸ Do you know how long the Thirty Year's War lasted? ❹ Bavaria is twice as big as North Rhine Westfalia, but North Rhine Westfalia has *(the most)* inhabitants. ❺ In China, there are *(live)* about fifteen times as many people as in the Federal Republic of Germany.

Übung 2 – Ergänzen Sie bitte

❶ My father is twice as heavy as I [am].
Mein vater ist in . . . . schwer . . . .

❷ My little sister is only half as heavy as you.
Meine kleine Schwester ist aber nur . . . .
. . . .

❸ Hamburg is also called the "Gateway to the World".
. . . . Hamburg auch „das Tor zur . . . . ".

❹ What can I do for you? I am at your disposal.
. . . . ich für Sie tun? . . . . zu
Ihrer . . . . !

79 Neunundsiebzigste Lektion

Ein Volk, aber viele Mund- ① und Eigenarten

1 Obw**o**hl es nur **ei**ne geschr**ie**bene d**eu**tsche Spr**a**che gibt,
2 gibt es v**ie**le verschi**e**dene ② Dial**e**kte, die mehr **o**der w**e**niger von dem geschr**ie**benen Deutsch **a**bweichen.
3 Verzw**ei**feln Sie nicht gleich, wenn Sie jemanden nicht verst**e**hen;

Notes

① **die Mundart** or **der Dialekt** is the spoken language of a region. When several compound nouns end with the same root-word you can avoid repetition in the following way: **die Damen- und Herrenkonfektion**, *ladies' and men's ready-to-wear*; **Sonn-und Feiertage**, *Sundays and public holidays.* ▸

❺ They had been speaking for more than three hours with each other.
Sie hatten . . . . drei Stunden
. . . . gesprochen.

❻ Have you already been to the Oktoberfest in Munich?
. . . . . Sie schon . . . . Oktoberfest in München?

Answers to exercise 2
❶ – doppelt so – wie ich ❷ – halb so schwer wie du ❸ Man nennt – Welt – ❹ Was kann – Ich stehe – Verfügung ❺ – länger als – miteinander – ❻ Waren – beim –

Second Wave: 29th Lesson

79th Lesson 79

One People *(n.)* but a Lot of Dialects and Peculiarities

1 Although there is only one written German language *(f.)*,
2 there are a lot of different dialects which differ to varying degrees from written German.
3 Don't despair immediately if you don't understand someone;

▸ ② **verschieden** or **anders**, *different*; **er trägt heute zwei verschiedene Schuhe**, *Today he is wearing two different shoes.* But: **Das ist etwas anderes**, *That is something different.*

79 **4** auch ein Deutscher versteht nicht immer einen Deutschen.

5 (Ganz zu schweigen von den Österreichern oder Schweizern!) ③

6 Das liegt jedoch manchmal nicht nur am Dialekt, sondern auch an den verschiedenen Temperamenten. (N.4)

7 Die Bayern ④ sind zum Beispiel nicht nur für ihre kurzen Lederhosen und ihre Weißwürste ⑤ bekannt, sondern auch für ihr schnell aufbrausendes Temperament,

8 die Schwaben ④ für ihre sprichwörtliche Sparsamkeit ⑥,

9 und die Westfalen für ihren Dickschädel ⑦, über den man sich einerseits lustig macht, ihn aber andrerseits fürchtet.

10 Am schlechtesten kommen jedoch bei diesen Klischees die Ostfriesen weg ⑧, die ganz oben an der Nordseeküste wohnen.

11 Es gibt unzählige Witze über ihre sogenannte Schwerfälligkeit,

12 aber wir können sie Ihnen heute leider nicht erzählen. □

5 … *erster'ri-ghern* … *shvi-tsern* **9** … *dikkshaidel* … **10** … *klichayss* …

Notes

③ The dialect spoken in Austria is similar to Bavarian; the **Schweizerdeutsch**, *Swiss-German*, however, is closer to the dialect spoken in **Baden-Württemberg**. Anyway, don't worry, everybody can speak **Hochdeutsch**, *Standard German* too. ▶

4 even a German does not always understand a German.
5 (To say nothing of the Austrian and the Swiss!)
6 This, however, is not only due to the dialect *(m.)* but also to the different characters.
7 The Bavarians, for example, are not only known for their leather shorts and their white sausages but also for their hot-headed character *(n.)*;
8 the Swabians for their proverbial thriftiness *(f.)*;
9 and the Westphalians for their pig-headedness *(m.)*, of which people make fun on the one hand but fear on the other.
10 Those who come off worst in these cliches are the East Frisians, who live high up on the coast of the North Sea.
11 There are innumerable jokes about their so-called clumsiness *(f.)*,
12 but unfortunately we cannot tell them to you today. □

④ **Die Bayern leben in Bayern** (*Bavaria*), **die Schwaben in Baden-Württemberg, und die Westfalen in Nordrhein-Westfalen.**

⑤ **die Weißwurst** is a sausage made of pork and as its name indicates, it is white.

⑥ **die Sparsamkeit**, *the thriftiness, economy*; **sparsam**, *economical*; **sparen**, *to economize; to save* and **die Sparkasse**, *the saving bank.*

⑦ **der Dickkopf** (or even stronger **der Dickschädel**) is a *pig-headed person (***dickköpfig**) person. **Der Schädel**, *the skull.*

⑧ **gut oder schlecht wegkommen**, *to come off well or badly.*

79 **Übung 1 – Übersetzen Sie bitte**

❶ Man spricht in Deutschland viele verschiedene Mundarten. ❷ Ein Hamburger versteht nicht immer einen Bayern, und ein Bayer versteht nicht immer einen Berliner, und ein Berliner... ❸ Die Sparsamkeit der Schwaben ist sprichwörtlich. ❹ Einerseits ist er ein Dickschädel, aber andrerseits macht er immer, was seine Frau will. ❺ Heute bekommst du ein besonders großes Stück Fleisch. Du bist das letzte Mal am schlechtesten weggekommen.

Übung 2 – Ergänzen Sie bitte

❶ Although he is German he does not always understand the people of the village.
. . . . . . er Deutscher ist, ... er die Leute aus dem Dorf . . . .

❷ They are known for their hospitality.
. . . . für ihre Gastfreundschaft.

❸ The youngest is always the hardest done by.
. . . . kommt immer . . . . weg.

❹ On the one hand I am afraid of these people and on the other [hand] I find them very nice.
. . . . fürchte ich mich vor diesen Leuten, ... finde ich sie sehr nett.

❺ Have you already worn leather shorts?
Haben Sie schon einmal kurze . . . . getragen?

Answers to exercise 1

❶ In Germany we speak a lot of different dialects. ❷ A Hamburger does not always understand a Bavarian, and a Bavarian does not always understand a Berliner, and a Berliner... ❸ The thriftiness of the Swabians is proverbial. ❹ On the one hand he is pig-headed, but on the other hand he does what his wife wants [him to do]. ❺ Today you will get a particulary big piece of meat. You came off worst last time.

❻ He is at his wits' end *(completely desperate)* because he doesn't understand anything.
Er ist ganz ...., weil er ....

Answers to exercise 2

❶ Obwohl – versteht – nicht immer ❷ Sie sind bekannt – ❸ Am schlechtesten – der Jüngste – ❹ Einerseits – andrerseits – ❺ – Lederhosen – ❻ – verzweifelt – nichts versteht

EIN HAMBURGER VERSTEHT NICHT IMMER EINEN BAYERN

Second Wave: 30th Lesson

80 Achtzigste Lektion

Der Aberglaube ①

1 – Kommen Sie! Nehmen Sie es nicht so tragisch!
2 – Sie haben gut reden! Sie haben nichts verloren ②!
3 – Na ja ③, Sie hatten eben Pech ④. Das kann jedem mal passieren.
4 – Pech, sagen Sie? Nein, wegen heute morgen hätte ⑤ ich es wissen müssen; es ist meine Schuld.
5 – Seien Sie doch nicht so hart zu sich selbst!…
6 – Trinken Sie noch einen kleinen?
7 – Ja, bitte!… Wissen Sie, als ich heute morgen die Augen aufschlug ⑥, sah ich über mir eine fette, schwarze Spinne.
8 – Na, nun machen Sie aber mal einen Punkt! Sie sind doch nicht etwa ⑦ abergläubisch?
9 – Ich? Abergläubisch? Nein, das wäre ⑧ ja noch schöner!
10 – Na, sehen Sie! Also: Prost und auf bessere Tage!

Pronunciation Key
7 … shpinne 8 … abergloybish

Notes

① **der Glaube**, *the belief*; **glauben**, *to believe*; **gläubig**, *believing*.

② **verlieren**, *to lose*.

Superstition *(m.)*

1 – Come on! Don't take it so tragically!
2 – It's easy for you to talk! You didn't lose anything!
3 – Oh, never mind, you were unlucky. That can happen to anybody.
4 – Bad luck *(n.)* you say? No, because of this morning I should have known [it]; it's my fault.
5 – Don't be so hard on yourself!…
6 – Will you have another small [drink]?
7 – Yes, please!… You know, when I opened my eyes this morning I saw a fat black spider *(f.)* [hanging] above me.
8 – Well? that's enough! Are you possibly superstitious?
9 – Me? Superstitious? No, that'd take the cake!
10 – Well, you see! So: cheers and [let's drink] to better days!

③ **na ja + eben** are translated by *never mind*. **Er ist noch nicht da**, *He hasn't arrived yet (he is not here yet)*. **Na ja, dann warte ich eben**, *Never mind, I'll wait.*

④ **das Pech**, *bad luck*. **Pech** is the opposite of **Glück**.

⑤ **hätte** is a form of the **Konjunktiv II**. The **Konjunktiv** is used in conditional clauses (see lesson 84, paragraph 1).

⑥ **aufschlagen**, *to open* (eyes, books…).

⑦ **etwa** expresses astonishment; in negative sentences it is translated by *surely* and in positive sentences by *possibly*: **Du willst doch nicht etwa schon gehen?**, *You surely don't want to go already?*

⑧ **wäre**, *would be*, is the **Konjunktiv II** form of **sein**, *to be* (see note 5 and lesson 84, paragraph 1).

11 – Prost!… Das tut gut!

12 Trotzdem… ich bin sicher, daß alles gut gegangen wäre, wenn nicht diese verfluchte schwarze Katze gerade vor mir die Straße überquert hätte,

13 und wenn heute nicht Freitag, der dreizehnte wäre ⑨. □

***12** … überkvert …*

Notes

⑨ Notice that, in conditional clauses, the verb of the main clause and that of the subordinate clause introduced by **wenn** are in the **Konjunktiv : Wenn ich Geld hätte**, **wäre ich glücklich**, *If I had money I would be happy.*

***

Übung 1 – Übersetzen Sie bitte

❶ Er hätte es wissen müssen; es ist seine eigene Schuld. ❷ Ich habe gestern beim Kartenspielen kein Glück gehabt. ❸ Hast du etwa mehr als fünfzig Mark verloren? ❹ Ja, leider! Aber wenn nicht Freitag, der dreizehnte wäre, wäre das nicht passiert. ❺ Er ist sehr abergläubisch und sammelt Glückskäfer. ❻ Als ich heute morgen die Augen aufschlug, sah die Welt ganz anders aus.

11 – Cheers! That does [one] good!
12 Nevertheless… I am sure that everything would have turned out well if this damned black cat had not crossed the street in front of me
13 and if it wasn't Friday13th today. □

HAST DU ETWA MEHR ALS FÜNFZIG MARK VERLOREN?

***

Answers to exercise 1

❶ He should have known [it]; it is his own fault. ❷ I had no luck at [playing] cards yesterday. ❸ Did you possibly lose more than 50 Marks? ❹ Yes, unfortunately! But if it wasn't Friday 13th it would not have happened. ❺ He is very superstitious and collects ladybirds. ❻ When I opened my eyes this morning the world looked completely different.

Übung 2 – Ergänzen Sie bitte

❶ Stop! You just crossed the street when the lights were red!
Halt! . . . . gerade bei Rot die Straße . . . . !

❷ Oh, don't be so hard; that can happen to anybody.
Ach . . . . . Sie doch nicht so . . . .; das kann . . . .

❸ It wouldn't be as bad as that *(half as bad)* if he hadn't lost everything.
Es . . . . ja auch nur halb so schlimm, ... er nicht alles . . . . hätte.

❹ Cheers, and don't take it so tragically!
. . . . . und nehmen Sie's nicht so . . . . !

81 Einundachtzigste Lektion

Die Lorelei und ihre Nachkommen

1 – Hör 'mal, was hier steht ①: „K**u**rzurlaub auf dem Rhein mit **a**llem Komf**o**rt…
2 Die Deutsche B**u**ndesbahn und die Köln-D**ü**sseldorfer – das ist wohl so 'ne ② Sch**i**ffahrtsges**e**llschaft – m**a**chen es m**ö**glich:

Pronunciation Key
***1** … kommf**o**r **2** … sh**i**ffahrtss-ges**e**llshaft …*

❺ She is afraid of fat black spiders.
Sie fürchtet sich ... ., ...
....

❻ That couldn't work *(go well)*; I should have known it.
Das konnte nicht gutgehen; ... .
....

Answers to exercise 2
❶ – Sie haben – überquert ❷ – scicn – hart – jedem passieren ❸ – wäre – wenn – verloren – ❹ Prost – tragisch ❺ – vor fetten – schwarzen Spinnen ❻ – ich hätte es wissen müssen

Second Wave: 31st Lesson

81st Lesson 81

The "Lorelei" and her Descendants

1 – Listen to what is written there: "Short holiday on the Rhine with all conveniences.
2 The "Deutsche Bundesbahn" and the "Köln-Düsseldorfer" – that must be one of these shipping companies – make it possible.

Notes

① We say: **Ein Artikel steht in der Zeitung**, *There is an article in the newspaper.* – **Was steht dort?**, – *What does it say/what is written there?*

② Do you remember that we sometimes leave out the **ei** of the indefinite article in spoken language?: **so 'ne Art Fisch**, *some kind of fish.*

3 Mod**e**rne Z**ü**ge der B**u**ndesbahn br**i**ngen Sie dir**e**kt zum Rhein ③, nach B**a**sel oder D**ü**sseldorf.

4 Dort st**ei**gen Sie um auf **ei**nes der „schw**i**mmenden F**e**rienhotels“

5 mit komfort**a**blen **Au**ßenkabinen, **ei**nem beh**ei**zten ④ Schw**i**mmbad und **ei**ner r**ei**chhaltigen Sp**ei**sekarte…“

6 Klingt echt gut, nicht? Was hältst du dav**o**n?

7 – Oh ja, das w**ä**re toll! Ich k**ö**nnte ⑤ **e**ndlich den F**e**lsen s**e**hen, auf dem die Lorel**ei** ihr l**a**nges, g**o**ldenes Haar gek**ä**mmt hat, ⑥

8 und **a**lle Sch**i**ffer, die vorb**ei**kamen, h**a**ben nur sie **a**ngesehen

9 und sind d**e**shalb g**e**gen den F**e**lsen gef**a**hren und **u**ntergegangen ⑦.

Notes

③ **Ich gehe zum Rhein** or **an den Rhein**, *I go to the Rhine*. **Die Bundesbahn**, *Federal Railways* (**die Bahn**, **der Zug**, *the train*).

④ **heizen**, *to heat*; **geheizt** or **beheizt**, *heated*; **die Heizung**, *the heating*.

⑤ **könnte**, *could*, is the **Konjunktiv** of **können**. **Konnte** (without the **Umlaut**) is the form of the **Imperfekt**. (See lesson 84, paragraph 1).

⑥ **Die Lorelei ist eine Rheinnixe** (**die Nixe**, *mermaid*). **Der Loreleifelsen** is situated on the right bank of the Rhine near **Sankt Goarshausen**.

3 The modern trains of the "Bundesbahn" take you directly to the Rhine, to Basel or Düsseldorf.
4 There you change [and you get] on one of the "floating holiday hotels"
5 with comfortable outer cabins, a heated swimming-pool and an abundant menu *(f.)*…"
6 That really sounds good, doesn't it? What do you think of it?
7 – Oh yes, that'd be great! I could finally see the rock on which "Lorelei" was combing her long golden hair *(n.)*,
8 and where all the sailors who came by only looked at her
9 and thus crashed into the rock and sank.

▸ ⑦ **untergehen**, *to sink, to drown*; but *to set (sun)*. **Die Sonne geht im Westen unter und im Osten auf**, *The sun sets in the West and rises in the East.*

81 **10** Als mir m**e**ine Gro**ß**mutter das Ged**i**cht von H**ei**nrich H**ei**ne ⑧ zum **e**rsten Mal v**o**rgelesen hat, h**a**be ich n**ä**chtelang ⑨ dav**o**n getr**äu**mt.

11 – Ja, mein Schatz, es hat dich **o**ffensichtlich sehr be**ei**ndruckt.

12 K**ö**nntest du viell**ei**cht **au**fhören, dich zu k**ä**mmen? □

***10** … h**i**ne'rich h**i**-n<u>e</u> …*

Notes

⑧ **Heinrich Heine** (1797-1856) wrote the famous poem on the legendary character **Lorelei**: **„Ich weiß nicht, was soll es bedeuten**…**"** A beautiful woman was said to be sitting on a rock on the right bank of the Rhine near **Goarshausen** combing her long golden hair. As all the sailors passing by only paid ▸

***

Übung 1 – Übersetzen Sie bitte

❶ Hören Sie mal, was heute in der Zeitung steht. ❷ Ein Schiff ist gegen einen Felsen gefahren und untergegangen. ❸ Wenn du endlich stillsitzen würdest, könnte ich dich kämmen. ❹ Er hat wochenlang an diesem Projekt gearbeitet. ❺ Das Resultat hat alle offensichtlich sehr beeindruckt. ❻ Der Felsen, auf dem Lorelei ihr langes, goldenes Haar' gekämmt hat, befindet sich auf dem rechten Rheinufer bei Sankt Goarshausen in Hessen.

10 When my grandmother read the poem by Heinrich Heine to me for the first time I dreamed of it for nights. 81
11 – Yes, my dear, it obviously impressed you a lot.
12 Maybe you could stop combing your hair? □

▸ attention to the woman they crashed into the rock. It was said that this woman had magical power. **Lur** (middle high German for **Lore**) means *elf* and **Lei**, *rock*.

⑨ **Tagelang**, *for days*; **wochenlang**, *for weeks*; **monatelang**, *for months;* **jahrelang**, *for years*.

***

Answers to exercise 1

❶ Listen to what they say in the newspaper today. ❷ A ship crashed into a rock and sank. ❸ If you finally sat still, I could comb your hair. ❹ He has been working on this project for weeks. ❺ Apparently everybody was very impressed by the result. ❻ The rock on which the Lorelei combed her long golden hair is situated on the right bank of the Rhine near Sankt Goarshausen in Hessia.

Übung 2 – Ergänzen Sie bitte

❶ My husband takes me to the office every morning.
Mein Mann . . . . jeden Morgen zum Büro.

❷ What do you think of it? – That would be great!
Was . . . . . . Sie . . . . . ? – Das . . . . !

❸ Could you stop singing please?
. . . . Sie bitte . . . . zu singen?

❹ Everybody who passed by stopped for a moment.
. . . . , blieben einen Moment stehen.

82 Zweiundachtzigste Lektion

Im Wartezimmer

1 – Mensch, guck ① mal! Da sind mindestens sechs Personen vor uns dran ②,
2 dabei haben wir unseren Termin jetzt um halb sechs.
3 – Ja, wollen wir gehen oder bleiben?
4 – Wieder gehen hat auch keinen Zweck ③; morgen ist es sicher nicht besser.
5 – Also gut, setzen wir uns und lesen die alten Zeitschriften!

Notes

① **gucken** is synonym of **sehen**, *to look*, in spoken language. ▸

⑤ Our train does not stop at Hagen; we have to change.
Unser Zug .... in Hagen; wir müssen ....

⑥ How *(where)* do you know that? – It was written in the newspaper this morning.
..... weißt du das? – Das ..... heute morgen in der Zeitung.

Answers to exercise 2
① – bringt mich – ② – halten – davon – wäre toll ③ Könnten – aufhören – ④ Alle Leute, die vorbeikamen – ⑤ – hält nicht – umsteigen ⑥ Woher – stand –

Second Wave: 32nd Lesson

82nd Lesson 82

In the Waiting-Room

1 – Hey, look! There are at least six persons before us,
2 though we have our appointment *(m.)* [now] at half past five.
3 – Yes. Are we going to leave or to stay?
4 – It's no use leaving; it won't be better tomorrow.
5 – Well, so let's sit down and read the old magazines!

② **dran sein** is the short form for **an der Reihe sein**, *to have one's turn(row)*. **Ich bin dran/an der Reihe**, *It's my turn.*

③ **der Zweck**, *the purpose, object, point*: **Was ist der Zweck dieser Sache?** *What is the point of it?* – **Das ist zwecklos**, – *That is useless, of no use; aimless.*

82

6 – Hei, hier ist ein Ps**y**cho-Test! Komm, den m**a**chen wir!

7 1. Fr**a**ge: Was w**ü**rden Sie m**a**chen, wenn Sie F**eu**erwehrmann w**ä**ren und ein kl**ei**ner J**u**nge dir**e**kt n**e**ben **I**hnen **ei**nen Benz**i**nkanister **an**zünden w**ü**rde ④?

8 a) dem J**u**ngen hinterh**e**rlaufen b) **ei**nen F**eu**erlöscher ⑤ s**u**chen c) die Z**ü**ndschnur **au**streten ⑥ d) S**o**nstiges.

9 – Ich w**ü**rde die Z**ü**ndschnur **au**streten und dann dem J**u**ngen hinterh**e**rlaufen.

10 – Du mußt dich für **ei**nes von b**ei**den entsch**ei**den!

11 – **A**lso gut: „c“!

12 – 2. Fr**a**ge: Was w**ü**rden Sie m**a**chen, wenn das Licht **au**sgehen ⑦ w**ü**rde, wenn Sie ger**a**de mit **ei**ner h**ei**ßen S**u**ppenschüssel auf der Tr**e**ppe sind?

13 a) l**a**ngsam w**ei**tergehen b) sich s**e**tzen c) den L**i**chtschalter s**u**chen.

14 – Ich gl**au**be, ich w**ü**rde mich h**i**nsetzen ⑧ und w**a**rten, bis die S**u**ppe kalt w**ä**re.

(Fortsetzung folgt) □

Pronunciation Key
6 *... psücho-test!* **7** *... bennts**ee**nkannister ...*

Notes

④ In German the **Konjunktiv** is also used in sentences beginning with **wenn** (*if*), **Wenn ich reich wäre, würde ich ein Auto kaufen**, *If I was rich I would buy a car.* The **Konjunktiv** is often formed with **würde** + infinitive. (See lesson 84, paragraph 1). ▸

6 – Hey, here is a psychological test *(m.)*! Come on, we'll do it!
7 First question: what would you do if you were a fireman and just next to you, a little boy set a petrol can *(m.)* on fire?
8 a) run after the boy b) look for a fire extinguisher *(m.)* c) tread out the match *(f.)* d) anything else.
9 – I would tread out the match and then run after the boy.
10 – You have to decide on one of the two!
11 – Well, "c" then!
12 – Second question: what would you do if the light went out just when you are going upstairs with a bowl *(f.)* of hot soup [in your hands]?
13 a) walk on slowly b) sit down c) look for the light switch.
14 – I think I would sit down and wait for the soup to cool down *(until the soup would be cold)*.
(To be continued) □

⑤ **löschen**, *to extinguish (fire)*; **die Feuerwehr**, *the fire brigade*.

⑥ **austreten**, *to tread out*; **eintreten**, *to enter*; **auf etwas treten**, *to step on something*; **treten**, *to kick*.

⑦ **Das Licht geht aus**, *The light goes out*. **Ich mache das Licht aus**, *I turn the light off*. (See lesson 84, paragraph 2).

⑧ **sich setzen** or **sich hinsetzen**, *to sit down*; but, **sitzen**, *to sit*. **Ich setze mich auf die Treppenstufe**, *I sit down on the step*. But, **Ich sitze auf der Treppenstufe**, *I sit on the step*. Have a look at lessons 43, note 6 and 49, paragraph 2.

82 **Übung 1 – Übersetzen Sie bitte**

❶ Ich kann morgen leider nicht kommen; ich habe einen Termin beim Zahnarzt. ❷ An deiner Stelle würde ich nicht mehr mit ihm sprechen. Das hat keinen Zweck. ❸ Muß ich lange warten? – Es sind noch fünf Personen vor Ihnen dran. ❹ Die Feuerwehr kam sehr schnell und hat das Feuer gelöscht. ❺ Wenn das Licht jetzt ausgehen würde, würde ich die Treppe hinunterfallen.

Übung 2 – Ergänzen Sie bitte

❶ Where is the light switch? – Just next to the door on the left.
. . . . ? – Gleich neben der Tür . . . . . .

❷ Could you give me an appointment for Tuesday please?
Könnten Sie mir bitte . . . . für Dienstag geben?

❸ Which train do you want to take? You have to decide on one of the two!
Welchen Zug . . . . nehmen? Sie müssen sich . . . . entscheiden!

❹ I would sit down and wait for him to come.
. . . . und warten, . . . er käme.

❺ Whose turn is it? – I think it is my turn.
Wer ist . . . . ? – Ich glaube, ...

❻ Don't go there! It is of no use.
Geh nicht dorthin! . . . .

Answers to exercise 1

❶ Unfortunately I cannot come tomorrow; I have an appointment at the dentist's. ❷ If I were you *(in your place)* I would not talk to him any more. It is of no use. ❸ Do I have to wait for a long time? – There are another five people before you. ❹ The fire brigade came very quickly and extinguished the fire. ❺ If the light went out now, I would fall down the stairs.

Answers to exercise 2

❶ Wo ist der Lichtschalter – links ❷ – einen Termin – ❸ – wollen Sie – für einen von beiden – ❹ Ich würde mich hinsetzen – bis – ❺ – an der Reihe – ich bin dran ❻ – Es hat keinen Zweck

Second Wave: 33rd Lesson

83 Dreiundachtzigste Lektion

Im Wartezimmer (Fortsetzung)

1 – Sieh mal, jetzt ist nur noch **ei**ne Pers**o**n vor uns! Das ging ja schn**e**ller, als wir d**a**chten.

2 – Na ja, wir sind auch schon **über ei**ne St**u**nde ① hier. **A**ber hör zu ②:

3 3. Fr**a**ge: Was w**ü**rden Sie m**a**chen, wenn **I**hnen Ihr Fris**eu**r aus Vers**e**hen **ei**ne Gl**a**tze geschn**i**tten ③ h**ä**tte ④?

4 a) w**ei**nen b) **ei**ne Per**ü**cke verl**a**ngen ⑤ c) ihn **o**hrfeigen ⑥ d) S**o**nstiges.

5 – Ich w**ü**rde ihn **o**hrfeigen und **ei**ne Per**ü**cke verl**a**ngen.

6 – Ich h**a**be dir schon mal ges**a**gt, du mußt dich entsch**ei**den!

7 – Gut, wenn es so ist, dann w**ü**rde ich nur w**ei**nen.

Notes

① **über eine Stunde**, *over an hour*, is an expression meaning, **mehr/länger als eine Stunde**, *more than an hour.*

② **hören**, *to hear* or *to listen to*; **jemandem zuhören**, *to listen to someone.* **Ich habe heute morgen Radio gehört**, *I have been listening to the radio this morning.* But, **Hören Sie bitte zu, wenn ich spreche!**, *Please listen when I am talking!* **Ich höre ihn singen**, *I hear him singing.*

③ **die Glatze**, *the bald head*; **eine Glatze schneiden**, *to shave a head (to cut a head bald).* **Schneiden, schnitt, geschnitten**, *to cut, cut, cut.* Have a look at the irregular verbs in the grammatical appendix at the end of the book, p. 477-481. ▸

In the Waiting-Room (continued)

1 – Look, there is only one person before us! It was quicker than we thought.
2 – Well, we have already been here for more than an hour. But listen:
3 Third question: what would you do if the hairdresser *(m.)* [had] shaved your head by mistake?
4 a) cry b) ask for a wig *(f.)* c) slap him d) anything else.
5 – I would slap him and ask for a wig.
6 – I have already told you that you have to decide!
7 – Well in this case, I would only cry.

④ The **Konjunktiv** is also used after **wenn** (*if*), introducing a hypothesis the realization of which is impossible or uncertain: **Wenn er seine Haare geschnitten hätte**, *If he had cut his hair...* (See lesson 84 paragraph 1).

⑤ **verlangen**, *to ask*, *to demand*, is stronger than **bitten**: **Ich verlange, daß Sie mir mein Geld zurückgeben**, *I demand that you give me my money back*.

⑥ **das Ohr**, **die Ohren**, *the ear, ears*; **die Feige**, *the fig;* but **die Ohrfeige**, *the slap*; **jemanden ohrfeigen**, *to slap someone*.

83

8 – 4. Frage: Was w**ü**rden Sie m**a**chen, wenn Sie schon mehr als **ei**ne St**u**nde beim Arzt gew**a**rtet h**ä**tten,

9 und man w**ü**rde **I**hnen pl**ö**tzlich s**a**gen: „K**o**mmen Sie b**i**tte m**o**rgen w**ie**der!“

10 – Entsch**u**ldigen Sie b**i**tte, **a**ber der Herr D**o**ktor muß dr**i**ngend **ei**nen Pati**e**nten ⑦ bes**u**chen. K**ö**nnten Sie b**i**tte m**o**rgen w**ie**derkommen?

11 – Ich w**e**rde verr**ü**ckt; das kann doch nicht wahr sein! Sag schnell, was sind die drei M**ö**glichkeiten?

12 – a) nach H**au**se g**e**hen b) Krach ⑧ schl**a**gen c) laut **a**nfangen zu st**ö**hnen,

13 – Komm, ich hab’s satt ⑨! G**e**hen wir! □

Pronunciation Key
***10** … pats'**ye**nnten … **12** … KracH … sht**er**hnen*

***

Übung 1 – Übersetzen Sie bitte

❶ Sie kam schneller zurück als ich dachte. ❷ Wir warten schon über eineinhalb Stunden. ❸ Die Lehrer dürfen die Schüler nicht ohrfeigen. ❹ Einige tun es trotzdem. ❺ Was würdest du machen, wenn ich verrückt würde? ❻ Er muß dringend zum Zahnarzt. ❼ Das kann doch nicht wahr sein! Ich hab’s wirklich satt!

8 – Fourth question: What would you do if you had already been waiting for more than an hour at the doctor,
9 and you were suddenly told: "Come again tomorrow please!"?
10 – Please excuse us but the doctor has to go and see a patient urgently. Could you come again tomorrow please?
11 – I am going mad; that can't be true! Tell me quickly the three possibilities?
12 – a) go home b) kick up a fuss *(m.)* c) start groaning aloud.
13 – Come on, I am fed up. Let's go! □

Notes

⑦ **der Patient**, **die Patientin**, *the patient* (m./f.) is a weak noun and therefore ends in **-en** in the accusative masculine: **Er besucht einen Patienten**, *He goes to see a patient*. Also: **Der Beamte**, **die Beamtin**, *the civil servant* (m./f.). **Ich frage einen Beamten**, *I ask a public servant*.

⑧ **der Krach**, *the crash, noise, row*. **Krach schlagen**, *to protest vehemently, to kick up a fuss*.

⑨ **Ich habe es satt, Ich habe genug davon**, *I am fed up*. Literally **satt** means "full, satisfied". **Ich bin satt**, *I have eaten my fill*.

***

Answers to exercise 1

❶ She came back more quickly than I thought. ❷ We have already been waiting for them for an hour and a half. ❸ Teachers don't have the right to slap the pupils. ❹ Nevertheless some do [it]. ❺ What would you do if I went mad? ❻ He really must go to see the dentist. ❼ That can't be true! I am really fed up!

83 Übung 2 – Ergänzen Sie bitte

1. What would you do if your neighbour was a saxophonist?
   ... . wenn Ihr Nachbar Saxophonist wäre?

2. Where would you go if you hadn't got a house any more?
   .... wenn Sie kein Haus mehr hätten?

3. What would you think if I didn't come home for a week?
   ... . wenn ich eine Woche nicht nach Hause käme?

4. If he wasn't so stupid he would have understood more rapidly.
   .... er nicht so dumm ...., ... er schneller verstanden.

5. Excuse me please but I really must talk to Mr. Meier.
   .... bitte, aber ich muß .... Herrn Meier sprechen.

6. He asks me to make up my mind *(decide)* before tomorrow.
   .. .. ich mich bis morgen entscheide.

❼ We have already been waiting for your answer for more than a week.
Wir warten schon .... auf ihre Antwort.

Answers to exercise 2

❶ Was würden Sie machen – ❷ Wohin würden Sie gehen – ❸ Was würdest du denken – ❹ Wenn – wäre – hätte – ❺ Entschuldigen Sie – dringend – ❻ Er verlangt, daß – ❼ – über eine Woche –

Second Wave: 34th Lesson

84 Vierundachtzigste lektion

Wiederholung und Erklärungen

1 The *Konjunktiv II*

In German, we use the **Konjunktiv II** in conditional clauses, in the subordinate (introduced by **wenn**, *if*), and in the main clause. As the **Konjunktiv I** is not very widely used in spoken language, we will introduce it later.

1.1 Hypothesis

Wenn er größer wäre, könnte er die Tür öffnen.
If he were taller he could open the door.

Wenn ich mehr Geld hätte, würde ich nicht arbeiten.
If I had more money I would not work.

1.2 An Action Which Has Not Been Realized in The Past

Wenn wir das gewußt hätten, wären wir früher gekommen.
If we had known that we would have come earlier.

The **Konjunktiv II** of irregular verbs is formed with the **Imperfekt**; you add **-e** to the end and if necessary the **Umlaut**:

Imperfekt	Konjunktiv II
ich kam, *I came*	**ich käme**, *I would come*
du kamst, *you came*	**du käm(e)st**, *you would come*
er kam, *he came*	**er käme**, *he would come*
wir kamen, *we came*	**wir kämen**, *we would come*
ihr kamt, *you came*	**ihr käm(e)t**, *you would come*
sie kamen, *they came*	**sie kämen**, *they would come*
Sie kamen, *you came/formal*	**Sie kämen**, *you would come*

Also: **ich war**, *I was* → **ich wäre**, *I would be*, **du wär(e)st**, **er wäre**, **wir wären**, **ihr wär(e)t**, **sie/Sie wären**

Ich hatte, *I had* → **ich hätte**, *I would have*, **du hättest**, **er hätte**, **wir hätten**, **ihr hättet**, **sie/Sie hätten**
Ich konnte, *I could* → **ich könnte**, *I could*, **du könntest**, **er könnte**, **wir könnten**, **ihr könntet**, **sie/Sie könnten**.

The **Konjunktiv II** of the regular verbs is however identical to the **Impertekt**.
To avoid ambiguity the **Konjunktiv II** is also formed with **würde** + infinitive:

Ich würde das nicht machen, wenn ich an deiner Stelle wäre.
I would not do that if I were in your shoes (place).

Sie würden das Haus kaufen, wenn sie Geld hätten.
They would buy the house if they had the money.

In spoken language this form is even used with irregular verbs. Only with **sein** and **haben** and the **auxiliary verbs** do we prefer the real **Konjunktiv**: **Wenn er mehr Zeit hätte, könnte er mehr lesen**, *If he had more time he could read more.*
Wenn du nicht so schreien würdest, würde ich dich besser verstehen, *If you did not shout I would understand you better.*

The **Konjunktiv II** is also used in sentences expressing a wish (we leave out **wenn** and add **doch** or **nur**.) **Würde ich doch nur schon fließend Deutsch sprechen (= Wenn ich doch nur schon fließend Deutsch sprechen würde)**, *If only I could already speak German fluently!*

2 The Verbs and Their Prefixes

Once again we are going to talk a little more about the verbs and their prefixes. Today, let's have a look at the different prefixes used with the verb **machen**: **Machen Sie bitte das Fenster auf! Nein, nicht „zu"! „Auf"**, **bitte**, *Open the window please! No, don't close it! Open it please!*
Könnten Sie bitte das Licht anmachen? Nein, nicht ausmachen! Anmachen, bitte! Himmel, diese Ausländer verstehen immer

85 **alles falsch!**, *Could you turn on the light please? No, don't turn it off! Turn it on, please! Heavens, these foreigners always get (understand) everything wrong!*

Pay attention to the following verbs:
aufmachen, *to open* ; **zumachen**, *to close*
anmachen, *to turn on* ; **ausmachen**, *to turn off.*

3 Die Bundesländer

Here are the names of the ten **Länder** (**Bundesländer**) that make up the Federal Republic of Germany. **Baden-Württemberg**, **Bayern** (*Bavaria*), **Bremen**, **Hamburg**, **Hessen**, **Niedersachsen**, **Nordrhein-Westfalen**, **Rheinland-Pfalz**, **Saarland**, **Schleswig-Holstein**.

85 Fünfundachtzigste Lektion

Die Pessimistin und der Egoist ①

1 – Ich kann's **i**mmer noch nicht gl**au**ben.
2 Wir s**i**tzen im Zug und die T**ü**ren werden ② geschl**o**ssen.
3 Wir f**a**hren **a**lso w**i**rklich **e**ndlich nach Par**i**s.

Notes

① A lot of nouns have a feminine form (in **-in**): **der Egoist**, but **die Egoistin**; **der Professor**, but **die Professorin** (a **Professor** only teaches at university, otherwise we say **Lehrer** or **Lehrerin**).

② You already know that **werden**, *to become*, is also used for the **Konjunktiv II** and the **future** (see lesson 42, paragraph 2). In this lesson **werden** is used to form the passive voice: **Das Kind wird von der Mutter angezogen**, *The child is (being) dressed by the mother.* Or: **Die Mutter zieht das Kind an**, *The mother dresses the child.*

If you want to know where they are situated, consult the map: **Bayern** (*Bavaria)* in the South*,* **Schleswig-Holstein** in the North and the *Ruhr area (***das Ruhrgebiet**) is situated in **Nordrhein-Westfalen**...

4 Another story

Woran liegt es, daß Sie so müde sind?, *Why are you so tired?* **Es liegt an den langen Grammatikparagraphen**, *This is due to the long grammar lessons...*
Remember this expression:
Woran liegt es...?, *What is the reason for.../Why...?*
Es liegt an..., *The reason is/It is due to...*
But: **Es liegt mir nichts daran**, *It does not matter/ It does not mean anything to me.*

85th Lesson 85

The Pessimist *(f.)* and the Egotist *(m.)*

1 – I still can't believe it.
2 We are sitting in the train and the doors are [being] closed.
3 We really are going to Paris after all.

4 – Ja, siehst du! Du bist **i**mmer so pessim**i**stisch! Hab' **e**twas mehr Vertr**au**en ③ in mich und die Z**u**kunft!
5 – Du bist gut! Verg**i**ß b**i**tte nicht, daß mir d**ie**se R**ei**se vor zw**a**nzig J**a**hren zum **e**rsten Mal verspr**o**chen ④ wurde.
6 – Ja, und wie **i**mmer h**a**be ich Wort geh**a**lten!
7 – Oh, laß uns b**i**tte nicht d**a**rüber diskut**ie**ren! H**au**ptsache: Wir r**o**llen.
8 Wie l**a**nge h**a**ben wir **Au**fenthalt ⑤ in Köln?
9 – Fast **ei**ne Stunde. Wir k**ö**nnen **u**nser Gepäck in **ei**nem Schl**ie**ßfach ⑥ l**a**ssen und den Dom bes**i**chtigen, der gleich n**e**ben dem B**a**hnhof steht.
10 – Au ja! Ich h**a**be n**eu**lich gel**e**sen, daß man sich be**ei**len muß, wenn man ihn noch s**e**hen will.
11 Es scheint, daß er l**a**ngsam **a**ber s**i**cher von dem Schw**e**feldioxyd in der Luft zerst**ö**rt wird ⑦.

Pronunciation Key
11 *... shvayfeldi'oxüt ...*

Notes

③ We can say: **ich habe Vertrauen in dich**, *I have confidence in you*, or **ich (ver)traue dir**, *I trust you*. The opposite is: **Ich mißtraue dir. Miß-** is a prefix expressing the negative opposite of a verb, an adjective or a noun: **verstehen**, *to understand* → **mißverstehen**, *to misunderstand*; **das Verständnis**, *the understanding* → **das Mißverständnis**, *the misunderstanding*; **billigend**, *approving* → **mißbilligend**, *disapproving*. ▸

4 – Yes, you see! You are always so pessimistic! Have a little bit more confidence in me and the future *(f.)*!
5 – You must be joking! Don't forget that I was promised this trip *(f.)* for the first time twenty years ago.
6 – Yes, and as usual I kept my word!
7 – Oh, please don't let us argue about that! All that matters is that: we are leaving *(rolling)*.
8 How long do we stop at Cologne?
9 – Nearly an hour. We can leave our luggage in a locker and visit the cathedral *(m.)* which is just next to the station.
10 – Oh, yes! I recently read that you have to hurry if you still want to see it.
11 It seems that it is slowly but surely being destroyed by the sulphur dioxide *(n.)* [contained] in the air.

▸ ④ **Es wurde mir versprochen**, *I was promised.* You noticed that we form the passive with **werden** + the past participle (in English, be + past participle), **Es wurde Ihnen nichts vorgeschwindelt**, *You were not told lies.*

⑤ **der Aufenthalt**, *the stay, the residence, the delay*; **die Aufenthaltsgenehmigung**, *the residence permit.*

⑥ **das Schließfach**, *the automatic luggage locker*; **die Gepäckaufbewahrung**, *the left luggage office* (**aufbewahren**, *to deposit for safe keeping; to keep*).

⑦ Pay attention to the passive: **Der Dom wird vom Schwefeldioxyd zerstört = Das Schwefeldioxyd zerstört den Dom**, *The sulphur dioxide destroys the cathedral.*

85 **12** – Na, ja, bis zum **E**nde des Jahrh**u**nderts wird er ja wohl noch h**a**lten, **o**der? Du und d**ei**ne Gr**ü**nen!

13 – Ego**i**st! Denkst du **ei**gentlich nie an d**ei**ne K**i**nder? □

***

Übung 1 – Übersetzen Sie bitte

❶ Sie kann es immer noch nicht glauben, daß sie endlich wirklich nach Paris fahren. ❷ Die Tür wird von dem Schaffner geschlossen. ❸ Der Dom wird von vielen Leuten besichtigt. ❹ Das wurde mir schon oft versprochen. Ich glaube nicht mehr daran. ❺ Er hat gelesen, daß man sich beeilen muß, wenn man noch Eintrittskarten für das Konzert kaufen will.

Übung 2 – Ergänzen Sie bitte

❶ The doors close automatically.
Die Türen . . . . . . automatisch . . . .

❷ She was promised this journey ten years ago.
Diese Reise . . . . . ihr vor zehn Jahren . . . .

❸ We stop in Frankfurt for half an hour.
Wir haben eine halbe Stunde . . . . in Frankfurt.

❹ We leave our suitcases in a locker.
Wir lassen unsere Koffer in . . . .

12 – Pooh, it'll doubtless last until the end of the century *(n.)*, won't it? You and your [ecologists] Greens!

13 – How selfish you are *(egotist)*! Do you really never think of your children? □

***

Answers to exercise 1

❶ They still can't believe that they are really going to Paris after all. ❷ The door is closed by the conductor. ❸ The cathedral is visited by a lot of people. ❹ This has already been promised to me so often. I don't believe in it any more. ❺ He read that you must hurry if you still want to buy tickets for the concert.

❺ He never thinks of his children.
Er denkt . . . . seine Kinder.

❻ Why don't you have confidence in me?
Warum haben Sie kein . . . . ?

Answers to exercise 2

❶ – werden – geschlossen ❷ – wurde – versprochen ❸ – Aufenthalt – ❹ – einem Schließfach ❺ – niemals an – ❻ – Vertrauen in mich

Second Wave: 36th Lesson

86 Sechsundachtzigste Lektion

Eigentum muß geschützt werden ①

1 – Weißt du **ei**gentlich, daß d**ei**ne **E**nkelkinder wahrsch**ei**nlich k**ei**nen Wald mehr s**e**hen werden?
2 – Sieh doch nicht **i**mmer **a**lles so schwarz!
3 – Wenn die L**u**ftverschmutzung so w**ei**tergeht wie bish**e**r, stirbt der Wald in den k**o**mmenden zehn bis f**ü**nfzehn J**a**hren. ②
4 Vor **ei**nem Jahr hat man acht Proz**e**nt kr**a**nke B**äu**me registr**ie**rt,
5 und h**eu**te w**u**rde f**e**stgestellt ③, daß schon ein V**ie**rtel des W**a**ldes ruin**ie**rt ④ ist.
6 – Dann m**ü**ssen eben neue M**ä**rchen geschr**ie**ben werden. F**ee**n und H**e**xen k**ö**nnen auch im Industr**ie**gebiet l**e**ben!
7 – Du bist w**i**rklich unverb**e**sserlich ⑤!
8 – Nein, **a**ber ich h**a**be die N**a**se voll von d**ie**sem Ger**e**de.
9 **A**lle Welt ⑥ spricht vom W**a**ldsterben und n**ie**mand denkt an die L**eu**te,
10 die f**ü**nfzig St**u**nden **o**der mehr pro W**o**che **a**rbeiten und sowies**o** k**ei**nen Wald s**e**hen.

Notes

① A lot of nouns ending in **-tum** are neuter. The infinitive of the passive voice: **geschützt werden**, *to be protected.*

② **die Umweltverschmutzung**, *the pollution*; **schmutzig**, *dirty*; **sterben**, **starb**, **gestorben**, *to die, died, died.*

③ **feststellen**, *to discover, to state.* ▸

Property *(n.)* Must be Protected

1 – By the way, do you know that your grandchildren will probably see no more woods?
2 – Don't always look on *(see)* the dark side of things!
3 – If pollution *(f.)* goes on [spreading] like this *(as up to now)* the woods will be dying within the next ten to fifteen years.
4 One year ago it was discovered that 8% of the trees [were] sick,
5 and today they discovered that already one quarter of the woods is destroyed *(ruined)*.
6 – Then new fairy-tales have to be written. Fairies and witches can live in industrial areas too!
7 – You really are incorrigible!
8 – No, but I am fed up *(have the nose full)* with all this babble.
9 Everybody talks of the death of the woods and nobody thinks of the people
10 who work 50 hours or more a week and don't see any woods anyway.

▸ ④ Verbs ending in **-ieren** don't take the prefix **ge-** in the past participle, **ruinieren**, *to ruin*; **ruiniert**, *ruined*.

⑤ **verbessern**, *to correct, to improve*; **die Verbesserung**, *the correction, improvement*. We also say: **korrigieren** and **die Korrektur**.

⑥ **alle Welt**, *all the world*, i.e. *everybody*.

11 – Mm, und wie steht's mit ⑦ d**ei**nem H**o**bby, F**i**schen?
12 Was w**ü**rdest du s**a**gen, wenn es **ei**nes T**a**ges, **o**der s**a**gen wir b**e**sser, in **a**bsehbarer Zeit, k**ei**ne F**i**sche mehr in d**ei**nem B**a**ggersee ⑧ g**ä**be?
13 – Komm, jetzt mal **a**ber nicht den T**eu**fel an die Wand! An m**ei**nen B**a**ggersee l**a**sse ich n**ie**manden ran ⑨!
14 Ach, das h**a**be ich dir **ü**brigens noch gar nicht erz**ä**hlt: Gestern m**u**ßte ich da w**ie**der fünf N**a**cktbader ⑩ wegjagen! □

Notes

⑦ Remember the following expression: **Wie steht's mit...**, *What about...*; **Wie steht's mit deinen Geschäften?** *How is business?*

⑧ **der Bagger**, *the excavator*. In Germany there are a lot of **Baggerseen**, generally artificial private lakes used for fishing or swimming. ▸

***

Übung 1 – Übersetzen Sie bitte

❶ Wenn es so weitergeht wie bisher, werden in den nächsten zwanzig Jahren alle Bäume sterben. ❷ Die Flüsse und Seen sind so verschmutzt, daß die Fische nicht mehr leben können. ❸ Es gibt immer mehr Leute, die gegen die Umweltverschmutzung kämpfen. ❹ Die gute Waldfee weiß bald nicht mehr, wo sie wohnen soll. ❺ Es wurde festgestellt, daß das Schwefeldioxyd unbestreitbar schädlich ist.

11 – Mm, and what about your hobby, fishing?
12 What would you say if one day, or let's say *(rather)* in the near future, there were no more fish in your artificial lake?
13 – Come on, don't take such a dim view of things *(don't paint the devil (m.) on the wall)*; I won't let anybody [come] near my lake!
14 By the way, I haven't told you yet: yesterday I had to chase away five nudists again! □

▸ ⑨ **Er läßt niemanden an seinen Fernsehapparat ran**, *He won't let anybody come near his TV set.*

⑩ **nackt**, *naked*; **baden**, *to bathe*; you can also say: **die Nudisten**.

***

Answers to exercise 1

❶ If it goes on as in the past *(up to now)* all the trees will die within the next twenty years. ❷ Rivers and lakes are so polluted that the fish cannot live any longer. ❸ There are more and more people who fight against pollution. ❹ The good fairy of the woods soon won't know any longer where to live *(where she is to live)*. ❺ It was discovered that sulphur dioxide is incontestably noxious.

86 Übung 2 – Ergänzen Sie bitte

1. He always look on [the] dark [side of things] whereas she is always optimistic.
   Er sieht immer . . . . während sie immer . . . . ist.

2. One year ago unemployment stood at 8% *(One year ago 8% of the unemployed were registered).*
   . . . . wurden acht . . . . Arbeitslose registriert.

3. What would you say if there were no more fish ever?
   . . . . , wenn es keine Fische mehr . . . . ?

4. I have never liked eating fish anyway.
   Ich habe Fische . . . . nie . . . . gegessen.

5. Everyone *(all the world)* is talking about the atomic bomb and nobody thinks about me and my fear of spiders.
   . . . . spricht . . . der Atombombe und . . . . denkt mehr . . mich und meine Angst . . . Spinnen.

❻ Don't take such a dim view of things *(don't paint the devil on the wall)*! Life is already hard enough.
Mal nicht . . . . an die . . . . ! . . . .
ist so schon schwer . . . . . .

Answers to exercise 2

❶ – alles schwarz – optimistisch – ❷ Vor einem Jahr – Prozent – ❸ Was würden Sie sagen – gäbe ❹ – sowieso – gern – ❺ Alle Welt – von – niemand – an – vor – ❻ – den Teufel – Wand – Das Leben – genug

Second Wave: 37th Lesson

87 Siebenundachtzigste Lektion

Der Spaßvogel ①

1 – Hallo Oskar! Wie schön, daß du doch noch gekommen bist!

2 Wir hatten schon beinahe die Hoffnung aufgegeben… Gott sei Dank! Der Abend ist gerettet!

3 – Was für eine herzliche Begrüßung! Womit habe ich denn das verdient ②?

4 – Komm, sei nicht so bescheiden! Du weißt gut, daß wir uns ohne dich zu Tode langweilen ③!

5 – Ah ja? Das ist das erste, was ich höre! Ich wußte bis heute nicht, daß meine Anwesenheit so geschätzt ④ wird.

6 Gerade gestern hat man mir noch das Gegenteil zu verstehen gegeben.

7 Man hat mich höflich aber bestimmt gebeten ⑤, den Sitzungssaal zu verlassen.

8 – Warum das denn? Was hast du denn da wieder angestellt ⑥?

Notes

① **Der Spaßvogel**, lit.: "the bird of fun"; someone who amuses the others.

② We already know that **verdienen** means *to earn money*: **Er verdient 2.000 Euro pro Monat**, *He earns 2,000 euros a month*. **But verdienen** also means *to deserve*. **Er hat das nicht verdient**, *He hasn't deserved it.* ▸

87th Lesson 87

The Jester

1 – Hello Oscar! How nice of you to have come *(that you have come)* after all.
2 We had almost given up hope *(f.)*. Thank God! The evening is saved!
3 – What a hearty welcome *(f.)*! What have I done to deserve that *(with what did I deserve that)*?
4 – Come on! Don't be so modest! You know very well that we are bored to death *(m.)* without you!
5 – Ah, do you? That's the first [time] I have heard that! Until today I didn't know that my presence was so appreciated!
6 Only yesterday I was given to *(made)* understand the contrary *(n.)*.
7 I was asked in a polite but firm way to leave the conference room *(m.)*.
8 – Why *(that)*? What have you been up to again?

③ **sich langweilen**, *to be bored*; **lang** cannot be separated from **weilen**, **ich habe mich gelangweilt**, *I was bored*.

④ **schätzen**, *to appreciate*, *to esteem*. You have already encountered **der Schatz**, *the treasure*, or **mein Schatz**, *my darling*.

⑤ **gebeten** is the past participle of **bitten**, *to ask* (see lesson 73, note 2).

⑥ **anstellen** has several meanings; in this text it is used in an idiomatic expression: **etwas anstellen**, *to do something (silly)*. Otherwise **anstellen** means
a) *to employ, to engage*: **Sie ist bei einer Bank angestellt**, *She is employed with a bank*;
b) *to turn on*: **Stell bitte das Radio an!**, *Please turn the radio on!*

87

9 – Nichts, ich schwöre es euch! Ich bin nur etwas eingenickt [7] und hatte anscheinend einen fürchterlichen Alptraum, an den ich mich nur noch sehr schwach erinnere, Gott sei Dank, denn er war wirklich entsetzlich.

10 Ich fand mich eingeschlossen in einem Saal ohne Fenster mit vielen anderen Personen, deren Gesichter ich nicht erkennen konnte wegen [8] des dichten Rauchs, der im Saal verbreitet war.

11 Und plötzlich bekam ich keine Luft mehr, und da sah ich in der Ferne meine Mutter, die mir winkte und mir zurief:

12 „Komm, wir gehen ans Meer! Es ist gerade Ebbe, und wir werden Krebse suchen!“

13 Und ganz zufrieden bin ich richtig eingeschlafen und… fing an zu schnarchen… □

***

Übung 1 – Übersetzen Sie bitte

❶ Sein Humor und seine Freundlichkeit werden von allen sehr geschätzt. ❷ Sie hat schon fast die Hoffnung aufgegeben, ihn jemals wiederzusehen. ❸ Er wurde sehr herzlich begrüßt, aber er wußte nicht, womit er das verdient hatte. ❹ Man hat ihm höflich zu verstehen gegeben, daß seine Anwesenheit nicht erwünscht war. ❺ Ich sah in meinem Traum in der Ferne eine Person, deren Gesicht ich nicht erkennen konnte. ❻ Sie haben ihn gebeten, den Sitzungssaal zu verlassen, weil er so entsetzlich schnarchte.

9 – Nothing, I swear it! I was only dozing a little and apparently I had an awful nightmare *(m.)* which I only remember very faintly, thank God, for it really was horrible.

10 I found myself locked up in a room *(hall)* without windows with a lot of other persons whose faces I could not make out because of the thick smoke *(m.) (which was spread over)* in the room.

11 And suddenly I couldn't breathe any more *(I got no more air)* and there I saw my mother waving at me and shouting in the distance:

12 "Come on, we will go down to the sea! The tide is out and we will look for crabs!"

13 And, completely happy, I really fell asleep and… started snoring.

Notes

⑦ **einnicken**, *to doze off*, is a familiar expression; **nicken**, *to nod*.

⑧ **wegen** + genitive, *because of*... **Wegen des Alptraums bin ich aufgewacht**, *I woke up because of the nightmare*.

***

Answers to exercise 1

❶ His humour and friendliness are appreciated by everybody. ❷ She has already given up hope of seeing him again. ❸ He was welcomed very heartily but he didn't know what he had done to deserve that. ❹ He was made to understand in a polite way that his presence was not desired. ❺ In my dream I saw a person in the distance whose face I could not make out. ❻ They asked him to leave the conference room because he was snoring so horribly.

87 Übung 2 – Ergänzen Sie bitte

❶ Are you a joker or are you always serious?
Sind Sie . . . . oder sind Sie . . . . .
. . . . . ?

❷ Were you very bored last night?
. . . . . Sie sich gestern abend . . . .
. . . . ?

❸ Have you ever fallen asleep during a conference?
. . . . schon einmal bei einer Sitzung
. . . . ?

❹ Have you already been asked to leave the room?
. . . man . . . schon einmal . . . . den
Saal . . . . ?

❺ Can you swear that you didn't do anything silly?
. . . . . . Sie . . . . daß Sie nichts . . . .
. . . . . ?

❻ Do you remember your nightmares or do you forget them immediately?
. . . . an ihre Alpträume
oder . . . . sie sofort?

Answers to exercise 2

❶ – ein Spaßvogel – immer ernst ❷ Haben – sehr gelangweilt ❸ Sind Sie – eingeschlafen ❹ Hat – Sie – gebeten – zu verlassen ❺ Können – schwören – angestellt haben ❻ Erinnern Sie sich – vergessen Sie –

Second Wave: 38th Lesson

88 Achtundachtzigste Lektion

Verschiedenes

1 Sichtlich schockiert erschien auf dem Polizeirevier in Friedrichshafen am Bodensee ein Urlauber ①

2 und präsentierte ② den Beamten ein Brot, in dem er beim Frühstück einen Finger gefunden hatte.

3 Die Polizei ermittelte, daß das Brot in einer Großbäckerei in Hechingen hergestellt worden war. ③

4 Dort hatte Tage zuvor ein Bäcker bei einem Unfall einen Finger verloren,

5 der aber trotz ④ intensiver Suche nicht wiedergefunden werden konnte.

Notes

① **der Bodensee**, *The Lake of Constance*. **Der Urlaub**, *holidays*, **Urlaub** is used with the working population. In the case of students we say **Ferien**. **Der Urlauber**, *holiday-maker*; *tourist*.

② **präsentieren** means *to show, to display*. Thus, you mustn't say: **Ich präsentiere Ihnen meine Frau**, but: **Ich stelle Ihnen meine Frau vor**, *Let me introduce my wife*. You can say, however: **Die Rechnung wird Ihnen bald präsentiert werden**, *You will have the bill soon (the bill will be presented to you soon)*.

③ the **Perfekt** and **Plusquamperfekt** of the passive voice: **Das Brot ist in Bonn hergestellt worden**, *The bread was (has been) made in Bonn*. And: **Das Brot war in Bonn hergestellt worden**, *The bread had been made in Bonn*. The prefix **ge-** is not added to the past participle of **werden** when it is used for the passive voice, in this case **worden** is always placed at the ▸

Miscellaneous

1 A holiday-maker appeared, visibly shocked, at the police station *(n.)* in Friedrichshafen on the Lake of Constance.
2 and showed *(presented)* the policemen *(officials)* a [loaf of] bread *(n.)* in which he had found a finger *(m.)* at breakfast *(n.)*.
3 The police *(f.)* found out that the bread had been made in an industrial bakery *(f.)* in Hechingen.
4 A baker *(m.)* had lost a finger in an accident the day before
5 which could not be found despite intense search *(f.)*.

WARME UND KALTE GETRÄNKE KÖNNEN AUS DEM AUTOMATEN GEHOLT WERDEN

end of the sentence: **Er ist von der Polizei verhaftet worden**, *He was arrested by the police.* (See lesson 91, paragraph 1).

④ **trotz**, *despite* (preposition) is followed by the genitive: **Trotz des schlechten Wetters pflanzt er Radieschen**, *He plants radishes despite the bad weather.*

6 Auf ihrer **Ho**chzeitsreise ⑤ hat **ei**ne dr**ei**undzw**a**nzig J**a**hre **a**lte Amerik**a**nerin in Las V**e**gas mit drei D**o**llar ⑥ **Ei**nsatz die Rek**o**rdsumme von 1.065.358 D**o**llar gew**o**nnen.
7 Dies ist der h**ö**chste Gew**i**nn, der j**e**mals im Gl**ü**cksspielerparad**ies** ⑦ Nev**a**da aus **ei**nem Sp**ie**lautomaten geh**o**lt w**u**rde.
8 Die j**u**nge Frau h**a**tte **ei**gentlich schon auf ⑧ ihr H**o**telzimmer zur**ü**ckgehen w**o**llen,
9 ließ sich dann **a**ber von Fr**eu**nden überr**e**den ⑨, noch ein l**e**tztes Spiel zu vers**u**chen. □

Pronunciation Key
*6 … i-ne millyo**h**n fünnf-oo**n**t-zeçhtsiçh-**tow**zennt-dr**y**-hoondert-**a**cHt-oont-f**ü**nftsiçh …*
*7 … gl**ü**kks'shpeelerparad**ee**ss …*

Notes

⑤ **die Hochzeit**, *the wedding.* ▸

***

Übung 1 – Übersetzen Sie bitte

❶ Konstanz ist eine alte Stadt am Bodensee, die heute ungefähr 70.000 Einwohner hat. ❷ Warme und kalte Getränke können aus dem Automaten geholt werden. ❸ Mein Vater war über meinen neuen Minirock sichtlich schockiert. Meinem Großvater gefiel er aber sehr gut. ❹ Ein etwa fünfundfünfzig Jahre alter Mann wurde tot auf einer Parkbank gefunden. ❺ Die Polizei ermittelte, daß er keinen festen Wohnsitz hatte. ❻ Die höchste Summe, die ich jemals im Lotto gewonnen habe, war zwölf Mark sechzig.

6 On her honeymoon a 23-year-old American won with a 3-dollar stake *(m.)* the unequalled amount of 1,065,358 dollars in Las Vegas.
7 This is the highest win *(m.)* ever made with a slot-machine *(m.)* in the gambling paradise *(n.)* of Nevada.
8 Actually the young woman had intended to go back to her hotel room,
9 but finally she let herself be persuaded to have a last try *(to try a last play)*. □

⑥ Please note that there is no plural ending with the words **Mark**, **Dollar**, etc.

⑦ **ein Spieler**, *a player*; **ein Glücksspieler**, *a gambler.*

⑧ **auf sein Zimmer gehen**, *to go, withdraw to one's room*, but: **Ich gehe in mein Zimmer**, *I go into my room.*

⑨ **jemanden überreden**, *to persuade someone*: **Er hat mich überredet, mit ins Kino zu gehen**, *He persuaded me to go to the cinema with [him]*; **über-** cannot be separated from **reden**!

***

Answers to exercise 1

❶ Konstanz is an old town on the Bodensee which has about 70,000 inhabitants today. ❷ Hot and cold drinks can be obtained from the drink dispenser. ❸ My father was visibly shocked by my mini-skirt but my grandfather liked it very much. ❹ A man about 55 years old was found dead on a park bench. ❺ The police found out that he had no fixed place of residence. ❻ The highest amount I have ever won in the lotto is *(was)* 12 Marks 60.

89 **Übung 2 – Beantworten Sie bitte die folgenden Fragen nach dem Text**
(Please answer the following questions basing your answers on the text)

❶ Where did the young holiday-maker appear visibly shocked?
Wo erschien der junge Urlauber sichtlich schockiert? . . . . Friedrichshafen.

❷ Why was he shocked?
Warum war er schockiert? Weil er in seinem Brot . . . .

❸ Where was the bread made?
Wo ist das Brot hergestellt worden?
Es . . . in . . . . in Hechingen . . . .

89 Neunundachtzigste Lektion

Ein gemütliches Abendessen ①

1 – M**a**hlzeit ②! Ihr habt schon **a**ngefangen?
2 – Na, kl**a**r! Wer n**i**cht k**o**mmt zur **re**chten Z**ei**t, der m**u**ß n**eh**men, was **ü**brigbleibt ③.

Notes

① **gemütlich**, *comfortable*, *cosy*, *pleasant*, e.g.: Sitting at the fireside is **gemütlich**. It is said that **gemütlich** is a very German state of mind; it describes a cosy atmosphere or a friendly, very sociable person.

② **Mahlzeit** (f.), *meal*. Before we start eating we wish each other **Guten Appetit** or **Mahlzeit** the short form of **gesegnete** ▶

❹ How old is the American?
Wie alt ist die Amerikanerin? Sie . . . 23 . . . .

❺ Why was she in Las Vegas?
Warum war sie in Las Vegas? Sie . . . auf ihrer . . . .

Answers to exercise 2
❶ – Auf dem Polizeirevier in – ❷ – einen Finger gefunden hatte ❸ – ist – einer Großbäckerei – hergestellt worden ❹ – ist – Jahre alt ❺ – war – Hochzeitsreise

Second Wave: 39th Lesson

89th Lesson 89

A Pleasant Dinner *(n.)*

1 – Have a nice meal! You have already started [eating]?
2 – Of course! He who does not come on time must eat the remainders.

▸ **Mahlzeit** (**gesegnet**, *blessed*), which means: *Have a nice meal, enjoy your meal.*

③ **übrig**, *remaining, left over*; **übrigbleiben**, *to remain.* **Ist noch was von dem Schinken übrig?**, *Is there some ham left?*

89

3 – Mensch, sei still! Es ist ja schl**ie**ßlich nicht m**ei**ne Schuld, wenn ich 'nen Pl**a**tten h**a**be ④.

4 Typisch! Du hast nat**ü**rlich den g**a**nzen Sch**i**nken schon **au**fgegessen ⑤!

5 – Kommt, hört auf, euch zu str**ei**ten! Es ist noch w**e**lcher in der K**ü**che.

6 – Oh, das ist gem**ei**n! Du hast mir ges**a**gt, das w**ä**re die l**e**tzte Sch**ei**be.

7 – Die l**e**tzte für dich! Das ist **e**twas **a**nderes. Du hast d**ei**nen Teil geh**a**bt.

8 – Du legst ⑥ für ihn **i**mmer die b**e**sten St**ü**cke zur**ü**ck ⑥!

9 Erst kommt er zu spät und dann wird er auch noch verw**ö**hnt.

10 – Tue nicht so ⑦, als ob du verh**u**ngern ⑧ w**ü**rdest!

11 Wenn ich r**i**chtig gez**ä**hlt h**a**be, hast du m**i**ndestens drei Sch**i**nkenbrote, **ei**nen R**o**llmops und zwei s**au**re ⑨ G**u**rken geg**e**ssen.

12 – Mach doch mal ⑩ das F**e**rnsehen an! Es ist fünf vor acht.

13 Die T**a**gesschau ⑪ beg**i**nnt gleich! □

Notes

④ **einen Platten haben**, *to have a flat tyre.* **Der Reifen**, *the tyre.*

⑤ **aufessen**, *to eat up, to finish.* **Iß dein Butterbrot**, *Eat your bread and butter.* But, **Iß dein Butterbrot auf**, *Finish your bread and butter.*

⑥ **zurücklegen**, *to put aside, to hold in reserve.* ▸

3 – Oh, be quiet! It isn't my fault if I have a flat tyre, is it?
4 That's typically you! Of course you have already finished the ham *(m.)*!
5 – Come on, stop quarrelling! There is still some left in the kitchen.
6 – Oh, that isn't nice of you! You told me that it was the last slice *(f.)*.
7 – The last one for you! That is different *(something else)*. You have had your share *(m.)*.
8 – You always put aside the best parts for him!
9 He not only *(first)* comes late but what is more *(and then)* he is *(even)* spoilt.
10 – Don't pretend to be starving! *(Don't do as if)*
11 If I counted right you ate at least three ham sandwiches, one pickled herring and two pickled cucumbers.
12 – [Won't] you turn the TV on, [please]! It is five to eight.
13 The news is about to start. □

▸ ⑦ **so tun als ob**, *to pretend (to do as if)*. The conjunction **als ob** requires the **Konjunktiv** because it introduces a supposition: **Er tut so, als ob er uns nicht kennen würde**, *He pretends not to know us*. (See lesson 91, paragraph 2).

⑧ **verhungern**, *to starve (to death)*; **hungern**, *to suffer hunger, to fast*. Pay attention to the prefixes: they often change the sense of a word.

⑨ **sauer**, *sour, acid*; the opposite is **süß**, *sweet*.

⑩ Notice that: **Mach doch mal...** is a suggestion rather than an imperative; this is reinforced by **mal**.

⑪ **die Tagesschau** is the *news* on the first channel, otherwise we say die **Nachrichten**, *the news*. In Germany we have three main channels and some lesser ones varying from one region to another.

89 **Übung 1 – Übersetzen Sie bitte**

❶ Das Restaurant, das wir gestern in der Altstadt entdeckt haben, ist sehr gemütlich und gar nicht teuer. ❷ Haben Sie noch was von dem guten Braten übrig? ❸ Ja, ich habe Ihnen etwas davon zurückgelegt. ❹ Sie tut so, als ob sie davon nichts wüßte. ❺ Machen Sie doch bitte mal das Licht aus! Vielleicht bleiben dann die Mücken draußen. ❻ Erst sagt er, er hätte keinen Hunger, und dann ißt er den ganzen Kuchen auf.

Übung 2 – Ergänzen Sie bitte

❶ They pretend to have no money.
. . . . sie kein Geld hätten.

❷ If we are not mistaken *(saw well)*, he smoked at least two packets of cigarettes.
. . . . wir richtig . . . . , hat er . . . . zwei Päckchen Zigaretten geraucht.

❸ My sister's child is very spoilt.
Das Kind . . . . ist sehr . . . .

❹ A lot of children don't eat up their spinach.
Viele Kinder . . . . . ihren Spinat nicht . . . .

❺ Don't give anything to the man! He has had his share.
. . . . dem Mann nichts . . . . ! Er hat . . . . gehabt.

❻ Oh, now I understand! That is completely different.
Ah, jetzt . . . . ! Das ist etwas ganz . . . . !

Answers to exercise 1

❶ The restaurant we discovered yesterday in the old part of the town is very pleasant and calm, and not expensive at all. ❷ Is there some roast meat left? ❸ Yes, I put some of it aside. ❹ She pretends not to know anything about it. ❺ [Won't] you turn the light off! Maybe the flies will stay out then. ❻ First he said that he wasn't hungry and then he ate up all the cake.

Answers to exercise 2

❶ Sie tun so, als ob – ❷ Wenn – gesehen haben – mindestens – ❸ – meiner Schwester – verwöhnt ❹ – essen – auf ❺ Geben Sie – mehr – seinen Teil – ❻ – verstehe ich – anderes

EIN GEMÜTLICHES ABENDESSEN

Second Wave: 40th Lesson

90 Neunzigste Lektion

Der Krimi am Freitagabend

1 – Also das hätte ich nun ja wirklich nicht vermutet!
2 Ich habe die ganze Zeit die alte Hausangestellte ① verdächtigt.
3 – Nein, die konnte es nicht gewesen sein, weil sie keinen Schlüssel hatte.
4 – Den hätte sie sich doch besorgen können ②! Nichts leichter als das!
5 – Ja, aber sie hat's nun mal nicht getan, und außerdem hatte sie kein Motiv.
6 – Doch, klar! Dasselbe wie alle anderen: das Geld!
7 – Das hätte sie doch nicht gekriegt. Da hätte sie sich etwas anderes einfallen ③ lassen müssen.
8 – Na ja, das ist jetzt ja auch egal. Wir kennen ja den wahren Schuldigen ④.

Notes

① **der Angestellte**, *the employee*; but **ein Angestellter**, *an employee*, ends in **-r** as if it were an adjective, because it is a **weak noun** (see lesson 83 note 7 and the declension of weak nouns in the grammatical appendix).

② Do you remember the "double infinitive"? **Er hätte sich den Schlüssel besorgen können**, *He could have got the key* (see lesson 56 paragraph 2). **Besorgen**, *to procure*, *to look after*; **Besorgungen machen**, *to go shopping*. ▸

Friday Night's Thriller *(on Friday evening)*

1 – I'd never have thought of that!
2 I have suspected the house-maid all along *(the whole time)*.
3 – No, she couldn't have done *(been)* it, because she didn't have a key.
4 – But she could have got it! Nothing easier than that!
5 – Yes, but she didn't do it, she doesn't have any motive *(n.)*.
6 – Of course she has! The same as everybody else: money!
7 – She wouldn't have got it. She should have thought of something else.
8 – Well, it doesn't matter now. We know the true culprit.

▸ ③ **der Einfall**, *the idea.* **Es fällt mir etwas ein**, *Something comes to my mind.* **Ich lasse mir etwas einfallen**, *I'll think of something (find a solution).*

④ **schuldig**, *guilty*; **unschuldig**, *innocent, not guilty.*

9 – Ich bin noch, ganz zittrig ⑤! Ich dachte, ich würde einen Herzschlag kriegen, als die Hand plötzlich hinter dem Vorhang hervorkam…!
10 – Ja, mir ging's auch so! Sieh doch mal nach, was im ersten ⑥ Programm kommt.
11 Ich brauche noch etwas zum Entspannen, bevor ich ins Bett gehe. □

Notes

⑤ **zittern**, *to tremble*; **zitterig** or **zittrig**: *trembly, shaky.*

⑥ We say: **Was kommt im ersten/zweiten/dritten Programm?** or simply: **Was kommt im ersten/zweiten/dritten**, *What's on the first/second/third channel?*

***

Übung 1 – Übersetzen Sie bitte

❶ Der wahre Schuldige ist also der Chauffeur. Hättest du das vermutet? ❷ Ja, ich habe ihn von Anfang an verdächtigt. ❸ Du brauchst eine neue Sekretärin? Nichts leichter als das! Die kann ich dir besorgen. Meine Freundin sucht gerade eine Stelle. ❹ Sie dürfen ihn nicht so erschrecken. Er hätte einen Herzschlag bekommen können! ❺ Als die Sonne hinter den Wolken vorkam, wurde es sehr warm.

9 – I am still trembling all over! I thought I'd suffer a heart attack when the hand suddenly emerged [from] behind the curtain. 90
10 – Yes, I felt the same way! Won't you go and see what's on the first channel?
11 I need something to relax before going to bed. □

DER KRIMI AM FREITAGABEND

***

Answers to exercise 1

❶ The driver is the true culprit. Would you have thought that? ❷ Yes, I suspected him from the beginning. ❸ You need a new secretary? Nothing easier than that! I can get you one. My girlfriend is looking for a job. ❹ You mustn't frighten him so. He could have had *(suffered)* a heart attack! ❺ When the sun rose [from] behind the clouds, it became very warm.

Übung 2 – Ergänzen Sie bitte

❶ He was suspected although he had no motive.
Man . . . ihn . . . . obwohl er . . . . hatte.

❷ On Thursday night they're showing "The Blue Angel" on the second channel.
Am . . . . kommt . . . . „Der blaue Engel".

❸ I have already told you I didn't do it.
Ich . . . . schon, ich . . . . es nicht . . . . . .

❹ My father is an employee of an electrical company.
Mein Vater ist . . . . einer Elektrofirma.

91 Einundneunzigste Lektion

Wiederholung und Erklärungen

1 *Das Passiv*

1.1 *Werden* and Past Participle

The passive voice expresses an action in progress. It is formed with **werden** + the past participle of the verb:
Ich werde vom Arzt untersucht, *I am (being) examined by the doctor.*
Von + dat. introduces the doer of the action (person or animal): **vom/von dem Arzt**.

Das Kind wird von dem Hund gebissen, *The child is bitten by the dog.*
Die Pakete werden von dem Briefträger gebracht, *The parcels are brought by the postman.*
Sie wird durch das Schreien ihres Kindes geweckt, *The crying of her baby wakes her up (she is woken up by the...).*

⑤ He needs another drink *(something else to drink)* before going to bed.

. . . . noch etwas . . . . , ... er . . . . geht.

⑥ What can we do? Can't you think of anything?

Was . . . . . . wir denn . . . ? . . . . . dir nichts . . . ?

Answers to exercise 2

❶ – hat – verdächtigt – kein Motiv – ❷ – Donnerstagabend – im zweiten Programm – ❸ – sagte Ihnen – habe – getan ❹ – Angestellter – ❺ Er braucht – zum Trinken – bevor – ins Bett – ❻ – können – tun – Fällt – ein

Second Wave: 41st Lesson

91st lesson 91

Durch + acc. is used when the doer is a thing; nowadays we say **von** in spoken language, even in the case of things.

Das Haus wird verkauft, *The house is (being) sold.*
Hier wird nicht geraucht, *No smoking here.*

In the grammatical appendix you will find the complete conjugations for the different tenses.

Imperfekt:
Ich wurde von einer Mücke gestochen, *I was bitten by a gnat.*
Es wurde viel darüber gesprochen, *It was much talked about.*

Perfekt and **Plusquamperfekt**:
Er ist gestern entlassen worden, *He was dismissed yesterday.*
Er war schon lange erwartet worden, *He had been expected for a long time.*

91 Please note that the participle **worden** is put at the end of the sentence and that it bears no prefix.

Future:
Er wird erwartet werden, *He will be expected.*

1.2 *Sein* and Past Participle

Pay attention to the following sentences. They express a state and not an action. They are formed with **sein** + past participle (as in English).
Das Haus ist verkauft, *The house is sold.*
Der Arm ist gebrochen, *The arm is broken.*
Die Kirche war zerstört, aber sie ist wieder aufgebaut worden, *The church was destroyed but it has been rebuilt.*
Das Haus ist verkauft, *The house is sold.*

2 The Conjunction *als ob*

The conjunction **als ob**, *as if*, requires the **Konjunktiv**:

Er tut so, als ob er der König von Frankreich wäre, *He acts as if he was king of France.*
Sie fährt, als ob es um Leben und Tod ginge, *She is driving as if it was a matter of life and death.*
Du ißt, als ob du den ganzen Tag nichts gegessen hättest, *You are eating as if you hadn't eaten anything today.*
When we leave out **ob**, the meaning is still the same, but the position of verb and subject has to be inverted:
Du ißt, als hättest du den ganzen Tag nichts gegessen, *You are eating as if you hadn't eaten anything today.*

3 The Conjunctions *solange* and *während*

The conjunctions **solange**, *as long as*, and **während**, *while*:

Macht keinen Unsinn, solange ich nicht hier bin, *Don't do anything foolish as long as I am away.*
Während ich weg war, tanzten die Mäuse auf den Tischen, *While I was away the mice danced on the tables.*

Während + genitive is also used as a preposition meaning *during.*

Während der Tagesschau darf er nicht gestört werden, *He mustn't be disturbed during the news.*

4 *Erst*

Do you remember the different meanings of **erst**?

4.1 *erst (zuerst)*: (at) first

Zuerst nahm er ein Aspirin und dann, als das Kopfweh immer noch nicht besser wurde, nahm er ein zweites, *First he took one aspirin and then, when his headache did not get better, he took another (second) one.*

4.2 *erst*: only

Erst, *only* refers to **time**:
Er hat erst ein Bier getrunken, *He has only had (drunk) one beer (up to now).*
Compare this with the word **nur**, which refers to quantity:
Er hat nur ein Bier getrunken, *He has only had one beer (that's all).*

4.3 *erst (-er, -e, -es)*: first (adjective)

Der erste Tag des Monat ist diesmal ein Donnerstag, *This time the first [day] of the month is a Thursday.*
Mein erstes Auto war ein Volkswagen, *My first car was a Volkswagen.*

4.4 Some Expressions With *erst*

Jetzt erst recht, *Now more than ever.*
Jetzt erst recht nicht, *Now less than ever.*
Ich mag keine Schnecken, und erst recht keine Froschschenkel, *I don't like snails and even less frogs' legs.*
Wie ich ihn liebe! Und dich erst! *How I love him! And you even more!*
But:
Sie hat den ersten besten (or **erstbesten) Mann geheiratet**, *She married the first man who came along.*

92 Zweiundneunzigste Lektion

Stille Wasser sind tief

1 – Haben Sie vielleicht Herrn Polsky gesehen, Frau Meier?
2 Die Milch steht seit heute morgen vor seiner Tür, und er hat mir nicht gesagt, daß er wegfahren würde ①.
3 – Ja, haben Sie denn nicht gehört, was passiert ist?
4 Er wurde in aller Frühe von der Polizei abgeholt ②!
5 – Von der Polizei? Herr Polsky? Das kann ich nicht glauben! Er war doch immer so nett und höflich.
6 – Ja, ja, so kann man sich täuschen. Stille Wasser sind tief.
7 – Jetzt erzählen Sie mal keine Märchen, Frau Meier!
8 Woher wissen Sie denn, daß er von der Polizei abgeholt wurde?
9 – Ich habe es mit eigenen Augen gesehen. Sie können mir glauben.
10 Wissen Sie, ich bin heute nacht durch laute Stimmen auf dem Flur geweckt ③ worden.

Notes

① The **Konjunktiv Form würde** is used because the sentence is in the indirect speech style. (See lesson 98, paragraph 1).

92nd Lesson 92

Still Waters Run Deep

1 – Maybe you've seen Mr Polsky, Mrs Meier?
2 The milk has been standing in front of his house since this morning, and he didn't tell me that he had left *(would leave)*.
3 – Why, didn't you hear what happened?
4 The police came early this morning to get him *(He was got by)*.
5 – The police *(by the police)*? Mr Polsky? I cannot believe it! He always was so kind and polite.
6 – Yes, yes, we were mistaken *(one can be mistaken)*. Still waters run *(are)* deep.
7 – You are telling stories, Mrs Meier *(don't tell fairytales)*[aren't you]!
8 How [where] do you know that the police came to get him?
9 – I saw it with my own eyes. You can believe me.
10 You know, last night *(I was woken up by loud voices)* loud voices in the corridor woke me up.

② **abholen**, *to fetch, get a person who is waiting.* **Holen**, *go and get* (see lesson 43, note 5). **Ich habe meinen Mann vom Büro abgeholt**, *I went to meet my husband at the office.* In the passive voice: **Mein Mann ist von mir vom Büro abgeholt worden**.

③ **jemanden wecken**, *to wake someone up.* **Wecken Sie mich bitte um halb acht**, *Please wake me at half past seven.* But: **aufwachen**, *to wake up*; **Ich bin um 6 aufgewacht**, *I woke up at 6 o'clock.*

11 Vor der Tür von Herrn P**o**lsky st**a**nden zwei Polize**i**beamte in **U**niform und kl**i**ngelten und kl**o**pften **o**hne **au**fzuhören ④.

12 Und er hat sich nat**ü**rlich l**a**nge nicht gem**e**ldet ⑤, **a**ber ich w**u**ßte, daß er da war, denn ich h**a**tte am **A**bend v**o**rher M**u**sik und St**i**mmen geh**ö**rt.

13 Schl**ie**ßlich h**a**ben sie gedr**oh**t ⑥, die Tür **au**fzubrechen ⑦, falls er sie nicht **ö**ffnen w**ü**rde…

14 Na, und da ist er **e**ndlich ⑧ **rau**sgekommen, und sie h**a**ben ihn m**i**tgenommen. □

Notes

④ **aufhören**, *to stop*. **Ohne**, *without*. If **ohne** is used as a conjunction, it is followed by **zu**: **Sie verließen das Restaurant ohne zu bezahlen**, *They left the restaurant without paying.* **Es regnete 2 Tage lang ohne aufzuhören**, *It has been raining continuously for 2 days.* **Ohne aufzuhören**, *continuously, incessantly.*

⑤ See lesson 71 note 5; **sich melden**, *to show oneself, to register*; **etwas melden**, *to announce something, to report.* **Er hat seine Ankunft gemeldet**, *He announced his arrival.* **Anmelden**, *to enrol, to register*: **Er hat sein Kind in der Schule angemeldet**, *He registered his child for school.*

⑥ **drohen**, *to threaten*: **Die Polizei droht dem Autofahrer mit einer Geldstrafe**, *The police threatened the driver with a fine.* **Er droht seinen Eltern, nie mehr wiederzukommen**, *He threatened his parents not to come back any more.*

⑦ **aufbrechen**, *to break down, force open down.* **Brechen**, *to break.* ▸

11 Two policemen in uniform *(f.)* stood in front of Mr. Polsky's door ringing and knocking incessantly. **92**
12 And of course, he didn't show himself for quite a while, but I knew that he was there, for I had heard music and voices the night before.
13 Finally they threatened to break down the door if he didn't open it...
14 Well, and then he came out after all and they took him with [them]. □

▸ ⑧ The difference between **endlich** and **schließlich**: **Endlich** is used when we wait for something to happen. **Endlich bist du da!**, *Here you are after all!* **Schließlich**: on the other hand indicates the end of an action. **Schließlich ist er gegangen, ohne etwas zu sagen**, *Finally, he left without saying anything.*

Übung 1 – Übersetzen Sie bitte

❶ Wissen Sie vielleicht, wo die Müllers sind? Die Zeitung liegt schon seit zwei Tagen in ihrem Briefkasten, und sie haben mir nicht gesagt, daß sie wegfahren würden. ❷ Oh, das ist aber schade! Er war doch so ein netter und höflicher Mann! ❸ Ich bin heute nacht dreimal durch Schreie auf der Straße geweckt worden. ❹ Sie wußte genau, daß er zu Hause war; aber er hat sich nicht gemeldet. ❺ Sie haben ihn in aller Frühe mitgenommen. Sie hat es mit eigenen Augen gesehen.

Übung 2 – Ergänzen Sie bitte

❶ What is [standing] in front of Mr. Polsky's door?
Was steht vor der Tür von Herrn Polsky? . . . .

❷ Who came to get Mr. Polsky? (*By whom Mr. Polsky...*).
Von wem wurde Herr Polsky abgeholt? . . . .

❸ When did they come to get Mr. Polsky?
Wann wurde Herr Polsky abgeholt? . . . .

❹ Why did Mrs Meier wake up during the night (*by what was Mrs Meier...*).
Wodurch wurde Frau Meier in der Nacht geweckt? . . . .

Answers to exercise 1

❶ Maybe you know where the Müllers are? The newspaper has been *(lying)* in their letterbox for two days already and they didn't tell me that they had left. ❷ Oh, what a pity! He was such a nice [and] polite man. ❸ Last night I was woken up three times by shouts coming from the street. ❹ She was well aware that he was at home but he didn't turn up. ❺ They took him with [them] early in the morning. She saw it with her own eyes.

❺ What did the policemen threaten to do?
Womit drohten die Polizeibeamten? (... ....) ... ...

❻ How *(why)* did Mrs. Meier know that Mr. Polsky was at home?
Warum wußte Frau Meier, daß Herr Polsky zu Hause war? ... ...

Answers to exercise 2

❶ – Die Milch ❷ – Von der Polizei ❸ – In aller Frühe ❹ – Durch laute Stimmen ❺ – (Sie drohten,) die Tür aufzubrechen ❻ – Sie hat Musik und Stimmen gehört

Second Wave: 43rd Lesson

93 Dreiundneunzigste Lektion

„Aktenzeichen XY ungelöst" ①

1 – Sch**ö**nen g**u**ten **A**bend, Frau M**ei**er! Was für **ei**ne ents**e**tzliche H**i**tze, nicht?
2 Na, h**o**ffentlich ist m**ei**ne Milch nicht s**au**er!
3 – Sie, Herr Polsky? Ich d**a**chte ②, Sie w**ä**ren…
4 – Im Gef**ä**ngnis für **i**mmer? Nein, ganz so weit ist es gl**ü**cklicherweise noch nicht ③!
5 – Da bin ich **a**ber froh! Ich h**a**be mir ja gleich ges**a**gt: Das muß ein **I**rrtum ④ sein!
6 **A**ber s**a**gen Sie mal, war**u**m sind Sie **ei**gentlich verh**a**ftet w**o**rden?
7 – Tja, st**e**llen Sie sich vor, **i**rgend j**e**mand muß mich mit **i**rgend j**e**mandem ⑤ verw**e**chselt h**a**ben.
8 Man hat mich für **ei**nen der in „**A**ktenzeichen XY" ges**u**chten Verbr**e**cher geh**a**lten ⑥.
9 Und ich muß z**u**geben, die **Ä**hnlichkeit ⑦ war frapp**ie**rend.

Notes

① **Aktenzeichen XY ungelöst** is a TV programme where unsolved crimes are reconstructed. The actors are chosen to resemble the criminals, thus the police appeal to the public for any information about the persons wanted.

② **denken**, *to think*, *to believe*. Its **Imperfekt** and past participle are irregular: **dachte**, **gedacht**. **Bringen**, *to bring* → **brachte**, **gebracht**.

③ **So weit sind wir noch nicht**, *It has not gone so far yet.* You already know the expression: **Wie weit bist du?**, *How far have you got?* ▶

"Reference *(n.)* XY Unsolved"

1 – *(Nice)* good evening, Mrs. Meier! What [an] awful heat *(f.)*, isn't it?
2 I hope my milk is not sour!
3 – You, Mr Polsky? I thought you were…
4 – In prison *(n.)* for ever? No, fortunately it has not gone so far yet!
5 – I am really glad then! I told myself at once: it must be a mistake *(m.)*!
6 But tell me, why were you actually arrested?
7 – Well, imagine, somebody must have mistaken me for someone else.
8 I was taken for a criminal who was looked for in "Reference XY".
9 And, I must admit, the resemblance *(f.)* was striking.

▸ ④ **der Irrtum**, *the error, mistake.* **Sich irren, sich täuschen**, *to be mistaken.*

⑤ **jemand**, *someone*; **irgend jemand**, *anybody.* **Irgend** translates *any,* **irgend etwas**, *anything*; **irgendeiner/eine/eines**, *any.* **Besteht irgendeine Hoffnung?**, *Is there any hope?*

⑥ **halten für** + acc., *to take for.* **Er hält sich für den intelligentesten Menschen auf der Welt**, *He takes himself for the most intelligent man in the world.* **Für wen hält er sich eigentlich?**, *What does he actually take himself for?*

⑦ **ähnlich**, *similar, alike.* Adjectives ending in **-lich** form their nouns by adding **-keit**: **ähnlich → Ähnlichkeit**; **freundlich → Freundlichkeit**, *friendliness*; **persönlich → Persönlichkeit**, *personality.* Remember that nouns ending in **-heit**, **-keit**, **-ung** are feminine.

93 **10** – Ja, nicht wahr? Das fand ich auch!

11 Zunächst wollte ich ja meinen Augen nicht trauen, aber dann habe ich meine Schwester angerufen, und sie hat mir auch gesagt, daß das sicherlich Sie wären, (N.1)

12 und ihr Mann und meiner und die Frau aus dem ersten Stock waren auch ganz sicher, verstehen Sie…

13 – Ja, ja, Frau Meier, ich verstehe schon, aber seien Sie ⑧ das nächste Mal vorsichtiger, denn so können Sie große Wellen in stillen Wassern schlagen. □

Note

⑧ Do you remember the imperative of **sein? Sei vorsichtig**! *Be cautious!*; **Seid vorsichtig**! *Be cautious!* (used when you are talking to more than one person, and **Seien Sie vorsichtig**! *Be cautious!* (formal address).

***

Übung 1 – Übersetzen Sie bitte

❶ Sie dachte, er wäre für immer weggegangen. ❷ Die Polizei hat Herrn Müller verhaftet? Das ist sicher ein Irrtum gewesen! ❸ Meine Schwester sieht mir sehr ähnlich. Man verwechselt mich oft mit ihr. ❹ Er mußte zugeben, daß er sich geirrt hatte. ❺ Sie dachten, ich wäre im Krankenhaus? Nein, so weit ist es glücklicherweise noch nicht! ❻ Diese Nachricht hat große Wellen geschlagen.

10 – Yes, wasn't it? That's what I found, too.
11 First I did not want to believe my eyes, but then I phoned my sister and she also told me that it was certainly you;
12 and her husband and mine and the woman upstairs were completely sure about it too, you understand…
13 – Yes, yes Mrs Meier, I understand, but be more cautious next time, for [acting] like that you can raise big waves in still waters! □

***

Answers to exercise 1

❶ She thought he had left for ever. ❷ The police arrested Mr. Müller? It is certainly a mistake! ❸ My sister looks very much like me. I am often taken for her. ❹ He had to admit that he was wrong. ❺ You thought I was in hospital? No, fortunately it hasn't gone so far yet! ❻ This news created a stir *(raised big waves)*.

Übung 2 – Ergänzen Sie bitte

1. What awful weather isn't it?
   . . .   .   entsetzliches Wetter, ... ?
2. He thought that I wasn't at home *(yet)*.
   . . . . noch nicht zu Hause.
3. Why was he actually arrested?
   Warum . . . er . . . . verhaftet . . . . . . ?
4. He was taken for a wanted criminal.
   Man . . . ihn . . . einen gesuchten Verbrecher . . . .

94 Vierundneunzigste Lektion

Hatschi ①!

1 – Gesundheit! Sind Sie erkältet ②?
2 – Na, hören Sie mal! Das würde mir ja gerade noch fehlen ③! Hatschi!
3 – Na also, da niesen Sie ja schon wieder!

Pronunciation Key
***3** ... neezen ...*

Notes

① Onomatopoeia differs from one language to another. Sneezing is expressed by **hatschi** in German, and the cock's crow by **kikeriki**. If we hurt ourselves we cry **au** *[ow]* or **auweh** or **aua**. ▸

❺ The resemblance between you and your brother is striking.
. . . . zwischen Ihnen und Ihrem Bruder ist . . . .

❻ He told me that you didn't have the time.
. . . . daß Sie keine Zeit . . . .

Answers to exercise 2

❶ Was für ein – nicht wahr ❷ Er dachte, ich wäre – ❸ – ist – eigentlich – worden ❹ – hat – für – gehalten ❺ Die Ähnlichkeit – frappierend ❻ Er hat mir gesagt – hätten

Second Wave: 44th Lesson

94th Lesson 94

Atishoo!

1 – Bless you *(health)*! Have you got a cold?
2 – Oh, *(listen)* think of that! That's all I wanted! Atishoo!
3 – There you are, you are sneezing again!

② **erkälten**, *to catch a cold/chill*; **eine Erkältung**, *a cold*. Some nouns are formed by adding **-ung** to the root of the verb: **Verzeihen**, *to pardon* → **die Verzeihung**, **wohnen**, *to live* → **die Wohnung**...

③ Remember the following expression: **(na), hören Sie mal**, *That's enough/Think of that*; **Das fehlt ja noch**, **That's all I wanted! Fehlen**, *to lack*, *be wanting*.

4 Sehen Sie, das ist sicherlich der Anfang einer Erkältung!

5 – Ich versichere Ihnen, ich bin noch nie krank gewesen und ich habe auch nicht die Absicht ④, es zu werden.

6 – Na, dann haben Sie eben einen Heuschnupfen ⑤.

7 – Einen Heuschnupfen? Ich? Das ist ja die Höhe! Jetzt soll ⑥ ich auch noch allergisch sein!

8 – Aber da ist doch nichts Schlimmes dran ⑦! Das passiert vielen Leuten.

9 – Was gehen mich die Leute an? Kümmern Sie sich um Ihre eigenen Angelegenheiten! (N.2) Hatschi!

10 – Gesundheit! Und ich bin sicher, daß es ein Heuschnupfen ist.

11 – Hören Sie, könnten Sie mich nicht endlich in Ruhe lassen?

12 – Aber natürlich! Wenn Sie es vorziehen, allein zu sein...

13 Ja, ja, so ist es immer: Je ⑧ netter man zu den Leuten ist, desto ⑧ unfreundlicher werden sie! □

***6** ... hoy'shnoopfen **7** ... allergish ...*

Notes

④ **die Absicht haben**..., *to plan, to intend, to mean to...*

⑤ **der Schnupfen**, *the cold (illness)*, **das Heu**, *the hay*. **Eben** here means: *Well, in that case...* **Die Busfahrer streiken? Dann gehe ich eben zu Fuß**, *The bus drivers are on strike? Well, I'll (in that case) go on foot then.* ▸

4 You see, it is certainly the beginning of a cold *(f.)!*
5 – I assure you I have never been ill and I don't mean to fall ill *(it)*.
6 – In that case you have got hay fever *(m.)*.
7 – Hay fever? Me? That's the limit! Now, you are even saying that I am allergic *(I am said to be)*!
8 – But there's nothing bad about it! It happens to a lot of people.
9 – What do I care for people? *(do people concern me?)* Mind your own business! Atishoo!
10 – Bless you! And I am sure it is hay fever!
11 – Listen, couldn't you leave me alone *(quiet)* after all?
12 – Certainly! If you prefer being alone...
13 Yes, it's always like that: the kinder you are with people the more unfriendly they get! □

⑥ **sollen** here is used in an idiomatic expression: **Er soll Millionär sein**, *He is said to be/They say he is a millionaire.*

⑦ **Daran** (adverb) - (**dran** in spoken language) stands for a part of the sentence introduced by **an**, In the above text: **Was ist Schlimmes an dieser Sache? → Was ist da Schlimmes dran?**, *What is bad about it?*

⑧ **Je... desto**, *the more... the more*. Please note that **je** and **desto** are followed by a comparative: **Je mehr ich verdiene, desto mehr gebe ich aus**, *The more I earn, the more I spend.*

94 **Übung 1 – Übersetzen Sie bitte**

❶ Hermann niest schon den ganzen Tag. Ich glaube, er hat sich gestern beim Schwimmen erkältet. ❷ Ihr Mann soll einen neuen Direktor bekommen. Stimmt das? ❸ Was? Das würde ihm ja gerade noch fehlen! ❹ In diesem Fall zieht er es sicher vor, die Arbeit zu wechseln. ❺ Je länger wir warten, desto kälter wird das Essen. ❻ Ich habe die Absicht, um acht Uhr dorthin zu gehen. Glaubst du, daß das möglich ist? – Natürlich! Je früher desto besser!

Übung 2 – Ergänzen Sie bitte

❶ Could you leave him alone please? He is ill.
. . . . du ihn bitte . . . . . . lassen? Er ist . . . . . .

❷ That is none of my business. Take care of it yourself!
. . . . geht mich nichts an. . . . . selbst darum!

❸ I assure you I didn't mean to annoy you.
Ich . . . ., daß ich nicht . . . . hatte, Sie zu ärgern.

❹ The more people talk the less they think.
. . . . . . die Leute sprechen . . . . . weniger denken sie nach.

Answers to exercise 1

❶ Hermann has been sneezing all day long. I think he caught a cold yesterday when [he was] swimming. ❷ It is said that your husband will have a new boss. Is that right? ❸ What? That's all he wanted! ❹ In this case he will certainly prefer to change his job. ❺ The longer we wait, the colder the meal will get. ❻ I intend to go there at eight o'clock. Do you think that this is possible? – Certainly! The earlier [you go] the better [it'll be].

❺ He has never been seriously ill, but he has had hay fever for years.
Er . . . nie ernsthaft krank . . . . , aber er hat seit Jahren . . . .

❻ The later the evening the kinder the guests!
. . . . der Abend, ... die Gäste!

Answers to exercise 2

❶ Könntest – in Ruhe – krank ❷ Diese Angelegenheit – Kümmere dich – ❸ – versichere Ihnen – die Absicht – ❹ Je mehr – desto – ❺ – ist – gewesen – einen Heuschnupfen ❻ Je später – desto netter –

Second Wave: 45th Lesson

95 Fünfundneunzigste Lektion

Ein Zeitungsbericht - Überfall auf Heidener Tankstelle geklärt

1 Der Überfall auf eine Tankstelle in Heiden, bei dem der Täter 5.200 Mark erbeutet ① hat, ist aufgeklärt.

2 Der Räuber hatte ② – wie berichet – den allein anwesenden Tankstellenpächter mit einem Revolver bedroht

3 und zur Herausgabe der Tageseinnahmen ③ gezwungen.

4 Als ④ Täter konnte jetzt ein 28jähriger Maurer aus Heiden ermittelt

5 und in seiner Wohnung festgenommen werden.

6 Dort wurde auch der größte Teil des geraubten ⑤ Geldes und die Waffe gefunden.

7 Als Tatmotiv gab ⑥ der Täter an ⑥, daß er hoch verschuldet sei,

8 da ⑦ er zum dritten Mal verheiratet sei und

Notes

① **die Beute**, *the loot*; *prey*; **erbeuten**, *to capture, to take.*

② **anwesend**, *present*; **abwesend**, *absent.*

③ **die Einnahme**, *the takings, money taken* (e.g. shop, cinema). **Die Ausgabe**, *the expenditure, the distribution.*

④ **als**, *as*: **Er arbeitet als Verkäufer in einem Kaufhaus**, *He works in a department store as a shop assistant.*

A Newspaper Report *(m.)* - The Hold-Up *(m.)* at the Heiden Petrol Station *(f.)* *(has been)* Solved

1 The hold-up at a petrol station in Heiden where the perpetrator *(m.)* took 5,200 Marks has been solved.
2 The robber *(m.)* had – as [already] reported – threatened the *(alone present)* station attendant *(m.)*, who was alone, with a revolver *(m.)*
3 and forced him to hand over the day's takings.
4 Now a 28-year-old mason has been identified as the perpetrator
5 and has been arrested in his flat.
6 There, most of stolen money *(the largest part)* and the weapon *(f.)* were found, too.
7 The robber said that the motive *(n.)* for this crime was his high level of debt *(the robber gave as a motive that he was highly indebted)*
8 because he was married for the third time and

⑤ **rauben** or **stehlen**, *to rob* or *to steal*; the past participles are **geraubt** and **gestohlen**.

⑥ **angeben**, *to give*, *to state*, introduces the indirect speech; that's why we have the **Konjunktiv I** in the subordinate clause. (See lesson 98, paragraph 1).

⑦ **da** (in the above text) means *as*, *for*, *because*.

95 **9** den gesch**ie**denen ⑧ Fr**au**en für s**ei**ne vier K**i**nder aus den **e**rsten b**ei**den **E**hen h**o**he **U**nterhaltskosten ⑨ z**a**hlen müsse. □

Notes

⑧ **geschieden**, *divorced*; **sich scheiden lassen**, *to divorce*. **Sie haben sich letztes Jahr scheiden lassen**, *They divorced last year.*

⑨ **die Kosten**, *the costs, expenses*; **der Unterhalt**, *the maintenance, subsistance*. **Die Unterhaltung**, *the conversation, talk*. The verb **unterhalten** covers the two meanings: **Ich unterhalte mich gern mit dir**, *I like talking to you*. But, **Mein Mann unterhält mich zur Zeit, denn ich bin arbeitslos**, *My husband is supporting me at the moment because I am out of work.*

***

Übung 1 – Übersetzen Sie bitte

❶ Der Überfall auf die Sparkasse in Hannover konnte von der Polizei niemals aufgeklärt werden. ❷ Alle anwesenden Teilnehmer werden gebeten, ihre vollständige Adresse anzugeben. ❸ Er hat mir erzählt, daß er zum vierten Mal verheiratet sei und daß er sich wieder scheiden lassen wolle. ❹ Der größte Teil der geraubten Diamanten konnte unter dem Bett des Verbrechers gefunden werden. ❺ Sie hat zwei Jungen aus erster Ehe und ein kleines Mädchen aus der zweiten.

9 because he has to pay a lot of alimony to his divorced wives for the *(his)* four children by his first two marriages. ☐ 95

DER ÜBERFALL AUF DIE SPARKASSE IN HANNOVER KONNTE VON DER POLIZEI NIEMALS AUFGEKLÄRT WERDEN

***

Answers to exercise 1

❶ The hold-up at the savings bank in Hannover has never been solved by the police [the police have never been able to solve the hold-up...]. ❷ *(All)* the participants [here] present are asked to give their full address. ❸ He told me that he was married for the fourth time and that he wanted to divorce again. ❹ Most of the stolen diamonds *(the greatest part of)* have been found under the bed of the robber. ❺ She has two boys by her first marriage and a little girl by her second.

Übung 2 – Ergänzen Sie bitte

❶ The hold-up on the Deutsche Bank in F. has been solved.
... . die Deutsche Bank in F. ist ....

❷ In the hold-up the robbers took €200,000.
.... hatten die Täter

200.000 Euro ....

❸ They forced the cashier to put money into a suitcase.
.... den Kassierer .... in einen ...... zu packen.

❹ Meanwhile, they threatened the other bank employees with a gun.
Währenddessen ..... sie die anderen Bankangestellten .... Revolver ....

96 Sechsundneunzigste Lektion

Andere Länder, andere Sitten ①

1 – Reich mir doch bitte die Wurst, Liebling!
2 – Die Wurst? Igitt! Seit wann ißt du denn Wurst zum Frühstück?
3 – Ich habe beschlossen, da ② wir nun einmal in Deutschland sind, auch wie die Deutschen zu leben.

Notes

① **die Sitte**, *the habit*, *custom*, *manner*; **die Sitten**, *the habits*. ▸

❺ The police declared that one of the perpetrators was German; the other two, however, [were] foreigners.
Die Polizei . . . ., daß der eine Täter ein . . . . die beiden anderen aber Ausländer.

❻ As for the German, he is 35-year-old Bernd K.
Bei dem . . . . handele es sich . . . . . 35 . . . . Bernd K.

Answers to exercise 2

❶ Der Überfall auf – aufgeklärt ❷ Bei dem Überfall – erbeutet ❸ Sie haben – gezwungen, das Geld – Koffer – ❹ – haben – mit einem – bedroht ❺ – hat angegeben – Deutscher sei – ❻ – Deutschen – um den – jährigen –

Second Wave: 46th Lesson

96th Lesson 96

Other Countries, Other Habits

1 – Pass me the sausage please, darling!
2 – The sausage? Ugh! Since when have you been eating sausage for breakfast?
3 – As we are in Germany I have decided to live like the Germans.

▸ ② **da**, **weil**, *as*, *for*. **Da es nun einmal so ist**, *Since things are as they are...*

4 Das ist die beste Art, Land und Leute gründlich kennenzulernen ③.

5 – Na, meinetwegen ④! Mir soll es recht sein, solange du nicht von mir verlangst, das gleiche zu tun.

6 – Übrigens schmeckt das gar nicht so schlecht! Ich glaube, ich könnte mich daran gewöhnen. (N.2)

7 – Das wundert mich nicht. Du warst schon immer ein großer Fleischfresser ⑤.

8 Aber halte doch bitte dein Wurstbrot ⑥ nicht direkt unter meine Nase!

9 – Jetzt übertreibe mal nicht! So schlecht riecht ⑦ das auch nicht!

10 Nebenbei bemerkt, du tätest ⑧ vielleicht auch gut daran, einige Sitten und Bräuche zu übernehmen.

11 – Sieh da, sieh da! Denkst du an etwas Bestimmtes? (N.2)

12 – Nicht direkt... aber sind dir auf unserer Fahrt die vielen Blumenkästen vor den Fenstern und auf den Balkons aufgefallen ⑨?

13 – Ja, das sind sie. Sie sehen wirklich wunderschön aus.

Pronunciation Key
***10** ... bro**y**'che ... **12** ... balk**o**ngs ...*

Notes

③ **kennenlernen**, *to get to know* (lit. "to learn to know"). **Kennen-** is separable: **Ich lernte Herrn Schulze gestern kennen**, *I got to know Mr. Schulze yesterday.*

4 This is the best way to get to know the country and the people thoroughly.
5 – As you like! I don't mind, as long as you don't ask me to do the same.
6 – By the way, it doesn't taste as bad [as that]! I think I could get used to it.
7 – That doesn't surprise me. You have always been a great carnivore *(m.)*.
8 But please don't hold your sausage sandwich directly under my nose!
9 – Don't exaggerate *(now)*! It doesn't smell as bad [as that]!
10 By the way, maybe you'd better adopt some of the manners and customs too.
11 – Well, fancy that! Are you thinking of something special?
12 – Not exactly, but did you notice the numerous flower boxes in front of the windows and on the balconies on our way?
13 – Yes, of course! They look really beautiful.

▸ ④ **meinetwegen**, *on my behalf; because of me*: **Meinetwegen müssen Sie nicht hier bleiben**, *You needn't stay here because of me*. When used alone, it means: *It's alright by me. Do as you like*. **Gehen wir? – Meinetwegen**, *Let's go! – As you like.*

⑤ **fressen**, *to eat (greedily), to devour*. Generally **fressen** is used for animals. But, used colloquially, it means *to gorge*.

⑥ **das Wurstbrot**, *sausage sandwich* (lit. "sausage bread"); **das Käsebrot**, *cheese sandwich*; **das Marmeladenbrot**, *bread and jam*; **das Butterbrot**, *bread and butter*.

⑦ **riechen**, *to smell*; **schmecken**, *to taste*; **fühlen**, *to feel*.

⑧ **tun, tat, getan**, *to do, to make* (see grammatical appendix). **Ich täte gut daran, du tätest gut daran...**, *I, you... had better*.

⑨ **etwas fällt mir auf**, *something strikes me, I notice something*.

96 **14** – Und hast du auch bemerkt, wie die deutschen Fensterscheiben in der Sonne blitzen ⑩?

15 – Ja, und ich habe mich gefragt, ob wir unsere nächsten Fensterscheiben nicht in Deutschland oder der Schweiz bestellen sollten...

Note

⑩ **blitzen**, *to shine, to sparkle.* **Der Blitz**, *the lightning.*

***

Übung 1 – Übersetzen Sie bitte

❶ Würden Sie mir bitte das Salz reichen? ❷ Da wir nun einmal hier sind, haben wir beschlossen, auch davon zu profitieren. ❸ Sie hat sich gefragt, ob es nicht besser wäre, auf dem Balkon zu frühstücken. ❹ Ihm ist aufgefallen, daß die Deutschen viele Blumen vor ihren Fenstern haben. ❺ Er täte gut daran, mit Rauchen aufzuhören. ❻ Es ist schwierig, sich an die Sitten und Bräuche eines anderen Landes zu gewöhnen.

14 – And did you also notice how German window panes are glistening in the sun?

15 – Yes, and I have been wondering whether we shouldn't order our panes in Germany or Switzerland next time... □

ER TÄTE GUT DARAN, MIT RAUCHEN AUFZUHÖREN

***

Answers to exercise 1

❶ Could you pass me the salt please? ❷ As we are here, we have decided to make the most of it *(to profit by it)*. ❸ She has been wondering whether it wouldn't be better to have breakfast on the balcony. ❹ He noticed that the Germans have a lot of flowers in front of their windows. ❺ He'd better stop smoking. ❻ It is difficult to get used to the manners and habits of other countries.

96 Übung 2 – Ergänzen Sie bitte

1. What are you eating there? Ugh! It looks awful!
. . . . denn da? . . . . . ! Das . . . . . ja scheußlich . . . !

2. He decided to give up smoking.
. . . . , nicht mehr . . . .

3. Don't hold your hat directly in front of my nose please!
. . . . doch bitte Ihren Hut nicht . . . . !

4. Did you know that sausage for breakfast doesn't taste as bad [as that]?
. . . . , daß . . . . . zum Frühstück gar nicht so . . . . ?

5. Are you thinking of something special or are you dreaming?
Denken Sie . . . . oder träumen Sie?

❻ Did you notice that there are a lot of cigarette machines in Germany?

... Ihnen ...., daß .. in Deutschland ..... Zigarettenautomaten ....?

❼ But don't exaggerate! It isn't as bad [as that]!

.... doch nicht! .. schlimm ist ... doch .....!

Answers to exercise 2

❶ Was essen Sie – Igitt – sieht – aus ❷ Er hat beschlossen – zu rauchen ❸ Halten Sie – direkt vor meine Nase ❹ Wußten Sie – Wurst – schlecht schmeckt ❺ – an etwas Bestimmtes – ❻ Ist – aufgefallen – es – viele – gibt ❼ Übertreiben Sie – So – das – nicht

Second Wave: 47th Lesson

97 Siebenundneunzigste Lektion

Die Rede des Bürgermeisters

1 – Liebe Gem**ei**nde!
V**ie**le **u**nter **I**hnen w**i**ssen schon, welch ①
fr**eu**diges Er**ei**gnis uns h**eu**te hier
zus**a**mmenführt.

2 Seit zwei J**a**hren bet**ei**ligt ② sich **u**nser
Dorf an dem B**u**ndeswettbewerb „Unser
Dorf soll sch**ö**ner w**e**rden". (N.2)

3 Rund 5. 800 D**ö**rfer und St**a**dtteile h**a**ben
sich d**ie**ses Mal um die **Au**szeichnungen
bew**o**rben – **ei**ne nicht zu ver**a**chtende ③
Konkurr**e**nz!

4 G**e**stern hat nun das
B**u**ndesl**a**ndwirtschaftsminist**e**rium ④ die
endgültigen S**ie**ger bek**a**nntgegeben,

5 und ich bin höchst erfr**eu**t ⑤, **I**hnen
m**i**tteilen zu d**ü**rfen, daß **u**nser Dorf **ei**ne der
dr**ei**zehn G**o**ldmedaillen err**i**ngen k**o**nnte.

Pronunciation Key

***2** ... **boo**nd<u>e</u>s'vettbeverb ... **3** ... **ow**stsy'ghnoong<u>e</u>n ...*
***4** **boo**nd<u>e</u>s'**la**nntvirtshaftsminist**e**ryoomm ... **5** ... g**o**ltmedally<u>e</u>nn ...*

Notes

① After **welcher**, **welche**, **welches**, the declension of the adjective is weak. See lesson 35, paragraph 1: **Welches freudige Ereignis**, *What a happy event*. But we can also decline the adjective normally and leave out the ending of **welch-**: **Welch herrlicher Tag**! *What a beautiful day*! ▸

The Mayor's Speech

1 – Dear citizens! *(commune)*
A lot of you already know the happy event *(n.)* that *(what a happy)* brings us together here today.
2 Our village *(n.)* has been participating in the federal competition *(m.)* "Our village shall become more beautiful" for two years [now].
3 This time about 5,800 villages and *(town)* districts were competing for the prizes – a remarkable competition *(f.) (not to be despised)*.
4 Yesterday, the federal ministry *(n.)* of agriculture announced the definite winners,
5 and I am highly delighted to inform you that our village was able to carry off one of the thirteen gold medals –

▸ ② **sich beteiligen an** + dat., *to participate in*. In the following lesson you will find other verbs which are followed by a preposition.

③ **verachten**, *to despise*; **achten**, *to respect*.

④ **das Ministerium**, *the ministry;* **die Landwirtschaft**, *the agriculture*.

⑤ You can either say: **Ich bin erfreut** or **ich freue mich**, *I am glad, happy*.

97

6 Ein Erf**o**lg, der nur durch **ei**ne b**ei**spielhafte Zus**a**mmenarbeit und herv**o**rragende L**ei**stungen **ei**nes jeden **ei**nzelnen err**ei**cht ⑥ werden k**o**nnte.

7 Ja, j**e**der von **I**hnen hat d**a**zu b**ei**getragen und ich m**ö**chte **I**hnen **a**llen d**a**für von g**a**nzem H**e**rzen d**a**nken ⑦. (N.2)

8 L**a**ssen Sie uns auf **ei**ne gl**ü**ckliche Z**u**kunft **u**nseres D**o**rfes mit **ei**nem dr**ei**fachen „hipp, hipp, hurr**a**!“ **a**nstoßen! Hipp, hipp hurr**a**! Hipp, hipp, hurr**a**! Hipp, hipp, hurr**a**! ⑧

9 – Na, Herr und Frau M**ü**ller, was s**a**gen Sie zu **u**nserem Erf**o**lg? Ein sch**ö**nes Erg**e**bnis ⑨, nicht wahr?

10 – Ja, wir m**ü**ssen gest**e**hen, wir sind sehr stolz auf **u**nsere Gem**ei**nde. (N.2)

11 **A**ber **a**ndrerseits, w**i**ssen Sie, sind wir auch z**ie**mlich froh, daß d**ie**se g**a**nze **Au**fregung **e**ndlich vorb**ei** ist.

12 Jetzt k**ö**nnen wir **e**ndlich w**ie**der die M**ü**lleimer ganz norm**a**l vor das Haus st**e**llen und die K**i**nder d**ü**rfen w**ie**der den R**a**sen betr**e**ten... □

Notes

⑥ **etwas erreichen**, *to achieve, obtain something*: **Er hat in seinem Leben viel erreicht**, *He has achieved a lot in (his) life.*

⑦ **Ich danke jemandem**, *I thank someone.* ▶

6 a success *(m.)* which could only be achieved by the exemplary cooperation *(f.)* and excellent performance of each individual.
7 Yes, each of you contributed to it and I want to thank you with all my heart.
8 Let's drink to the happy future of our village with a threefold "Hip, hip, hurray!"

9 – Well, Mr. and Mrs. Müller, what do you think of our success? A nice result *(n.)*, isn't it?
10 – Yes, we must admit we are very proud of our commune *(f.)*.
11 But on the other hand, you know, we are happy that all this excitement *(f.)* is over *(finished)* after all.
12 We can put our dustbins in front of the houses as usual *(normally)* and the children can walk on the lawn again... □

▸ ⑧ Do you remember the imperative of the first person plural? **Wir wollen anstoßen** or **laßt uns anstoßen**, *Let's drink to...* **Einfach**, *single (and simple)*; **zweifach**, *twofold*; **dreifach**...

⑨ Be careful not to mix up: **das Ergebnis**, *the result* and **das Ereignis**, *the event.*

97 **Übung 1 – Übersetzen Sie bitte**

❶ Heute wurde von der Regierung bekanntgegeben, daß die Ölpreise im nächsten Monat erhöht werden. ❷ Tausende beteiligten sich an der Friedensdemonstration. ❸ Sie hat sich um die Stelle einer Sekretärin beworben. ❹ Wir sind höchst erfreut, Ihnen die Geburt unseres dritten Kindes mitteilen zu dürfen. ❺ Er ist mit Recht sehr stolz darauf, die Bronzemedaille gewonnen zu haben. Es war wirklich eine hervorragende Leistung. ❻ Die Fortschritte, die wir in Deutsch gemacht haben, sind nicht zu verachten, nicht wahr?

Übung 2 – Ergänzen Sie bitte

❶ Our commune has the youngest mayor in Germany.

. . . . hat den . . . . Bürgermeister Deutschlands.

❷ Everybody participated in the preparations for the great festivities *(feast)*.

Alle . . . . den Vorbereitungen für das Fest . . . .

❸ I am very glad to announce [you] that you have won the first prize in our competition.

. . . . . . sehr . . . . , ... mitteilen zu . . . . . . , daß Sie den ersten Preis in unserem . . . . gewonnen haben.

❹ The basis of our success is the good cooperation in our society.

Die Grundlage . . . . ist die gute . . . . in unserer Firma.

Answers to exercise 1

❶ Today the government announced that oil prices are going to increase next month. ❷ Thousands [of people] were participating in the demonstration for peace. ❸ She applied for the job of secretary. ❹ We are highly delighted to announce [you] the birth of our third child. ❺ He is justly *(with right)* proud of having won the bronze medal. It really was an excellent performance. ❻ The progress we made in German is considerable *(not to be despised)*, isn't it?

❺ Let's drink to that!
Darauf . . . . . . wir . . . . !

❻ I can't bear this excitement any longer, I hope that everything will be over soon!
. . . . ertrage ich nicht länger. Hoffentlich . . . bald alles . . . . . . !

❼ Keep off the lawn!
. . . . !

Answers to exercise 2

❶ Unsere Gemeinde – jüngsten – ❷ – haben sich an – beteiligt ❸ Ich bin – erfreut – Ihnen – dürfen – Wettbewerb – ❹ – unseres Erfolgs – Zusammenarbeit – ❺ – wollen – anstoßen ❻ Diese Aufregung – ist – vorbei ❼ Rasen betreten verboten

Second Wave: 48th Lesson

98 Achtundneunzigste Lektion

Wiederholung und Erklärungen

1 The *Konjunktiv I*

The **Konjunktiv I** is used in indirect speech.

Direct speech:
Mein Bruder sagt, „Ich habe kein Geld mehr“.
My brother says: “I have no money left”.

Indirect speech:
Mein Bruder sagt, daß er kein Geld mehr habe.
My brother says that he has no money left.

The first person in the direct speech becomes third person in the indirect speech.

The third person singular of the **Konjunktiv I** is formed by adding **-e** to the root of the infinitive; the third person plural is the same as the indicative:

	Indikativ	Konjunktiv I
3rd person singular	**er braucht**	**er brauche**
	er hat	**er habe**
	er gibt	**er gebe**
3rd person plural	**sie brauchen**	**sie brauchen**
	sie haben	**sie haben**
	sie geben	**sie geben**

When the forms of the **Konjunktiv I** are equivalent to those of the indicative, we use the **Konjunktiv II**. So you can say:

Sie sagen, daß sie kein Geld haben or **hätten**.
They say that they have no money left.

See the complete conjugation of the **Konjunktiv I** and **II** in the grammatical appendix.

2 Verbs Followed By a Preposition

• **denken an** + acc., *to think about.*

Ich denke nur noch an die Ferien, *I am only thinking about the holidays.*

When the complement of verb is a subordinate clause you have to use **da / dar** + preposition:

Ich denke nur noch daran, daß ich nächste Woche in Ferien fahre, *I am just thinking about going on holiday next week.*

• **abhängen von** + dat., *to depend on*:

Es hängt von meinen Eltern ab, *It depends on my parents.*
Es hängt davon ab, ob meine Eltern mich allein lassen, *It will depend on whether my parents are going to leave me alone.*

• **sich gewöhnen an** + acc., *to get used to*:

Ich habe mich an die neue Wohnung gewöhnt, *I have got used to the new flat.*
Er hat sich daran gewöhnt, jeden Morgen um 5 Uhr aufzustehen, *He got used to getting up at 5 o'clock every morning.*

• **bitten um** + acc., *to ask for*:

Er bittet um ihre Hand, *He asks for her hand.*

But:
• **fragen nach** + dat., *to ask*:

Er fragt nach dem Weg zum Bahnhof, *He asks the way to the station.*

• **sich erinnern an** + acc., *to remember*:

Erinnern Sie sich an Ihre Ferien in Deutschland?, *Do you remember your holidays in Germany?*
Erinnern Sie sich noch daran, daß Sie erst vor einigen Monaten anfingen Deutsch zu lernen?, *Do you remember that you only started learning German some months ago?*

3 *Imperfekt und Perfekt*

In German we generally use the **Imperfekt** in narratives and in formal written language, and the **Perfekt** in conversation.
Exception: for the verbs **sein** and **haben** and the auxiliaries **müssen**, **sollen**, **können** etc., we prefer the **Imperfekt** – this is however not a grammar rule.

99 Neunundneunzigste Lektion

Mein lieber Matthias!

1 Du bist s**i**cherlich **ü**ber d**ie**sen Brief sehr überr**a**scht. M**ö**ge ① es **ei**ne **a**ngenehme Überr**a**schung sein!
2 Seit 15 J**a**hren h**a**ben wir uns aus den **Au**gen verl**o**ren.
3 **A**ber das Spr**i**chwort „aus den **Au**gen, aus dem Sinn" trifft ② nicht **i**mmer zu ②.

Notes

① **mögen** in the **Konjunktiv I** expresses a wish: **Möge er nicht zu spät kommen**, *May he not be late!* **Mögen die Götter mit uns sein!**, *May the gods be with us!* Please note that the infinitive is placed at the end of the sentence. Otherwise **mögen** means *to like*: **Ich mag keine Wurst**, *I don't like sausage* (see lesson 21, paragraph 2.3).

Read the following story and pay special attention to the tenses: 99

Tut mir leid, daß du so lange warten mußtest. Aber ich habe eine tolle Geschichte gehört. Bei Karl wurde gestern nacht eingebrochen. Zwei Männer stiegen durchs Küchenfenster ein und leerten dort erst mal in aller Ruhe den Kühlschrank. Uns als sie dann wirklich ans Stehlen gehen wollten, kam Karl nach Hause.
– Na, dann war es ja nicht so schlimm, oder? – Doch, er hatte einen Bärenhunger!
I'm sorry for having kept you waiting for such a long time (that you had to wait...). But I've heard an incredible story. Last night Karl's house was broken into. Two men got in through the kitchen window and they calmly emptied the refrigerator first. And when they were about to steal, Karl came home. – So, it wasn't as bad as that, was it? – Indeed it was, he was famished!

99th Lesson 99

My Dear Matthias!

1 You will certainly be very surprised by this letter! I hope it is a nice *(pleasant)* surprise!
2 We have been losing sight *(eyes)* of each other *(ourselves)* for 15 years.
3 But the proverb *(n.)* "Out of sight, out of mind" does not always come true.

▸ ② **zutreffen**, *to come true*, *to be true of.* When followed by the preposition **auf** + acc., it means *to apply to.* **Das trifft auf ihn zu, aber nicht auf mich**, *That applies to him but not to me.*

99

4 Ich habe viel an Dich* gedacht und mich oft gefragt, was wohl aus Dir* geworden ist.

5 Durch einen glücklichen Zufall ③ habe ich gestern beim Aufräumen meines Schreibtisches Deine* Adresse wiedergefunden.

6 Das war für mich ein Geschenk des Himmels!

7 Ich lerne nämlich ④ gerade Deutsch, und das macht mir sehr viel Spaß.

8 Diesen Brief schreibe ich ganz allein, und ich bin gespannt ⑤ wie ein kleines Kind vor Weihnachten, ob Du* auch alles verstehen wirst.

9 Ich möchte Dich* sehr gern wiedersehen, und ich frage mich, ob ich nicht vielleicht sogar deinetwegen ⑥ angefangen habe, Deutsch zu lernen?

10 Was meinst Du* dazu? Laß bald von Dir* hören!

Sei herzlich gegrüßt
von Deiner* Patricia

* In a letter, the personal pronouns and possessive articles referring to our correspondent start with a capital letter.

Notes

③ **ein glücklicher Zufall**, *a coincidence, lucky chance.*

④ **nämlich** is always placed after the subject and the verb. It is used in a sentence which explains what has been said in the preceding one. There is no equivalent in English; we have to translate it by a subordinate introduced by *since* or *because*: **Ich kenne ihn gut. Ich habe nämlich 2 Jahre lang mit ihm gelebt**, *I know him well, since I have lived with him for two years.* ▸

4 I have been thinking of you a lot and have often been wondering what might have become of you.
5 Yesterday while tidying my desk, I accidentally *(by a happy accident)* found your address.
6 That was a godsend for me,
7 for I am learning German at the moment and I like it a lot.
8 I am writing this letter all by myself and I am as anxious as a little child before Christmas [to know] whether you will understand everything:
9 I would love to see you again and I am wondering whether I didn't *(maybe)* even start learning German because of you.
10 What do you think of this? I hope to hear from you soon *(let hear from you soon)*!

Love
(your) Patricia

EIN GLÜCKLICHER ZUFALL HAT SIE WIEDER ZUSAMMENGEFÜHRT

⑤ **gespannt sein auf etwas**, *to be anxious about something.* **Er is gespannt auf das Ende des Films**, *He is anxious [to see] the end of the film.* Or: **Er ist sehr gespannt, ob das gut enden wird**, *He is anxious [to know] if it will turn out (end) well.*

⑥ You already know **meinetwegen** (see lesson 96, note 4). The other forms are: **deinetwegen**, **seinetwegen**, **ihretwegen**, *because of you, of him, of her* and **unsretwegen**, **euretwegen**, **ihretwegen**, *because of us, of you, of them.*

11 Die Antwort kommt umgehend:
Komm, wann immer Du* willst Stop Habe 15 Jahre lang auf Dich gewartet Stop ohne es zu wissen Stop

12 Dein* Deutsch ist phantastisch Stop Freue mich sehr auf Dich* ⑦ Stop

13 Bin etwas älter, und dicker geworden Stop Ist das schlimm?

In Liebe
Dein* Matthias □

* In a letter, the personal pronouns and possessive articles referring to our correspondent start with a capital letter.

Note

⑦ **sich freuen**, *to be glad; to be looking forward to*, can be followed by two different prepositions. The meaning changes accordingly. **Sich freuen über** + acc., *to be glad/happy about, to be pleased with* (at the present moment): **Ich freue mich** ▸

***

Übung 1 – Übersetzen Sie bitte

❶ Sie haben sich sehr über unsere Einladung gefreut. ❷ Die Kinder freuen sich auf Weihnachten. ❸ Ich habe schon seit Wochen nichts mehr von ihm gehört. Möge der Himmel ihn schützen! ❹ Sie hat das Radio seinetwegen leiser gestellt. ❺ Ein glücklicher Zufall hat sie wieder zusammengeführt. ❻ Alle sind gespannt, wie es weitergehen wird. ❼ Sie hatten sich viele Jahre aus den Augen verloren. Aber eines Tages haben sie sich zufällig wiedergetroffen.

11 The answer arrives by return of post:
Come whenever you want Stop Have been waiting for you for 15 years Stop without realizing *(knowing)* it Stop
12 Your German is fantastic Stop Happy to see you Stop
13 Have grown a bit older and fatter Stop Is that bad [do you mind]?

With *(in)* Love
(your) Matthias □

▸ **über dein Geschenk**, *I am happy about your present* (the person has already got the present). **Sich freuen auf** + acc., *to be looking forward to*: **Ich freue mich auf ihren Besuch**, *I am looking forward to your visit.*

***

Answers to exercise 1

❶ They were very glad about our invitation. ❷ The children are looking forward to Christmas. ❸ I haven't heard anything of him for weeks. May [the] heaven keep him! ❹ She turned the radio down because of him. ❺ Pure *(lucky)* chance brought them together again. ❻ Everybody is anxious [to know] how it'll go on. ❼ They had lost sight of each other for many years. But one day they accidentally met [each other] again.

Übung 2 – Ergänzen Sie bitte

❶ He was very surprised by her letter.
Er war . . . . sehr . . . .

❷ But was very happy about it.
Aber er . . . . sehr darüber . . . .

❸ While tidying up she found a €100 note.
Sie hat . . . . einen Hunderteuroschein . . . .

❹ All their children were a godsend to them.
Alle ihre Kinder waren für sie . . . .

100 Hundertste und letzte Lektion

Trauen Sie niemandem!

1 – Sagen Sie, was ist **I**hnen denn **ü**ber die Leber gel**au**fen ①? Kann ich **I**hnen viell**ei**cht **i**rgendwie h**e**lfen?

2 – Nein, n**ie**mand kann mir h**e**lfen! **A**lles ist zu **E**nde!

3 – Na, na, nun mal l**a**ngsam! „**I**mmer wenn du denkst, es geht nicht mehr, kommt **i**rgendwo ein L**i**chtlein her.“ K**e**nnen Sie das?

Note

① **laufen** or **rennen**, *to run* (see line 13); **die Leber**, *the liver*. The question: **Was ist Ihnen über die Leber gelaufen?** comes from the expression: **mir/dir/ihr... ist eine Laus über** ▸

⑤ Today I have made *(baked)* pancakes for you *(because of you)*. Are you glad about that? **100**
. . . . habe ich heute Pfannkuchen gebacken. . . . . darüber?

⑥ This does not apply to me because I am [a] foreigner.
Das . . . . . . nicht auf mich . . . Ich bin . . . . Ausländerin.

Answers to exercise 2

❶ – über ihren Brief – überrascht ❷ – hat sich – gefreut ❸ – beim Aufräumen – gefunden ❹ – ein Geschenk des Himmels ❺ Deinetwegen – Freust du dich – ❻ – trifft – zu – nämlich –

Second Wave: 50th Lesson

100th and Last Lesson 100

Don't Trust Anybody!

1 – Tell me, what's wrong with you *(what has run across your liver [f.])*? Maybe I can help you in some way or other *(somehow)*?
2 – No, nobody can help me! Everything is over *(finished)*!
3 – Come on, take it easy *(slowly)*! "Each time you think it won't *(doesn't)* go on, a small light *(n.)* comes from somewhere." Do you know that?

▸ **die Leber gelaufen**, lit. "a louse has run across my/your/her... liver", *I am/you are... in a bad mood.*

100

4 Dieser Spruch hing ② bei uns zu Hause über dem Spiegel im Badezimmer und beim Zähneputzen mußte ich ihn immer ansehen.

5 So bin ich Optimist geworden, verstehen Sie? Also, was ist los?

6 – Ich bin an der letzten Lektion von meinem Deutschbuch angelangt!

7 – Na, wenn's weiter nichts ist! Werfen Sie's in die Ecke und freuen Sie sich!

8 – Nein, Sie verstehen mich falsch! Ich habe mich jeden Tag auf die nächste Lektion gefreut und jetzt gibt's keine mehr!

9 – Na, so etwas ist mir mein Leben lang noch nicht begegnet! Und ich bin weit rumgekommen ③!

10 Zeigen Sie mir mal das Buch! Wir wollen mal sehen, ob da nichts zu machen ist!

11 Ha, ha, lustige Bildchen... Mmm, ich habe auch mal ein bißchen Deutsch in der Schule gelernt... Ah, das hier verstehe ich... und das da auch!

12 – Hören Sie, das gilt nicht ④! Sie sollen nicht lesen, Sie sollen mir helfen!

13 Halt! Warten Sie! Was machen Sie denn da? Halt! Laufen Sie nicht weg! Mein Buch, Hilfe, mein Buch!

Notes

② **hängen**, *to hang*, is the infinitive of **hing**.

③ **Er ist viel herumgekommen** means *he has travelled/seen a lot*. We also say: **Diese Neuigkeit ist schnell herumgekommen**, *This news spread rapidly*.

4 This saying *(m.)* hung above the mirror in our bathroom at home and when I was brushing my teeth I couldn't help *(I had to)* looking at it.
5 That's how I became an optimist, you understand? So, what is the matter?
6 – I have come *(reached)* to the last lesson of my German manual *(n.)!*
7 – Well, if that's all *(if it isn't anything more)*! Throw it away *(in the corner)* and be happy!
8 – No, you misunderstand me! I was looking forward every day to the next lesson and now there aren't any [more] left!
9 – Think of that! I have never come across anything like that in my life! And I have done a lot of travelling!
10 Show me the book! Let's see whether there isn't anything to be done!
11 Ha, ha, funny pictures... mm, I also learnt *(once)* a little German at school. Ah, I can understand this... and that too!
12 – Listen, you are cheating! You shall not read, you shall help me!
13 Stop! Wait! What are you doing? Stop! Don't run away! My book, help, my book!

▸ ④ **Das gilt nicht**, *This is not fair (you are cheating)*. The infinitive is **gelten**, *to be valid* (see lesson 65, note 2).

14 – Guten Tag! Warum weinen Sie denn so? Kann ich irgend etwas für Sie tun?
15 – Nein, niemand kann mir mehr helfen! Alles ist zu Ende... □

***

Übung 1 – Übersetzen Sie bitte

❶ Er traut niemandem, am wenigsten sich selbst. ❷ Ich weiß nicht, welche Laus ihm heute wieder über die Leber gelaufen ist. Auf alle Fälle geht man ihm besser aus dem Weg. ❸ Es ist schwierig, beim Zähneputzen zu singen. Haben Sie es schon einmal versucht? ❹ Er ist mit seinem Latein am Ende. Jetzt ist alles zu Ende! ❺ Als ich klein war, habe ich mich jeden Abend auf das Frühstück gefreut. ❻ Jetzt freue ich mich beim Frühstück auf das Abendessen.

Übung 2 – Ergänzen Sie bitte

❶ Help! He ran away with my purse!
. . . . . ! Er . . . mit meinem Portemonnaie . . . . !

❷ Nobody can help us! Everything is over!
. . . . kann . . . helfen! . . . . !

❸ Of course *(but)* not, you get everything wrong! I only want to help you!
Aber nein, Sie . . . . ! Ich will . . . . . nur . . . . . . !

❹ You are cheating! You have seen my cards in the mirror!
. . . . ! Sie . . . . . meine Karten . . . . !

14 – Hello! Why are you crying like that? Is there anything I can do for you? **100**
15 – No, nobody can help me! Everything is over... □

***

Answers to exercise 1

❶ He doesn't trust anybody, least of all himself. ❷ I don't know what's wrong with him today. In any case it's better to get out of his way. ❸ It's difficult to sing while brushing your *(the)* teeth. Have you *(already)* tried it? ❹ He is at his wits' end. Everything is over now. ❺ When I was a little child I used to look forward to breakfast every evening. ❻ Now, I am looking forward to dinner during [while I am having] my breakfast.

❺ What are you looking forward to most: [to] Christmas, [to] Easter or [to] your birthday?
. . . . am meisten: . . . Weihnachten, . . . Ostern oder . . . Ihren Geburtstag?

❻ We have come *(reached)* to the end of our book and we hope that you enjoyed it very much!
Wir . . . . am Ende . . . . Buches . . . . und wir hoffen, daß . . . . viel . . . . !

Answers to exercise 2

❶ Hilfe – ist – weggelaufen ❷ Niemand – uns – Alles ist zu Ende ❸ – verstehen alles falsch – Ihnen – helfen ❹ Das gilt nicht – haben – im Spiegel gesehen ❺ Worauf freuen Sie sich – auf – auf – auf – ❻ – sind – unseres – angelangt – es Ihnen – Spaß gemacht hat

100 *Here we are at the end of our book.*
In the course of a few months, you have been able to acquire a basic knowledge of the German language. You are capable of understanding a conversation and of making yourself understood.
But don't stop here, carry on with the Second Wave: there are still 50 lessons to study.
After that, don't put the book aside. Keep reading it a little every day, and don't hesitate: you are now able to read German newspapers and even novels (possibly with the help of a dictionary).
Listen to the radio, try to meet Germans or, better still, go to Germany and enjoy the **gemütlich** *way of life!*

ES IST SCHWIERIG, BEIM ZÄHNEPUTZEN ZU SINGEN

Grammatical Appendix

1 Article + Adjective + Noun **457**

2 The Personal and Reflexive Pronouns **462**
2.1 The Personal Pronoun.. 462
2.2 The Reflexive Pronoun 463

3 Prepositions **463**
3.1 The Place to Which/Where You Go 464
3.2 The Place You Are In 464

4 Word Order **464**
4.1 Subject – Verb – Object 464
4.2 Verb – Subject – Object 464
4.3 The Verb at The End of The Sentence 465

5 Conjugations of *sein, haben, werden* **465**
5.1 *Sein*, to be 465
5.2 *Haben*, to have 467
5.3 *Werden*, to become, to get 468

6 Regular Verbs 470

7 An Irregular Verb: to speak **474**

8 Irregular Verbs **477**

Grammatical Appendix

1 Article + Adjective + Noun

- **Nominative**

Masculine

der (*the*)	**kleine Mann**	**ein** (*a*)	**kleiner Mann**
dieser (*this*)		**Kein** (*no*)	
jener (*that*)		**mein** (*my*)	
jeder (*every*)		**Ihr** (*your*)	

Feminine

die	**kleine Frau**	**eine**	**kleine Frau**
diese		**keine**	
jene		**meine**	
jede		**Ihre**	

Neuter

das	**kleine Kind**	**ein**	**kleines Kind**
dieses		**kein**	
jenes		**mein**	
jedes		**Ihr**	

- **Accusative**

Masculine

<table>
<tr><td>den</td><td rowspan="4">kleinen Mann</td><td>einen</td><td rowspan="4">kleinen Mann</td></tr>
<tr><td>diesen</td><td>keinen</td></tr>
<tr><td>jenen</td><td>meinen</td></tr>
<tr><td>jeden</td><td>Ihren</td></tr>
</table>

Feminine

<table>
<tr><td>die</td><td rowspan="4">kleine Frau</td><td>eine</td><td rowspan="4">kleine Frau</td></tr>
<tr><td>diese</td><td>keine</td></tr>
<tr><td>jene</td><td>meine</td></tr>
<tr><td>jede</td><td>Ihre</td></tr>
</table>

Neuter

<table>
<tr><td>das</td><td rowspan="4">kleine Kind</td><td>ein</td><td rowspan="4">kleines Kind</td></tr>
<tr><td>dieses</td><td>keine</td></tr>
<tr><td>jenes</td><td>mein</td></tr>
<tr><td>jedes</td><td>Ihr</td></tr>
</table>

- **Dative**

Masculine

dem	**kleinen Mann**	**einem**	**kleinen Mann**
diesem		**keinem**	
jenem		**meinem**	
jedem		**Ihrem**	

Feminine

der	**kleinen Frau**	**einer**	**kleinen Frau**
dieser		**keiner**	
jener		**meiner**	
jeder		**Ihrer**	

Neuter

dem	**kleinen Kind**	**einem**	**kleinen Kind**
diesem		**keinem**	
jenem		**meinem**	
jedem		**Ihrem**	

- **Genitive**

Masculine

des	kleinen Mannes	eines	kleinen Mannes
dieses		keines	
jenes		meines	
jedes		Ihres	

Feminine

der	kleinen Frau	einer	kleinen Frau
dieser		keiner	
jener		meiner	
jeder		Ihrer	

Neuter

des	kleinen Kindes	eines	kleinen Kindes
dieses		keines	
jenes		meines	
jedes		Ihres	

- **Plural: Nominative = Accusative**

die		
diese	**Männer**	**Männer**
jene	**kleinen Frauen**	**kleine Frauen**
alle	**Kinder**	**Kinder**
keine		
meine		
Ihre		

- **Plural: Dative**

den		
diesen	**Männern**	**Männern**
jenen	**kleinen Frauen**	**kleinen Frauen**
allen	**Kindern**	**Kindern**
meinen		
Ihren		

• **Plural: Genitive**

<table>
<tr><td>der</td><td rowspan="7">Männer
kleinen Frauen
Kinder</td><td rowspan="7">Männer
kleiner Frauen
Kindern</td></tr>
<tr><td>dieser</td></tr>
<tr><td>jener</td></tr>
<tr><td>aller</td></tr>
<tr><td>keiner</td></tr>
<tr><td>meiner</td></tr>
<tr><td>Ihrer</td></tr>
</table>

• **The Possessive Pronoun**

Its endings are the same as those of the possessive article, except for the nominative masculine: we have to add **-er**; nominative and accusative neuter: we have to add **-(e)s**.

Mein Wein ist ausgezeichnet. Und wie ist deiner?, *My wine is excellent. What about yours?*

Ich habe kein Taschentuch. Gib mir bitte dein(e)s, *I haven't got a handkerchief. Give me yours please.*

2 The Personal and Reflexive Pronouns

2.1 The Personal Pronoun

Nominative	Accusative	Dative	Genitive
ich	**mich**	**mir**	**meiner**
du	**dich**	**dir**	**deiner**

er	**ihn**	**ihm**	**seiner**
sie	**sie**	**ihr**	**ihrer**
es	**es**	**ihm**	**seiner**
wir	**uns**	**uns**	**unsrer**
ihr	**euch**	**euch**	**eurer**
sie	**sie**	**ihnen**	**ihrer**
Sie	**Sie**	**Ihnen**	**Ihrer**

2.2 The Reflexive Pronoun

The forms are the same as those of the personal pronoun, except for the third person of the singular and the plural, which are always **sich**.

3 Prepositions

The following prepositions can be followed by the accusative or the dative. The case depends on whether the preceding verb denotes movement (+ acc.) or not (+ dat.):

in	*in (to)*	**vor**	*in front of*
an	*at*	**hinter**	*behind*
auf	*on (to)*	**über**	*above, across*
neben	*near*	**unter**	*below, under*
zwischen	*between*		

Example:
Er ist im Garten, *He is in the garden* (dative)
Er geht in den Garten, *He goes into the garden* (accusative)
Das Buch liegt auf dem Tish, *The book lies on the table* (dative)
Wir legen das Buch auf den Tisch, *We lay the book on the table* (accusative)

Commonly used expressions:

3.1 The Place to Which/Where You Go

Ich gehe nach Hause, *I go home.*
Ich gehe nach oben, *I go upstairs.*
Ich gehe zu Bett, *I go to bed.*
Ich gehe zu meinem Freund, *I go to my friend's.*

3.2 The Place You Are In

Ich bin zu Hause, *I am at home.*
Ich wohne oben, *I live upstairs.*
Ich bin im Bett, *I am in bed.*
Ich bleibe bei meinem Freund, *I stay at my friend's.*

4 Word Order

4.1 Subject – Verb – Object

Generally the word order is the same as in English:

Subject – Verb – Object
Ich treffe meinen Freund, *I meet my friend.*

4.2 Verb – Subject – Object

When the sentence begins with the object, or an adverb of time or place, verb and subject are inverted:

Gestern waren wir im Kino, *Yesterday we were at the cinema.*

The **inversion** also takes place **after**:

deshalb, *therefore, that's why*
also, *so*
trotzdem, *despite*

dann, *then*
Sie möchte nach Paris gehen, deshalb muß sie Französich lernen, *She wants to go to Paris; that's why she has to learn French.*

4.3 The Verb at The End of The Sentence

The conjugated verb is placed at the end of the sentence preceded by the infinitive or the past participle, after:

weil, *because*
obwohl, *although*
wenn, *when*
als, *when*
daß, *that*
relative pronouns

Sie möchte nach Paris gehen, weil sie Frenzösich lernen will, *She wants to go to Paris because she wants to learn French.*
Der mann, den ich gestern getroffen habe, ist mein Freund, *The man (whom) I met yesterday is my friend.*

When the subordinate clause precedes the main clause the verb and the subject are inverted in the main clause:

Weil sie Französich lernen will, möchte sie nach Paris gehen, litt. "Because she wants to learn French, she wants to go to Paris."

5 Conjugations of *sein*, *haben*, *werden*

5.1 *Sein*, to be

- **Indicative**

Present	Imperfect
ich bin	**ich war**
du bist	**du warst**

er sie } ist es	**er sie } war es**
wir sind	**wir waren**
ihr seid	**ihr wart**
sie sind	**sie waren**
Sie sind	**Sie waren**

Perfekt: **sein** + past participle **gewesen**: *been*
Future: **werden** + infinitive **sein**.

Er ist sehr krank gewesen, *He has been very ill.*
Sie werden morgen hier sein, *They will be here tomorrow.*

- **Konjunktiv I and II**

Konjunktiv I	Konjunktiv II
ich sei	**ich wäre**
du sei(e)st	**du wär(e)st**
er sie } sei es	**er sie } wäre es**
wir seien	**wir wären**
ihr sei(e)t	**ihr wär(e)t**

sie seien	**sie wären**
Sie seien	**Sie wären**

- **Imperative**

Sei!, *be*, **Seien wir!**, *Let us be!* **Seid!**, *Be!* **Seien Sie!**, *Be!* (formal)

- **Present Participle**

seiend, *being.*

5.2 *Haben*, to have

- **Indicative**

Present	Imperfect
ich habe	**ich hatte**
du hast	**du hattest**
er / sie / es } hat	**er / sie / es } hatte**
wir haben	**wir hatten**
ihr habt	**ihr hattet**
sie haben	**sie hatten**
Sie haben	**Sie hatten**

Perfekt: **haben** + past participle **gehabt**: *had.*
Future: **werden**+ infinitive **haben**.

Er hat niemals Geld gehabt, *He has never had any money.*
Wir werden nicht genug Zeit haben, *We will not have enough time.*

- **Konjunktiv I and II**

Konjunktiv I	Konjunktiv II
ich habe	**ich hätte**
du habest	**du hättest**
er / sie / es } habe	**er / sie / es } hätte**
wir haben	**wir hätten**
ihr habet	**ihr hättet**
sie haben	**sie hätten**
Sie haben	**Sie hätten**

- **Imperative**

Hab(e)!, *have!* **Haben wir!**, *Let's have!* **Habt!**, *Have!* **Haben Sie!**, *Have!* (formal)

- **Present Participle**

habend, *having.*

5.3 *Werden*, to become, to get

- **Indicative**

This verb is used as an auxiliary to form the future and the passive voice.

Present	Imperfect
ich werde	**ich wurde**
du wirst	**du wurdest**
er **sie wird** **es**	**er** **sie wurde** **es**
wir werden	**wir wurden**
ihr werdet	**ihr wurdet**
sie werden	**sie wurden**
Sie werden	**Sie wurden**

Perfekt: **sein** + past participle **geworden**, *become*.
Future: **werden** + infinitive **werden**.

Er ist Arzt geworden, *He has become a doctor.*
Das Leben wird immer teurer werden, *Life will become more and more expensive.*

- **Konjunktiv I and II**

Konjunktiv I	Konjunktiv II
ich werde	**ich würde**
du werdest	**du würdest**
er **sie** } **werde** **es**	**er** **sie** } **würde** **es**

wir werden	**wir würden**
ihr werdet	**ihr würdet**
sie werden	**sie würden**
Sie werden	**Sie würden**

- **Imperative**

Werde!, *Become/get!* **Werden wir!** *Let's become/get!* **Werdet!** *Become/get!* **Werden Sie!**, *Become/get!* (formal).

- **Present Participle**

werdend, *becoming/getting.*

6 Regular Verbs

In the infinitive all verbs end in **-en** or **-n**. The endings are added to the root of the verb, i.e., the infinitive without **-en** or **-n**.

– **kaufen**, *to buy*

- **Indicative**

Present	Imperfect	Future
ich kaufe	**ich kaufte**	**ich werde kaufen**
du kaufst	**du kauftest**	**du wirst kaufen**
er / sie / es } kauft	**er / sie / es } kaufte**	**er / sie / es } wird kaufen**
wir kaufen	**wir kauften**	**wir werden kaufen**

ihr kauft	**ihr kauftet**	**ihr werdet kaufen**
sie kaufen	**sie kauften**	**sie werden kaufen**
Sie kaufen	**Sie kauften**	**Sie werden kaufen**

Perfect	Pluperfect
ich habe gekauft	**ich hatte gekauft**
du hast gekauft	**du hattest gekauft**
er / sie / es } hat gekauft	**er / sie / es } hatte gekauft**
wir haben gekauft	**wir hatten gekauft**
ihr habt gekauft	**ihr hattet gekauft**
sie haben gekauft	**sie hatten gekauft**
Sie haben gekauft	**Sie hatten gekauft**

• **Imperative**
Kauf(e)!, *Buy!* **Kaufen wir!**, *Let's buy!* **Kauft!**, *Buy!* **Kaufen Sie!**, *Buy!* (formal)

• **Present Participle**
kaufend, *buying.*

- **Konjunktiv I**

Present	Past tense
ich kaufe	**ich habe gekauft**
du kaufest	**du habest gekauft**
er / sie / es } kaufe	**er / sie / es } habe gekauft**
wir kaufen	**wir haben gekauft**
ihr kaufet	**ihr habet gekauft**
sie kaufen	**sie haben gekauft**
Sie kaufen	**Sie haben gekauft**

- **Konjunktiv II**

Present	Present/ Future	Past tense
ich kaufte	**ich würde kaufen**	**ich hätte gekauft**
du kauftest	**du würdest kaufen**	**du hättest gekauft**
er / sie / es } kaufte	**er / sie / es } würde kaufen**	**er / sie / es } hätte gekauft**
wir kauften	**wir würden kaufen**	**wir hätten gekauft**

ihr kauftet	**ihr würdet kaufen**	**ihr hättet gekauft**
sie kauften	**sie würden kaufen**	**sie hätten gekauft**
Sie kauften	**Sie würden kaufen**	**Sie hätten gekauft**

With regular verbs we use **würden** + infinitive in the present tense of the **Konjunktiv II** because its forms are the same as those of the **Imperfekt** of the indicative.

• **The Passive Voice**

(see also lesson 91, paragraph 1)

Present	Imperfekt
ich werde gekauft	**ich wurde gekauft**
du wirst gekauft	**du wurdest gekauft**
er / sie / es } wird gekauft	**er / sie / es } wurde gekauft**
wir werden gekauft	**wir wurden gekauft**
ihr werdet gekauft	**ihr wurdet gekauft**
sie werden gekauft	**sie wurden gekauft**
Sie werden gekauft	**Sie wurden gekauft**

Perfect	Pluperfect
ich bin gekauft worden	**ich war gekauft worden**
du bist gekauft worden	**du warst gekauft worden**
er / sie / es } ist gekauft worden	**er / sie / es } war gekauft worden**
wir sind gekauft worden	**wir waren gekauft worden**
ihr seid gekauft worden	**ihr wart gekauft worden**
sie sind gekauft worden	**sie waren gekauft worden**
Sie sind gekauft worden	**Sie waren gekauft worden**

Future	
ich werde gekauft werden	**wir werden gekauft werden**
du wirst gekauft werden	**ihr werdet gekauft werden**
er / sie / es } wird gekauft werden	**sie werden gekauft werden** **Sie werden gekauft werden**

7 An Irregular Verb: to speak

In the imperfect, the root vowel of the verb always changes. Sometimes it also changes in the second and third person singular of the present tense, **a** becomes **ä** and **e** becomes **i**. (There are however some exceptions as i.e. **Gehen**, **ich gehe**, **du gehst...**). Their past participles mostly end in **-en**.

– **sprechen**, *to speak*

• **Indicative**

Present	Imperfect
ich spreche	**ich sprach**
du sprichst	**du sprachst**
er **sie** } **spricht** **es**	**er** **sie** } **sprach** **es**
wir sprechen	**wir sprachen**
ihr sprecht	**ihr spracht**
sie sprechen	**sie sprachen**
Sie sprechen	**Sie sprachen**

Please note that the first and the third person singular of the imperfect have **no ending**!

Future: **werden** + infinitive (See conjugation of regular verbs)

• **Imperative**
Sprich!, *Speak!* **Sprechen wir!**, *Let's speak!* **Sprecht!**, *Speak!* **Sprechen Sie!**, *Speak!* (formal).

• **Present Participle**
sprechend, *speaking*.

• **Past Participle**
gesprochen, *spoken*.

Perfect and **Pluperfect** (see regular verbs).

Konjunktiv I	**Konjunktiv II**
Present	Present
ich spreche	**ich spräche**
du sprechest	**du sprächest**
er **sie** } **spreche** **es**	**er** **sie** } **spräche** **es**
wir sprechen	**wir sprächen**
ihr sprechet	**ihr sprächet**
sie sprechen	**sie sprächen**
Sie sprechen	

See the regular verbs for the past and the future. The passive is formed with the auxiliary **werden** + past participle.

8 Irregular Verbs

Backen (ä), **buk** (or **backtel**), **gebacken**, *to bake.*
Befehlen (ie), **befahl**, **befohlen**, *to command.*
Beginnen, **begann**, **begonnen**, *to begin.*
Beißen, **biß**, **gebissen**, *to bite.*
Bergen (i), **barg**, **geborgen**, *to hide, to save.*
Besitzen, **besaß**, **besessen**, *to possess.*
Betrügen, **betrog**, **betrogen**, *to deceive.*
Bewegen, **bewog**, **bewogen**, *to move.*
Biegen, **bog**, **gebogen**, *to bend.*
Bieten, **bot**, **geboten**, *to offer.*
Binden, **band**, **gebunden**, *to bind, to tie.*
Bitten, **bat**, **gebeten**, *to ask.*
Blasen (ä), **blies**, **geblasen**, *to blow.*
Bleiben, **blieb**, **geblieben**, *to stay.*
Braten (ä), **briet**, **gebraten**, *to fry, to roast.*
Brechen (i), **brach**, **gebrochen**, *to break.*
Brennen, **brannte**, **gebrannt**, *to burn.*
Bringen, **brachte**, **gebracht**, *to bring.*

Denken, **dachte**, **gedacht**, *to think.*
Dringen, **drang**, **gedrungen**, *to urge, to insist.*
Dürfen (**ich darf**, **du darfst**, **er darf**, **wir dürfen**), **durfte**, **gedurft**, *to be allowed /permitted, may.*

Empfangen (ä), **empfing**, **empfangen**, *to receive.*
Empfehlen (ie), **empfahl**, **empfohlen**, *to recommend.*
Empfinden, **empfand**, **empfunden**, *to feel.*
Erbleichen, **erblich**, **erblichen**, *to turn pale.*
Erschallen, **erscholl**, **erschollen**, *to resound.*
Erschrecken (i), **erschrak**, **erschrocken**, *to frighten.*
Essen (i), **aß**, **gegessen**, *to eat.*

Fahren (ä), **fuhr**, **gefahren**, *to drive.*
Fallen (ä), **fiel**, **gefallen**, *to fall.*
Fangen (ä), **fing**, **gefangen**, *to catch.*
Fechten (i), **focht**, **gefochten**, *to fence.*
Finden, **fand**, **gefunden**, *to find.*
Fliegen, **flog**, **geflogen**, *to fly.*
Fliehen, **floh**, **geflohen**, *to flee.*
Fließen, **floß**, **geflossen**, *to flow.*

Fressen (i), **fraß**, **gefressen**, *to devour.*
Frieren, **fror**, **gefroren**, *to freeze.*

Geben (i), **gab**, **gegeben**, *to give.*
Gedeihen, **gedieh**, **gediehen**, *to prosper.*
Gefallen (ä), **gefiel**, **gefallen**, *to please.*
Gehen, **ging**, **gegangen**, *to go.*
Gelten (i), **galt**, **gegolten**, *to be effective.*
Genesen, **genas**, **genesen**, *to recover.*
Genießen, **genoß**, **genossen**, *to enjoy.*
Geschehen (ie), **geschah**, **geschehen**, *to happen.*
Gewinnen, **gewann**, **gewonnen**, *to win.*
Gießen, **goß**, **gegossen**, *to pour.*
Gleichen, **glich**, **geglichen**, *to resemble.*
Gleiten, **glitt**, **geglitten**, *to glide.*
Graben (ä), **grub**, **gebraben**, *to dig.*
Greifen, **griff**, **gegriffen**, *to seize.*

Haben (ich habe, du hast, er hat, wir haben), **hatte**, **gehabt**, *to have.*
Halten (ä), **hielt**, **gehalten**, *to hold.*
Hängen, **hing**, **gehangen**, *to hang.*
Hauen, **haute (hieb)**, **gehauen**, *to strike.*
Heben, **hob**, **gehoben**, *to lift.*
Heißen, **hieß**, **geheißen**, *to be called, to mean.*
Helfen (i), **half**, **geholfen**, *to help.*

Kennen, **kannte**, **gekannt**, *to know.*
Klingen, **klang**, **geklungen**, *to sound.*
Kneifen, **kniff**, **gekniffen**, *to pinch.*
Kommen, **kam**, **gekommen**, *to come.*
Können (ich kann, du kannst, er kann, wir können), **konnte**, **gekonnt**, *to be able, can.*
Kriechen, **kroch**, **gekrochen**, *to creep.*

Laden, **lud**, **geladen**, *to load.*
Lassen (ä), **ließ**, **gelassen**, *to let.*
Laufen (äu), **lief**, **gelaufen**, *to run.*
Leiden, **litt**, **gelitten**, *to suffer.*
Leihen, **lih**, **geliehen**, *to lend.*
Lesen (ie), **las**, **gelesen**, *to read.*

Liegen, lag, gelegen, *to lie.*
Lügen, log, gelogen, *to lie.*

Mahlen, mahlte, gemahlen, *to grind.*
Meiden, mied, gemieden, *to avoid.*
Messen (i), maß, gemessen, *to measure.*
Mögen (ich mag, du magst, er mag, wir mögen), mochte, gemocht, *to like, may.*
Müssen (ich muß, du mußt, er muß, wir müssen), mußte, gemußt, *to be obliged, must.*

Nehmen (ich nehme, du nimmst, er nimmt, wir nehmen), nahm, genommen, *to take.*
Nennen, nannte, genannt, *to call.*

Pfeiffen, pfiff, gepfiffen, *to whistle.*
Pflegen, pflog or **pflegte, gepflogen** or **gepflegt**, *to attend to, to be used to.*
Preisen, pries, gepriesen, *to praise.*

Quellen, quoll, gequollen, *to swell, to emanate from.*

Raten (ä), riet, geraten, *to advise.*
Reiben, rieb, gerieben, *to rub.*
Reißen, riß, gerissen, *to tear.*
Reiten, ritt, geritten, *to ride.*
Rennen, rannte, gerannt, *to run.*
Riechen, roch, gerochen, *to smell.*
Ringen, rang, gerungen, *to fight.*
Rinnen, rann, geronnen, *to flow, to trickle.*
Rufen, rief, gerufen, *to call, to shout.*

Salzen, salzte, gesalzen, *to salt.*
Saufen (äu), soff, gesoffen, *to drink (a lot).*
Schaffen, schuf, geschaffen, *to create.*
Scheiden, schied, geschieden, *to part.*
Scheinen, schien, geschienen, *to shine, to seem.*
Schelten, schalt, gescholten, *to scold.*
Scheren, schor, geschoren, *to shear, to clip.*
Schieben, schob, geschoben, *to push.*
Schießen, schoß, geschossen, *to fire.*

Schlafen (ä), schlief, geschlafen, *to sleep.*
Schlagen (ä), schlug, geschlagen, *to beat.*
Schleifen, schliff, geschliffen, *to sharpen.*
Schließen, schloß, geschlossen, *to close.*
Schlingen, schlang, geschlungen, *to sling.*
Schmelzen (i), schmolz, geschmolzen, *to melt.*
Schneiden, schnitt, geschnitten, *to cut.*
Schreiben, schrieb, geschrieben, *to write.*
Schreien, schrie, geschrie(e)n, *to cry, to shout.*
Schreiten, schritt, geschritten, *to stride.*
Schweigen, schwieg, geschwiegen, *to be silent.*
Schwellen, schwoll, geschwollen, *to swell.*
Schwimmen, schwamm, geschwommen, *to swim.*
Schwinden, schwand, geschwunden, *to wane.*
Schwingen, schwang, geschwungen, *to swing.*
Schwören, schwur or **schwor, geschworen,** *to swear.*
Sehen (ie), sah, gesehen, *to see.*
Sein (ich bin, du bist, er ist, wir sind), war, gewesen, *to be.*
Senden, sandte, gesandt, *to send.*
Singen, sang, gesungen, *to sing.*
Sinken, sank, gesunken, *to sink.*
Sinnen, sann, gesonnen, *to meditate.*
Sitzen, saß, gesessen, *to sit.*
Sollen (ich soll, du sollst, er soll, wir sollen), sollte, gesollt, *shall.*
Spalten, spaltete, gespalten, *to split.*
Speien, spie, gespie(e)n, *to spit.*
Spinnen, spann, gesponnen, *to spin, to be mad.*
Sprechen (i), sprach, gesprochen, *to speak.*
Springen, sprang, gesprungen, *to spring.*
Stechen (i), stach, gestochen, *to sting.*
Stehen, stand, gestanden, *to stand.*
Stehlen (ie), stahl, gestohlen, *to steal.*
Steigen, stieg, gestiegen, *to climb.*
Sterben (i), starb, gestorben, *to die.*
Stinken, stank, gestunken, *to stink.*
Stoßen (ö), stieß, gestoßen, *to push.*
Streichen, strich, gestrichen, *to rub, to spread.*
Streiten, stritt, gestritten, *to quarrel.*

Tragen (ä), trug, getragen, *to carry.*
Treffen (i), traf, getroffen, *to meet.*

Treiben, trieb, getrieben, *to operate, to induce.*
Treten (i), trat, getreten, *to tread.*
Trinken, trank, getrunken, *to drink.*
Tun (ich tue, du tust, er tut, wir tun), tat, getan, *to do.*

Verderben (it), verdarb, verdorben, *to spoil.*
Verdrießen, verdroß, verdrossen, *to annoy, to gall.*
Vergessen (i), vergaß, vergessen, *to forget.*
Verlieren, verlor, verloren, *to lose.*
Verschwinden, verschwand, verschwunden, *to disappear.*
Verzeihen, verzieh, verziehen, *to pardon.*

Wachsen (ä), wuchs, gewachsen, *to grow.*
Waschen (ä), wusch, gewaschen, *to wash.*
Weben, wob, or **webte, gewoben** or **gewebt,** *to weave.*
Weichen, wich, gewichen, *to give way.*
Weichen, weichte, geweicht, *to soak.*
Weisen, wies, gewiesen, *to show.*
Wenden, wandte or **wendete, gewandt** or **gewendet,** *to turn.*
Werben (i), warb, geworben, *to recruit.*
Werden (i), wurde, geworden, *to become.*
Werfen (i), warf, geworfen, *to throw.*
Wiegen (or **wägen**), **wog, gewogen,** *to weigh.*
Winden, wand, gewunden, *to wind.*
Wissen (ich weiß, du weißt, er weiß, wir wissen), wußte, gewußt, *to know.*
Wollen (ich will, du willst, er will, wir wollen), wollte, gewollt, *to want.*

Ziehen, zog, gezogen, *to pull.*
Zwingen, zwang, gezwungen, *to force.*

ASSiMiL®

Germam
With Ease

Also available from Assimil:

German From The Word Go!

N° édition 2985 : GERMAN WITH EASE – mars 2011

Achevé d'imprimer par «La Tipografica Varese S.p.A.» Varese
Imprimé en Italie